BEDSIDE HOLLYWOOD

BEDSIDE HOLLYWOOD:

Great Scenes from Movie Memoirs

Edited by Robert Atwan and Bruce Forer
Foreword by Jack Kroll

MOYER BELL LIMITED/NIMBUS BOOKS
NEW YORK

For Harold and Gladys
For Allan and Ellen

Preface, notes and selection copyright © 1985 by Robert Atwan and Bruce Forer

Foreword copyright © 1985 by Jack Kroll

All photographs courtesy of the Film Stills Archive, Museum of Modern Art, New York

Designer: Thomas Ridinger
Editor: Laurance Wieder

Published by Moyer Bell Limited, Mount Kisco, New York,
and Nimbus Books, Inc., Brooklyn, New York

Printed in the United States of America

Library of Congress Cataloging-in-Publication Data

Main entry under title:

Bedside Hollywood.

    Includes index.
    1. Moving-picture actors and actresses—United
States—Biography—Addresses, essays, lectures.
I. Atwan, Robert. II. Forer, Bruce.
PN1998.A2B414 1985   791.43′028′0922 [B]   85-15337
ISBN 0-918825-11-3

CREDITS

BEDSIDE
HOLLYWOOD

Table of Contents

Foreword
by Jack Kroll

Is this book for intelligent, cultivated people? Of course. But why do intelligent, cultivated people want to read the memoirs of movie stars and other Hollywood fauna? Is it possible that intelligent, cultivated people (whatever that concept has come to mean in our culture, where high-, middle-, and lowbrows are now found in the same cranium, like intellectual Silly Putty) are slavering for Tinseltown gossip and checkout-counter revelations? Well, gossip has recently become an object of academic study, just like nuclear proliferation and the genesis of psychoanalysis. The clandestine shenanigans of strategically placed people have always attracted the lustful attention of concerned citizens, and in our Entertainment Society entertainers are strategically placed people.

Maybe reading the memoirs of show business superstars is for us what reading the Goncourts' journal or Samuel Pepys' diary was for previous generations. Trying to put the highest gloss on their intentions, the Goncourt brothers claimed that they wanted to capture "the face of woman and the voice of man." So what if the faces were those of George Sand and the Empress Eugènie, and the voices belonged to Flaubert and Rodin? We need not apologize for the face of Marilyn Monroe and the voice of Humphrey Bogart. The fact is that the movies have spawned a whole new species of creature for us to watch and care about. In one of John Berryman's poems James Cagney appears as the inventor of a new behavioral language, and John Ashbery once wrote a delightful (and serious) sestina about those indispensable movie stars Popeye, Olive Oyl and Wimpy.

So this anthology is serious (and delightful) business. For the committed connoisseur of movie memoirs is a true democrat: he or she may want to know about Eisenstein's montages or Buñuel's surrealism, but first things first. How did Bacall and Bogey get together? What really happened between Errol Flynn and those two "teenage" girls? Who was Jackie Cooper's "professor of love"? Why did Lana Turner's daughter stick a kitchen knife into hoodlum Johnny Stompanato? These matters are the stuff of Hollywood, but they are also the stuff of life and sometimes even of myth, the sort of mini-myths that move through our heads at twenty-four frames per second. Perhaps the most important thing about movies is that they provide the perfect context for that mixture of the transcendent and the trashy which seems to be the inescapable fatality of our culture. Whichever of the polar flavors attracts you more, these luscious samplings of movie memoirs add up to an irresistible *That's Entertainment* of the printed word.

Preface

They can be outrageously narcissistic, self-serving, untrustworthy. They are often tirelessly self-promotional, gooey with sentiment. They are master-pieces of selective memory. The sermonizing can be deadly; the espousal of good causes could drive any decent reader into misanthropy. And, through it all, the first person narrative glides along with a naive assurance that could set a literary critic's teeth on edge.

Yet, even the most demanding readers can find Hollywood memoirs irresistible. One of W. H. Auden's favorite books was *The Big Love*—Mrs. Florence Aadland's account of her daughter's notorious love affair with Errol Flynn. Her tale begins with a line that William Styron found worthy of Melville: "There's one thing I want to make clear right off, my baby was a virgin the day she met Errol Flynn." The Swashbuckler first laid eyes on the fifteen year-old "Woodsie" (short for his "little wood nymph") while she was dancing on the set of *Marjorie Morningstar*. And the rest is history—or, rather, memoir.

Flynn, of course, romped through his own autobiography, *My Wicked, Wicked Ways*, with a unique combination of lewdness and élan. Such spirit never carries an "X" rating. Capturing the moral climate of another era, Flynn's hardboiled story contains none of the sex-as-therapy boosterism that marks contemporary erotica. The star's 1943 trial for the statutory rape of two "minors" thrust World War II off the front pages, and gave "sparking" GI's a new term for scoring with the girls—"In like Flynn." His recollections of that trial, with its mix of politics, suspense and period prurience, stands up as one of the great scenes of the Hollywood memoir.

Movie star memoirs go back nearly as far as the movies themselves. Sarah Bernhardt published her life story (*Ma double vie*) in 1907; the following year she made an heroic effort to become the world's first movie star. While *La Tosca* (1908) was never released, her *Elizabeth, Queen of England* (1912) deserves its reputation as the first full-length feature film, though one hesitates to call this four-reel "photoplay" a *motion* picture. She made eight movies in all ("my last chance at immortality"), several after the amputation of her right leg. She succeeded as a silent film star, so perhaps her book—though its chronology never catches up with her film career—could be called the first movie star memoir. Her story certainly displays all the characteristics of the genre: a fastidious avoidance of serious self-assessment; a fascination with role-playing; and an energetic self-promotion. The last quality bothered Henry James so much that he rudely referred to the Divine Sarah as "an advertising genius."

Memoirs trickled out of the early movie industry. The "queen of the silent serials," Pearl White, survived such thrillers as *The Perils of Pauline* and *The Exploits of Elaine* to write *Just Me* in 1919. Not wanting to "include himself out," Samuel Goldwyn published an autobiography, *Behind the Screen*, in 1923. Two cowboy stars, even then, waxed nostalgic about the vanishing west: Tom Mix's *The West of Yesterday* appeared in 1923, and William S. Hart brought out *My Life East and West* in 1928. The prize for the most prestigious autobiography to come out of the silent era belongs to John Barrymore's *Confessions of an Actor* (1926). The most romantic early memoir is Rudolph Valentino's posthumous *Intimate Journal* (1931). But the most intelligent Hollywood story from those early days remains Harold Lloyd's *An American Comedy* (1928).

Lloyd's genius perhaps comes closer to today's comic sensibility than does his box-office rival, Charlie Chaplin's. The star and director of *Safety Last* was a consummate craftsman both on celluloid and on paper, where he shows far more interest in the filmic art of comedy than in his own career. John Updike has noted that, in their memoirs, actors and actresses seem most themselves—and most exciting—when they talk shop. That's when they reveal the details of craft, the hidden tricks of the trade, the inside dope. Ingrid Bergman's account of *Casablanca's* other ending, like Janet Leigh's descriptions of her wardrobe problem during the seventy-one setups required for the "nude" shower scene in *Psycho*, makes a real contribution to the history of film.

While shop talk may be the best part of Hollywood memoirs for fans who like their facts, few readers can resist the temptation to eavesdrop on movieland gossip. It's been said that autobiography is the greatest vehicle for telling the truth—about other people. Consider what catches a movie star's eye: Jackie Cooper sneaks a glimpse of George Raft's girdle; Cagney notices Humphrey Bogart's "nervous habit of picking his nose wherever he was"; Eddie Fisher recalls Elizabeth Taylor spending twenty minutes each evening fanatically brushing her teeth. "People. Wonderful, remarkable people," said Jimmy Cagney, "is what an autobiography should be rich in—the people who make up a person's real environment."

But Cagney is an exception. "All autobiographies are necessarily egotistical," P. T. Barnum observed. America's first great master of ceremonies invented the show business memoir in 1855. After the Bible, his *Struggles and Triumphs* was the most popular page-turner of the nineteenth century. Literary conventions precluded any talk of his sexual life, but Barnum did expound at length on that other great theme of American autobiography—money. From then on, popular autobiography told only one kind of story: success.

Hollywood autobiographies are tinselled success stories, with Frank Sinatra's "I Did It My Way" supplying the background music. The archetypal movie memoir progresses through five stages: Act I: *The Early Years*. Here we encounter the celebrity's real self; learn the real name; meet the family; discover the one or two events that have irrevocably shaped the personality. Act II: *The Big Break.* In pursuit of the dream, the star struggles until the lucky moment—"So much of a successful career," says Shelley Winters, "depends on standing on the right corner at the exact right moment"—when the unknown undertakes that Hollywood rite of passage, the screen test. Act III: *Making It.* The unexpected glamor; the new friends; the parties; the love affairs; and the contracts. Act IV: *The Crisis.* The deterioration of the perfect relationship; a tragic accident; breakdown; divorce, drugs, drink; contract problems; a new agent; Act V: *Final Triumph.* A new self-awareness; a hard-won philosophy of life that accepts the ups and downs; the new person—complete and self-accepting—now comes to realize that Hollywood betrays the real self when it fabricates a movie star.

Though few autobiographies run entirely true to form, most share a good portion of this composite Hollywood life cycle. Almost all memoirs are written from the perspective of Act V, and thus an authentic person—not a fake movie star—claims to be the author of the book. Now whole, and with the wisdom of retrospect, the star disavows his or her stardom. "I'm not *just* a movie star," the classic Memoir insists, "I'm a loving parent, a supportive spouse, an artist, a conscientious citizen, a sponsor of worthy charities, a connoisseur of the finer things, a serious Broadway actor, an athlete, a writer, director, producer—a complete individual." Given this drive to establish a non-Hollywood self, it is not surprising that many famous movie stars seem only partially interested in writing about movies. At times, they even dismiss the very talents that elevated them to stardom. In *Steps in Time* (1959), Fred Astaire concluded that he had nothing to say about dancing—did he really think that no one would be interested in that aspect of his career?

Identity crisis—the movie star in conflict with the "real self"—is the dramatic heart of the Hollywood memoir. How would readers react to the story of an aspiring actress from a small midwestern town who breaks into the movies and at last discovers her "real" self in her role as star? But the genre hasn't yet evolved that way. In memoir after memoir, the "real person" is the pre-Hollywood innocent. Kids who grew up as Hollywood stars, like Jackie Cooper or Shirley Temple, have an especially rough time trying to establish their true identity, but somehow they succeed. It's often said that movie stars are childlike; perhaps that's because their only image of themselves as "real people" derives from childhood.

A confusion of names often plays a key role in the theatrics of identity. Shelley Winters announces this central conflict in the opening line of her autobiography: "Who is Shirley Schrift? What happened to her, and what metamorphosis took place that changed her into Shelley Winters, movie star?" Throughout the entire lively account of her career, she attempts to reclaim an identity buried in adolescence. Her story ends with a Felliniesque episode in

Venice. The actress sees a poor young woman who looks "exactly like the adolescent Shirley Schrift." "Isn't this movie star business enough already?" the woman seems to ask. They commune with each other, and then: "I took her hand and as I did, I experienced, in some deep mysterious way, a merging of that long buried part of my self with the rest of me." Now at one with herself, Shelley Winters (or is it Shirley Schrift?) can rush back to the Taverna Fenice to rejoin her friend Maria Callas.

Occasionally, the star's identity problem grows extremely convoluted. Breaking into pictures at nineteen, Lauren Bacall (born Bette Joan Perske) felt that she, too, lost some part of herself to Hollywood. And her book also ends with a reaffirmation of her pre-Hollywood "real self": "What was not real in Howard Hawks' version of me is not real now. I remain as vulnerable, romantic, and idealistic as I was at fifteen, sitting in a movie theatre, watching, *being*, Bette Davis." The "real person" is not Lauren Bacall the movie star; it is instead a star-stuck teenager whose fragile identity momentarily merges with a prominent actress, someone who spent her own teenage years immersed in Greta Garbo movies. This is a story for Vladimir Nabokov.

The stars may question their identity—but the questions readers ask are: Is this the truth? And who really wrote the book anyway? Mark Twain (born Samuel Clemens) once gave his brother some advice about writing an autobiography: he encouraged him to "try to tell the straight truth . . . to refrain from exhibiting himself in creditable attitudes exclusively and to honorably set down all the incidents of his life . . . including those which were burned into his memory because he was ashamed of them." He reminded his brother that no writer had ever done this before; and that if he could pull it off his "autobiography would be a most valuable piece of literature." Twain's brother did write one, and Mark Twain was very disappointed. Then Twain tried to write one himself and he realized that he had given his brother impossible advice. "I have been dictating this autobiography of mine daily for three months; I have thought of fifteen hundred or two thousand incidents in my life which I am ashamed of but I have not gotten one of them to consent to go on paper yet."

Autobiographies, in other words, are only human. Yet if we can't expect the whole truth and nothing but, can we at least believe that movie stars write their own books? In a number of cases, the movie star does—or does to the point of rough draft. People at Alfred A. Knopf can recall how Lauren Bacall graced the offices for days at a time writing *By Myself*. Sometimes the star gets "grammaticized" (a euphemism for intensive rewriting); sometimes the work is heavily shaped and edited by the publishing house; in many instances a "ghost" does the dirty work—takes the notes and performs the actual writing. And in other instances, the authorship is shared by a respectful "and" or a less dignified "with," or the ambiguous "as told to." The variations are infinite; the problems are knotty; the jockeying for credit can be vitriolic. Nonetheless, once past the title page and acknowledgement credits, it's the movie star's book.

There's a certain justice in this. Movie stars have grown accustomed to a world where the written word is not exactly king. They've seen scripts savaged and talented writers reduced to pulp. They spend their work days in a collaborative environment where it's almost impossible to allocate proper credit. Why should the autobiography be any different from any other project? If it takes a staff to assemble a book, what's so special about that? It can take a full staff just to get a star on the set. The autobiography's a mess? Well, call in a rewrite specialist. After all, it's *only* writing.

By the time a book is finished, the movie star—no matter what the nature of the editorial contribution—will think he or she wrote it anyway. In *Giving Up the Ghost*, the highly entertaining memoir of a ghostwriter, Sandford Dody recalls how Bette Davis behaved after their "collaboration." It was the "usual syndrome," Dody, who has ghosted five celebrity books, reports: "Bette had unburdened herself and now I knew too much. I'm sure that in her confusion she believed—since she had told me everything—that she had now written it as well. All my subjects have felt this way." Dody then says something that should be inscribed in the sidewalk at Grauman's Chinese Theatre: "To live a life and to write it are of course two entirely different things."

It's probably beside the point to fault movie stars for not writing every word of their autobiographies. Few public figures—politicians, high-level corporate executives—actually write their own speeches and books. Comedians don't always write their own jokes. It's realistic to believe in ghosts, but we shouldn't forget that stars like Mary Astor, Louise Brooks, Dirk Bogarde, Groucho Marx, and Mae West became talented authors in their own right. Errol Flynn enjoyed writing, and as a young adventurer dashed off Jack London-style journalism to an Australian weekly. Remember, too, that the Hollywood memoir is not only a vehicle for movie stars. Successful screenwriters like Anita Loos and William Goldman, great directors like Frank Capra and Mack Sennett—even cameramen and film editors—have brought out fine, informative autobiographies. Sometimes it seems that the writing coming out of Hollywood is better than the movies themselves.

The constant stream of memoirs gives no indication of drying up. Every year about a dozen new ones make their debut. So many celebrity autobiographies have been written that the Hollywood memoir has truly evolved into a literary genre, perhaps the most durable version of the American success story. Over the past decade, the genre has become a staple of the publishing industry, leaving a permanent mark on our popular culture. For all their publicity, however, these books receive no literary prizes—no Pulitzers, no American Book Awards, and ordinarily no critical acclaim. Perhaps it's time for Hollywood to establish for the Oscar ceremonies an Academy Award for Best Autobiography.

R.A.
B.F.

BEDSIDE
HOLLYWOOD

Great Scenes from Movie Memoirs

"A true autobiography is almost an impossibility. . . .
man is bound to lie about himself."

—Fyodor Dostoyevsky
Notes From Underground

DESI ARNAZ

Lucille Ball and Desi Arnaz in The Long, Long Trailer *(1954), MGM.*

Born Desiderio Alberto Arnaz III on March 2, 1917 in Santiago, Cuba . . . Fled 1933 Cuban Revolution . . . Best high school friend in Miami: Al Capone, Jr. . . . Singer with Xavier Cugat . . . First Film: *Too Many Girls*, starring Lucille Ball (1940) . . . Married Lucille Ball 1940 . . . Divorced 1960 . . . Little Ricky (Desi Jr.) born 1953, appeared on the cover of the first issue of *TV Guide*.

The Birth of Little Ricky

W e were about to begin filming our second season, early in 1952, when Lucy came to me and said, "Hey, Father, I've got news for you. I'm pregnant again."

We were so happy we couldn't believe it. For ten years we had wanted children so much and all we were able to get were cats, dogs, bees, old chickens and The Duchess of Devonshire, and here it was nine months after our beautiful girl was born and Lucy was pregnant again.

After we calmed down, I said, "Jesus, I better tell Jess Oppenheimer* about it." I arranged a meeting with him and told him there was a situation we had to think about.

"What's that?" he asked.

"Lucy's pregnant again."

"Oh, my God," he said, "what are we going to do?"

I laughed and said, "What do you mean, what are we going to do? She's going to have a baby. Whatever there was to be done about it, Lucy and I have already done it."

"Yeah, but what about the show?" he asked. "You know how big she gets. There's no way we can hide it for more than a couple of months at the most."

"I know. So how about Lucy Ricardo having a baby as part of our shows this year?"

"They'll never let you do that," he answered.

"Why won't they? And who are 'they'?"

"You know—the sponsor, the network, the advertising agency."

"Well, I don't see why not," I said. "What's wrong with Lucy Ricardo having a baby? Lucy and Ricky are married. She's pregnant. There is no way we can hide that fact from the audience. We have already signed the contracts. This is the number-one show on the air. There is only one way to do it—Lucy Ricardo will have a baby."

"It'd be a hell of a gimmick," said Jess, "if they would let you do it."

I called the Biow agency and told them the situation. They said, "There's no way you can do that. You cannot show a pregnant woman on television."

I called CBS. They had the same answer, and so did the Philip Morris people. No matter how much I argued that Lucy and Ricky were married, that it was a natural thing for them to have a child, "What the hell could be wrong with that?"

*Writer of the *I Love Lucy* pilot, along with Bob Carroll, Jr. and Madelyn Pugh. He developed many scripts for the show.

They wouldn't agree to it. They wanted us to do the shows without showing she was pregnant.

They asked, "Can you hide her behind chairs or something or other?"

"There ain't no way I can hide Lucy's pregnancy. By the time fall comes around she'll be as big as the Goodyear blimp. And I still don't see what is so wrong if she has a baby in the show as Lucy Ricardo."

Well, I couldn't get anywhere.

They finally said, "Can you just do one or two shows about it?"

"No, it cannot be done that way. We need at least eight or ten shows to do them honestly and well, and have any kind of continuity in the series. First, she has to tell Ricky she's going to have a baby. Lucy and Ricky, in our story life, have been married for more than ten years without having a child, so that has to be great news in the Ricardo household and we couldn't do it justice without doing one whole show just about that. Then, even though we will cover the last six months of her pregnancy in eight or ten shows, we certainly could not make them fun and sentimental and honest and real in much less than at least eight shows."

Mr. Alfred Lyons, chairman of the board at Philip Morris, was not in the United States. He was in England. A wonderful, wise old gent, he had always been very kind to us and also very understanding.

He had visited the ranch at Chatsworth shortly after he bought our show. When he first met Lucy at our house she was not feeling too well. As he came into the bedroom, Lucy was propped up in bed, wearing a lovely bed jacket, reading a book and smoking a Chesterfield, a fact she could not hide because there was a whole carton of Chesterfields staring at Mr. Lyons from the night table next to her. He took it very gracefully and after the how-do-you-do's and how-do-you-feel's and hope-you're-on-your-feet-soon's, he said, "That's a very funny joke."

"What?" asked Lucy.

"Putting the carton of Chesterfields on your night table."

"Oh, my God!" said Lucy.

As we walked out of the room, he told me, "Look, if she must smoke Chesterfields, make sure you put them inside a Philip Morris package and inside a Phillip Morris carton."

We did this for some time, until one day I told our propman not to switch them and see if she would notice. She didn't. We didn't switch them anymore.

I decided to write a letter to Mr. Lyons and explain the whole situation about Lucy being pregnant and how I wanted to treat that in the show, how all these people were against it, including his own Philip Morris people, his advertising agency and the network.

> Mr. Lyons, I guess it all comes down to you. You are the man who is paying the money for this show and I guess I will have to do whatever you decide. There's only one thing I want to make certain that you understand. We have

given you the number-one show in the country and, up till now, the creative decisions have been in our hands. Your people are now telling us we cannot do this, so the only thing I want from you, if you agree with them, is that you must inform them that we will not accept them telling us what not to do unless, in the future, they will also tell us what to do.

At that point, and if this is your decision, we will cease to be responsible to you for the show being the number-one show on television, and you will have to look to your people, to the network and to the Biow Agency for that responsibility.

Thank you very much for all you have done for us in the past.

Sincerely yours.

About a week after I sent the letter, all arguments about the "pregnant" shows stopped. Nobody was squawking anymore about whether there should only be two shows or no shows or eight shows or whatever. I figured Mr. Lyons must have done something, but I wasn't about to find out what. The fact that the opposition had stopped was good enough for me.

A couple of years later I was in New York and, as usual, went to Mr. Lyon's office just to say hello to him and thank him again for all his trust and cooperation in the past. As I was leaving, I was stopped at the door by his secretary, the lady who had been with the old man for thirty or forty years, and with whom I had a very good relationship.

She asked, "Did you ever wonder why all the arguments stopped when you wanted to do those shows about Lucy being pregnant and everybody was against it?"

"Yes, I sure did. I figured Mr. Lyons must have said something to somebody, but I wasn't about to ask too many questions and maybe create some other problems. Let good enough alone, you know."

"I have a memo here I want to show you," she said, "but don't you ever tell anybody I showed it to you."

The memo, sent from England, read: "To whom it may concern: Don't fuck around with the Cuban! Signed, A.L."

I almost fell to the floor. What a great old man he was!

After the opposition to the "baby" shows stopped, we got together with Jess, Bob and Madelyn, and laid out what we all thought should be done, how we should introduce it, and how many shows we should do. We finally decided that in the first show Lucy should find out she was pregnant and tell Ricky about it. In the eighth show he would take her to the hospital and the baby would be born.

In between, we could do shows about Lucy having cravings for strange combinations of food, like chocolate ice cream, sardines and pickles, mixed together. Ricky would develop sympathetic labor pains and order the same horrible mixture, and other humorous things common to pregnancies, like Lucy not being able to get out of an easy chair or tie her own shoes. An obvious one was that Ricky should not talk to the baby, so he or she would not be handicapped by his accent.

If we needed a break or two from the pregnancy shows, or if we needed to extend the period of time to make the birth of the Ricardo baby coincide as close as possible with the actual birth of the Arnaz baby, we would use repeats of past shows as if we were reminiscing about what had happened. One short scene would be sufficient to lead us into each repeat.

One thing in our favor for the timing was that Lucie, our first child, was born by Caesarean operation. It wasn't supposed to be that way, but at the last minute Dr. Joe Harris found the child had turned the wrong way, and he didn't want to take a chance.

She was a nice big baby and he was very glad he decided to operate, because Lucy was about two weeks overdue. If we had lost that second child after losing the first, it would have been such a tragedy I don't think we could have taken it.

Every day of my life when I think of this gorgeous daughter of ours, I bless Dr. Harris and thank God.

Lucy, having had a Caesarean, would also have to have her next child by Caesarean. Knowing this, we asked Dr. Harris when he thought the baby would be born. He said it would be sometime in January of 1953. It was then sometime in August. We started counting back from the middle of January and decided that on one show in October of 1952 Lucy would tell Ricky that she was pregnant.

We didn't have to go week by week. In the writing we could say it was the next day or the next month.

We figured that, with eight shows about the baby and perhaps one, two or three repeats, we could cover the rest of the pregnancy leading to the birth of the Ricardo child and come pretty close to the birth of our own child.

And that's the way it was all laid out.

One other thing we wanted to make sure of was that we didn't do or say anything that would offend our television audience in any way whatsoever. So I called Cardinal James McIntyre, who was our top man out here. I also called Rabbi Edgar Magnin and the Protestant leader concerned with television, Rev. Clifton Moore of the Hollywood Presbyterian Church. I explained to each of them what we were doing and asked them to assign someone to be with us during this entire period to read the scripts, come to the rehearsals and see the filming.

They graciously agreed. We had a Catholic priest, Monsignor Joseph Devlin of St. Vincent's Catholic Church and head of the Catholic Legion of Decency; Rabbi Alfred Wolf, of the Wilshire Temple, representing the Jewish faith; and Mr. Moore himself. They were with us four days a week to see the rehearsals and filming. They used to have lunch and dinner together and became very good friends.

They never objected to anything. As a matter of fact, we had the word "pregnant" in one of the shows and the CBS censor would not let us say it, but the rabbi, the minister and the priest said, "Well, what's wrong with 'pregnant'? That's what it is."

I met with them and said, "Look, what's the difference? What else can we say?"

"Expecting," all three advised.

"Okay, we'll use 'expecting.' I'll probably get a laugh with that because I can't pronouce 'expecting' too well. It will probably come out 'specting' and Lucy will then be able to imitate my way of saying it. 'Yeah, like he says, I'm 'specting.'"

It is hard to believe in this day and age that CBS or anyone else could have been prudish about the word pregnant. Today they not only use the word but also show you how to get into that condition.

I didn't want Lucy to work beyond her fifth month of pregnancy, which would be in October, more than three months before the birth of our child.

We knew the child was going to be born sometime in January. That meant the last show had to be done at least three or four months before that.

By this time I had checked again with Dr. Harris and he had told me the second week in January.

So we had to film the show about Lucy Ricardo having the baby not later than the first of October, and then Lucy Arnaz could go home and wait for the birth of our child.

The next question was, Is it going to be a boy or a girl? As far as the show was concerned, we had to decide this three and a half months before the baby was actually born.

I asked Dr. Harris, "Can you tell me what it's going to be?"

"I can tell you it's going to be a boy or a girl."

"Yeah, but I've got to film the show in the next couple of weeks."

"You're a gambler," he said. "It's a fifty-fifty shot."

"Well, Joe, I've already discussed this with Lucy and we have agreed the Ricardos should have a boy, regardless of what the Arnazes have. We are thinking of our daughter, who has never been in the show. She wasn't even born when we started. So if the Ricardos have a boy, and we get an actor to play the part, our daughter will understand that he's only a member of the Ricardos' make-believe family and that she and the newborn baby are the only real members of the Arnaz family. It's all settled. Lucy Ricardo's child is going to be a boy, regardless of what Lucy Ball Arnaz gives birth to."

A couple of weeks after that we started rehearsing the eighth show in which little Ricky would be born. The writers had really outdone themselves for that one. The routine of rehearsing and timing how Ethel, Fred and Ricky would act when Lucy would tell us it was time to take her to the hospital, and how our very well-planned and *timed* procedure fell apart when the actual time came, has always been one of my favorites.

In the hospital scene when Ricky was shown the baby and was told "It's a boy," he fainted beautifully. I hope Ricky appreciates that I got a hell of a bump on my head doing that full-figure backward fall to portray his faint.

You probably couldn't see my tears through that crazy makeup and headdress of a tribal Indian chief that I had on, but my eyes were full. I was thinking that in ten or twelve weeks I would be in a real maternity ward waiting to hear our baby had been born and was healthy. Of course, I was really praying our baby would be a boy, but not for the sake of the show.

I was the only male of the Arnaz family in my generation. Both of my father's brothers had girls, and, as I mentioned before, the family was a very old family. If I didn't have a son, that would be the end of the Arnaz name. So, of course, I was extremely interested in having a son, and this was my last chance because, after this one, Lucy could not have another child. The doctor had already said, "She's not that young anymore and two Caesareans are enough. Another one would be dangerous."

I'll be the first to admit that Lucy Arnaz having a baby boy at 8:30 A.M. on Monday, the nineteenth of January, 1953, and Lucy Ricardo having a baby boy that same night on CBS was the most unbelievable piece of timing I know of. But, as Dr. Harris said, "It was a fifty-fifty shot."

One of the reasons it happened on the same day was that Dr. Harris always performed his Caesareans on Monday, unless there was an emergency of some kind. He had told me that if the baby cooperated and continued making the progress he was making, on Monday, January 19, he should be ready to make his debut and join the world.

All we had to do, to have the eighth show televised the same Monday, was to use two repeats of previous, non-baby shows on Christmas Eve and New Year's Eve.

A tremendous amount of lucky breaks and a hell of a lot of hardworking and dedicated people helped us to accomplish this. As the shows about the Ricardos' going to have a baby started to be shown on television, they created the most incredible interest all over the world, and it kept building up. When it was announced that the Arnaz baby would, in all probability, be born the same day, reporters from all over the world and every wire service in the United States and Latin America descended upon me. They all wanted to be with me in the fathers' waiting room at the hospital. Of course it was impossible to accommodate all of them. I asked them to pick one guy to represent the wire services and the newspapers and only he would be with me in the fathers' waiting room.

Lucy went to surgery at eight o'clock in the morning. James Bacon of the Associated Press, who is now writing a syndicated column appearing in the *Los Angeles Herald-Examiner,* was the one picked to be in the fathers' waiting room with me. It was a small room right next to the delivery room, where the surgery was being done. There was only a swinging door between me and Lucy, but they wouldn't let me go inside and be with her.

All the doctors, the nurses, everyone else who was in that room with Lucy had been looking at the shows and knew the Ricardos' baby was going to be born that same evening on television, and that it would be a boy.

Simultaneously, Jim and I heard a loud baby cry and a happy choir of voices sing out, "It's a boy!"

Bacon took off like a rocket, shouting "Congratulations!" Later on he told me that within ninety seconds the news was on Japanese radio. News services all over the world were standing by during the surgery.

"It's a boy!" I wish I had a recording of it, but I really don't need it—I can hear it today.

The national ratings on *I Love Lucy* the night the baby was born were the highest ever on television. Front pages carried the story that over two million more people saw our show that night than watched General Eisenhower being inaugurated as President of the United States the following day. I will never forget when Desi was nine or ten years old and he was spending a weekend with me in Palm Springs. We happened to run into General Eisenhower, who was about to tee off at El Dorado Country Club. The General looked up while we were watching and waiting to tee off after him, and then he asked me, "Is this the little fellow who knocked me off the front pages the day before I was inaugurated?"

"Yes, sir, General, that's him."

General Eisenhower seemed to get a kick out of meeting Desi, and afterward in the clubhouse bought him a banana split. Desi has never forgotten that day.

ELIZABETH ASHLEY

Elizabeth Ashley in Paternity *(1981), Paramount.*

Born August 30, 1939 in Ocala, Florida . . . Won Tony Award for *Take Her She's Mine* (1962) . . . Screen debut in *The Carpetbaggers* (1964) . . . *Ship of Fools* (1965) . . . Married James Farentino in 1962 . . . Affair with George Peppard in 1963 . . . Romance with writer Tom McGuane . . . Retired 1965 for personal reasons . . . Comeback in *The Marriage of a Young Stockbroker* (1971) . . . *Rancho Deluxe* (1975) . . . *92 in the Shade* (1975) . . . Picture on the cover of LIFE Magazine the day President Kennedy was shot in Dallas, Texas . . . Most famous movie line: "What do you want to see on your honeymoon?" "Lots of lovely ceilings."

"A Bad Girl"

After we finished shooting *Carpetbaggers*, it was time to pack my suitcase and head back to New York to start rehearsing *Barefoot in the Park*. George [Peppard] had just about settled his divorce by then and was beginning to talk about getting married. But there were certain conditions. During the months we lived together he made it perfectly evident he thought actresses were all unstable, neurotic, fucked-up women, and he wasn't about to marry one, no matter how much he loved her. The deal was that I give it up, turn in my SAG card, eyelashes, and tap shoes and settle down to become a proper wife and mother, the way Nature intended.

I didn't want to give it up.

Being an actress was the only thing I'd ever done that made me feel the least bit like a competent human being who deserved a place on the planet. Over the past year I had done *Take Her, She's Mine* and *Carpetbaggers*, and now I was about to go back to Broadway in a play Neil Simon had written for me. Not that I was so terrific, but I was hot and I hoped I would start to get better.

Besides, I wasn't all that sure about getting married again. My marriage to [James] Farentino was fun while it lasted, but it never made a whole lot of sense and we shortly went our separate ways. Why would it be any different with George? Yes, he was a lot different than Jimmy—older, wiser, more sure of himself. But I was still the same.

I kept thinking about what my mother always told me while I was growing up. She'd say, "Any stupid little nit that works in the ten-cent store can get married. It doesn't take any brains to get married. It takes brains to stay single. My God, girl, get yourself an education. Be independent so you can have some choices in your life."

But I didn't want to lose George either. I loved him too much to let him go. And maybe he was right about actresses.

I needed some time to figure it all out.

We agreed I would go do my play in New York and he would fly in to see me as often as he could, maybe once every couple of weeks. We would keep talking and see what happened.

He wasn't at all happy about it. He thought I was sitting on the fence, and I was. But he agreed to hang in with me.

When he flew in for the opening of *Barefoot*, it turned out to be an absolute nightmare. He had reached the point where he hated everything about my being an actress, and at the party at Sardi's afterward he got very drunk. Every time someone wanted to take my picture, he grabbed another drink off the tray. When the reviews came in and we knew the show was a hit, it only made it worse.

The next day we were taken to lunch at "21" to celebrate my being the hottest little piece of ass in show business for that five minutes. I was so stoned and miserable and spaced out I didn't even know where I was.

Years later, Freddy de Cordova, the producer of the *Tonight Show*, told me he'd been there that afternoon with Mary Livingston, Jack Benny's wife, and some other high rollers in the hierarchy of the business, and when they came over to the table to congratulate me I was vulgar and rude and mean. He said they were shocked. They had never seen anyone behave so badly. And after that, needless to say, he had never been much of a fan of mine. All I could say to him was, "Freddy, I can't even remember it. It's a total blank. But I know it's true."

The next time George came in, he took me to a party at Albert Finney's house. They had done a picture together and become friends. George liked him a lot and so did I, and the three of us took to meeting for drinks after the show. When George had to go back to California, he told Finney, "Well, keep an eye on my girl, will you?"

Finney was in New York touring with *Luther*. When he left England he announced he was planning to screw his way around the world. Every female in New York between fourteen and sixty was calling him on the phone, just begging to go to bed with him. I was probably the only actress in town who didn't have that in mind. I have always been pretty much of a one-man-at-a-time woman, and I was already in love with George. But I found Finney inspiring and exciting. I was very much in awe of him. We were almost the same age, and he was already a great, great actor. He was everything I wanted to be but wasn't.

I started hanging out at Finney's house during the afternoons I didn't have a matinee, spending hours with him listening to him talk about acting. There were always other performers around, people like Tom Courtenay and some of the other Brits working in New York. Sometimes after our shows we would all get together for drinks at Downey's. I was just one of the guys.

And then of course the inevitable happened. I fell in love with him. There is never anything more seductive than forbidden fruit. The one person you are not supposed to have is the one person you are going to want. I knew it was only a fantasy that couldn't come to anything. Finney made it absolutely clear he wasn't in love with me. But it didn't seem to make any difference.

For the first time in my life I was in love with two men at the same time. George was offering to take care of me, to solve my life and make it simple and good. But he wanted me to stop being an actress. Finney was offering me nothing at all except some of his time and body. But he didn't want me to stop being an actress. What I wanted was both things in one man. But you don't get that. It doesn't come that way. So I was being pulled in both directions at once. It's possible that had something to do with my falling apart and ending up in Payne Whitney [psychiatric pavilion at New York Hospital].

I came out of the hospital a cynical, angry, frightened person and went back to the play with a very different set of priorities. I was no longer so concerned about getting Bob Redford's approval. I stopped worrying about how to do it better. My only responsibility was to show up. It didn't matter if I was any good or not. Nobody seemed to care about that. All they wanted was my physical presence. As long as they had that, my personal problems couldn't have mattered less to them.

And they weren't wrong. Not at all. One of the first big lessons you have to learn is that whatever personal *angst* you may have comes second. And if your personal *angst* gets between you and the gig, then you don't have any right to be doing the gig.

The rules are simple: If you've got problems, go to an analyst. During the day. On your own time. And that's what I started to do. Four times a week I would trot over to the analyst's office and plop myself down on the couch for an hour, just the way I was supposed to. Then I'd go to the theater and get to work so I would have the money to pay him.

By the time I returned to *Barefoot in the Park*, Albert Finney had left town with his play and disappeared from my life. George never found out about him, and I never told him. He continued to work around his shooting schedule to be with me as much as he could, doing everything possible to make sure I was all right. He seemed to be the only person in the world who gave a damn whether I was dead or alive, other than those who worried whether I would show up at the theater.

I was still in *Barefoot* when George's mother suddenly died. When he called to tell me, I could hear in his voice how pained and distraught he was. I wanted to be with him, to help him the way he helped me, but I had to do the show. The only thing I could think to say was what I'd heard as a kid when something terrible like that happened. My mother always took a tough line about those things, and in the arrogance of my youth that's what I gave to George.

"Oh, man, I'm really sorry about it. But, look, everybody dies. Weeping and moaning won't bring her back. You never liked her much anyway. You're going to have to get past it."

Not a very sensitive response.

After the funeral, George called again and said he was flying to Europe to be by himself for a while. He had a lot of things to think about. He'd write me soon.

Every morning I ran down to the mailbox hoping his letter would be there. For weeks it wasn't, and then one day it was. I sat down on the stairs and tore it open. He said it was all over. He couldn't get past how callous I had been and didn't want to be with me any more. I think I was too dazed to cry.

Finally I climbed back up to my apartment and tried to reach him on the telephone. It took hours to find him, but when at last I got through it didn't change anything. He was through with me. And that made a terrible kind of sense. He was the one person who cared about me, and I'd blown it by being neurotic and emotionally unreliable. I got what was coming to me. It seemed like the final failure.

I started hitting the streets with a passion.

Instead of trying to improve myself and be a better person and a better actress, I began running with my good and true low-life buddies who didn't give a shit if I was neurotic or not. Everybody was crazy. Crazy was your currency. It wasn't something you tried not to be. It was something you were proud of and worked hard to embellish. After the show, instead of trying to hang out with the uptown grownups, I would head right back to my apartment, which would be full of people who were as lost, crazy, disillusioned, and pained as I was.

I smoked a lot of dope. I made it with a lot of guys. I tried every way I could think of to act just as bad and outrageously as I could. If I was invited to a party uptown, I would go, but I would make a great point of not putting on a dress. I'd wear my fatigues, and I'd be sure to take two or three of my buddies with me, who much of the time were in no condition to be let out of their cages much less turned loose on polite society.

Of course, there was vengeance in it, childish, self-destructive vengeance. All the grownups had been telling me I was a Bad Girl, and I was saying, "You think that's a Bad Girl? Hell, I'll show you what a Bad Girl is! . . . But I show up for the play. I'm not crazy. See? See me be there? I'm there. And that's all I'm gonna do." I was in a rage because somewhere in my head it seemed to me I had begged for help and all I had gotten was a good strong read-out on the rules. And if you break the rules you don't get help. You get punishment.

Stanley Kramer got me out of *Barefoot* to make *Ship of Fools* for him. The deal was I would leave the play for fifteen weeks over the summer and then when I finished the film come back to the play for fifteen weeks beyond the run of my contract. I was delighted. I wanted out so badly it didn't matter what the movie was. I didn't even have to read the script.

Elizabeth Ashley and José Greco in Ship of Fools *(1965), Columbia.*

MARY ASTOR

Mary Astor and Clark Gable in Red Dust *(1932), MGM.*

Born Lucille Vasconcellas Langhanke on May 3, 1906 in Quincy, Illinois . . . First feature film: *John Smith* (1922) . . . Last (and 109th) film: *Hush, Hush, Sweet Charlotte* (1964) . . . Won Academy Award for Best Supporting Actress in *The Great Lie* (1941) . . . In the same year also starred in *The Maltese Falcon* . . . Author of several novels . . . Romance with playwright George S. Kaufman led to a major scandal of the 1930s.

"What Was It Like to Kiss Clark Gable?"

Not long ago—a couple of years, maybe—I was in my local bank for the usual reasons, depositing a check or cashing one, and a sharp-eyed lady teller gave me a penetrating look and said, "Will you wait a moment, Miss Astor?" And when anyone looks at me that way or addresses me sharply, the old guilt pops right out: "What have I done now?"

But she emerged from behind the grill, and touching my elbow in a confidental manner, walked me to the entrance. "Tell me," she said, her voice warm with the overtones of a cello, "tell me, what was it like to kiss Clark Gable?"

I was startled into blurting the exact truth, "Good Lord, I've forgotten!"

"Oh, you couldn't have!" Her face pinked up and behind the mask of lady bank teller I saw yesterday's bobby-soxer.

"Well, it was a long time ago," I said.

"Yes, I know that, but there was a rerun on TV last night—didn't you *see* it? I should think that would remind you."

I hadn't seen it. I think I read in the TV listing about *Red Dust* being on around one in the morning.

I couldn't just walk away from that disappointed face, so I smiled confidentially. "It's a long story," said I. Let her read into that whatever she wanted.

Happily she fluttered her fingers in farewell as I went past the guard at the door.

In the car, my poodle, Jasper, was as usual pantomiming "What took you so long?" So I told him about it. I told him the lady had stirred up some memories:

Jean Harlow and that great introductory shot of her cleaning the parrot's cage and saying, "Whatcha been eatin', cement?" And during the production, the tragedy of the death of her husband, Paul Bern, a gentle person who had filled her dressing room daily with flowers and little presents like hand-embroidered handkerchiefs. And [director] Vic Fleming saying when she returned to work sometime after the funeral, "How are we going to get a sexy performance with *that* look in her eyes?"

Now I don't claim to have total recall, but bits and pieces of what people said come echoing back, and it's simpler to put it down as a sequence.

Stage 18—or was it 16?—where the interiors were filmed; hot, no air-conditioning then, just big fans; damp from the constant use of rain machines. Vic being tough about our complaints, "So what! Everybody sweats in the tropics. Let it show, that's the way it is."

The mason jar of moths released each scene to flutter and bat their way around kerosene lamps for realism. (Of course they preferred the brighter, hotter lights offstage and Props had to try and shoo them back into the scene.)

"Hi baby!" (Everybody was "baby" to Clark, male or female.) "Rhea [Gable, wife number two] wants you to call her tonight—some damn shindig or other on Sunday—wants you and Frank [Astor's husband]. O.K.?"

"O.K. with me," I said. "Frank may have a baby to deliver—always happens when you plan something."

Vic (butting in): "Don't forget we're working on the tiger blind Saturday night. *All* night. Outside."

Clark: (Unprintable.)

We had completed several days on the back lot on the rubber plantation set. Shots of Clark carrying me through the mud, gasping from the force of the monsoon.

We had just finished the continuation on the stage inside where he carries me up the veranda steps into my bedroom, soaking wet, breathless.

Fleming said, "O.K., let's move in on a tight two."

In the script it probably read something like this: "Close shot. He is about to dump her onto the bed, but her arms still cling. There's a look. A faint, cynical smile crosses his face. This is the wife of his partner, but she's been asking for it. He kisses her, gently at first, then fiercely."

Now Clark was a husky guy and a good sport, but it was not practical for him to be a hero and hold me up for the hour or so the shot would take to line up and shoot. So first of all, a stool had to be found which was the correct height to support most of my weight. Out of sight, of course; they were cutting about elbow high.

A prop man and a carpenter shoved a stool under my bottom as Clark hoisted me up, his right arm supporting me under my knees, his left under my shoulder.

From behind the camera: "Too high! Too high! Her head's gotta be lower than his." The carpenter started in with a saw on one of the legs.

"Wait a minute! Check it in the finder, first, Mac. Let's see where you're going to be, kids."

"Make it fifty-fifty to begin with, Clark, then just before you kiss her, swing her an inch or two, so we get you full face."

We tried it.

Vic said, "Too much, too much—back just a little."

Peering through the camera lens.

Clark said, "It's uncomfortable, I'll never hit it right."

"Yes, you will. Just clear the key light on her neck, see it?"

"Why don't you move the camera?" asked Clark.

"I don't want to move the camera. It's a natural move, Clark."

"O.K., O.K.!"

Meantime the carpenter was taking a tape measurement from the bottom of my fanny to the floor, and getting the legs sawed off the stool. Lighting was being blocked in. And in those days there were lots of lights. We were hedged in by them, in fact. It was getting very, very hot.

Harold Rosson, the head cameraman said, "You can step out for a minute, Clark and Mary. Give me the stand-ins."

We cooled off and had a smoke at the big open doorway. I had my usual bad-tempered argument with the makeup man about too much makeup. He pursued me, carrying a powder puff like an extension of his arm.

Soothingly he said, "The freckles are coming through on your forehead, Mary. Let me just touch it up with a *leetle* bit of pancake."

"O.K., but *no* lipstick, Harry—you know what Mr. Fleming said. All that rain, I'd never have any makeup left."

"Looks so naked."

"That's what he wants."

Half an hour or so later, "Ready to try it!" I went back onto the set.

"Clark's on the phone. Step out of the lights a minute, Mary, but don't go 'way."

One of the prop men—in a raincoat—yelled from somewhere, "You wanna wet 'em down?"

"Just a rehearsal—no rain."

"O.K., here's Clark—let's try it now. Everybody settle down. *Quiet!*" Bells rang, doors were closed. It wasn't very quiet. And it wasn't really important until that final moment when the sound man said authoritatively, "We are rolling." Then it was quiet.

I hoisted myself up onto the stool. As Clark took his position he cracked, "Hey, you've lost weight! That's a relief!"

The head gaffer, kneeling under the camera asked Clark, "This gonna be too hot?" Indicating an eyelight.

"Gee-sus it *is* hot," Clark replied. "It'll make me squint, Gus."

"No it won't. We really need it."

"Then it's not too hot. Whadja ask for?"

The gaffer grinned and said, "Got anything in the fifth on Saturday?"

"Yeah, I gotta honey."

"Lemme in on it, huh?"

"Sure, later."

Finally Vic came in from behind the camera so that he could talk to us quietly. And we started to think about the scene. What happened previously, relationships, emotional levels, etc.

"Let's just move through it once," Vic said. "The look needn't be very long, Clark—she's very vulnerable—if she caught it she might start thinking. Mary, keep it simple. Real. Just *want* him."

He turned and disappeared behind the lights.

"Let's make one, O.K.?" he called. "Don't need a rehearsal. Just mean it, kids. Think. Feel." To the camera crew, "Can we go?"

Hal Rosson didn't like that. "No rehearsal? Well, let me check their position when they kiss. We could move in, you know."

Vic said, "I don't *want* to move in, goddamn it! I don't want to move the camera. Let the *people* do it, not the camera."

Rosson interrupted to say, "Give us a look, people."

Clark leaned his head close to me and our lips were barely touching. Loudly, he asked, "How's this?" I jumped a little and he said, "Sorry, baby."

"No good. We're just getting the top of your head."

We maneuvered fractional changes, our noses getting in the way.

"Hold it, hold it! That's fine, if you raise her just a little—too much, too much. Right there, that's beautiful, perfect."

Clark whispered to me, "That's where we were in the first place."

The assistant director checked his watch. It was getting close to lunch time. "O.K., can we go? Let's wet 'em down!"

Clark said, "Here we go again, baby," as we unwound and he helped me down from the stool.

We went over and stood just off the set in a shallow bathtub arrangement made of tarpaper and two by fours, and the man in the raincoat turned the hoses on us. After the heat of the lights, the water felt icy and we gasped and yelled as it hit us.

The assistant said, "Let's go, let's go! Let's get 'em while they're wet!" The makeup man popped in to wipe a drop from the end of my nose. "Git outta there, Harry!"

Now it was quiet. Now we were ready to go. To do what they paid us all that money for. To use our acquired ability to concentrate, to focus all our thoughts and emotions on the scene.

It was pin-drop silence. Then somebody chuckled from behind the camera. Clark's head jerked up, shocked, mad. Then the whole crew started laughing.

Vic said, "Cut it! Cut it!" and came in to us. "It's a very hot scene, kids, but not *that* hot! You're steaming!"

And we were, literally. The hot lights had vaporized the water on our clothes and skin, and it was rising in waves.

After the laughter and kidding and the joke was over, the problem remained. Everybody made a suggestion to solve it.

Then there was a question of lunch time. After lunch we were scheduled to move to another set—a "dry" scene. During lunch time I was to have my hair set and a new makeup. If we waited until after lunch to get this sequence shot, the production would be held up for at least an hour for the hairset and makeup renewal. And time was valuable.

The problem was solved. The water had to be heated. Since the source for the hoses couldn't be heated, we simply stayed in position with the lights on until we stopped steaming. To prevent our drying off the prop man kept us wet by pouring teakettles of warm water over our head and shoulders.

And the scene was shot. According to the script: "He kisses her, gently at first and then fiercely." And it was a print. "Lunch everybody. One hour! Crew back in a half hour."

The weird part of it all is that it never occurred to anyone, including Clark and me, that all this might have had a bad effect on the mood, or on our ability to play a love scene convincingly. But that's the way it was. The way it always is. The way it is today, on any movie set.

So, dear Mrs. Bobby-Soxer, in answer to your question, "What was it like to kiss Clark Gable?" I'm sure you can understand that it wasn't much of a thrill. Of course if circumstances had been different and one afternoon he had grabbed me and pulled me behind a door where nobody would see us and said in that wonderful crumbly voice, "Baby, you're for me!" and (sigh) *kissed* me, why then I might have told you what it was like. And I'm positive I would never have forgotten.

GENE AUTRY

Champion, the Wonder Horse, and Gene Autry, ca. 1946.

Born Ovon Gene Autry on September 29, 1907 in Tioga, Texas . . . Discovered by Will Rogers while working as an Oklahoma railroad telegrapher . . . Movie debut: *Old Santa Fe* (1934) . . . Lead role in serial: *The Phantom Empire* (1935) . . . *Tumblin' Tumbleweeds* (1935) . . . *Back in the Saddle* (1941) . . . Sidekicks: Smiley Burnette and Champion, the Wonder Horse . . . Close friend of Richard Nixon . . . Won platinum record for "Rudolph the Red-Nosed Reindeer."

"The Most Famous Reindeer of All"

After the war, the music industry began a massive hunt to find a new Christmas number that would appeal to the kids. "Jingle Bells" was wearing thin. In 1946 I was the grand marshal for the annual Hollywood Christmas parade, an event that combines the spirit of the season with all the trimmings the fantasy factory can muster. It had been a tradition for cowboy stars to appear. I had ridden in my first one with Tom Mix.

The parade route jangled right on down Hollywood Boulevard, leading to what the promoters called Santa Claus Lane. The curbs and sidewalks were lined with kids, thick as church bugs, craning their necks, some perched on the shoulders of their dads. Santa was in the big sleigh a few rows back and as I rode past each block I could hear the kids, already looking behind me, shouting to each other, "Here he comes, *here comes Santa Claus.*"

With that as a title, and a few scribbled notes, I went to work with Oakley Haldeman, then the manager of my music publishing company (set up after the war). In August of 1947, well ahead of the holiday season, we recorded "Here Comes Santa Claus." That winter it swept the country, as the first new Christmas song in years.

Now the rush was on. Everyone wanted to do a Christmas novelty. "Here Comes Santa Claus" was an even bigger hit in 1948, with new versions out by Bing Crosby, Doris Day, and the Andrews Sisters, among others.

The next year I was in the market for another Christmas song as a follow-up to "Santa," and I sifted through dozens of lead sheets and demo records that came through the mail, most of them unsolicited. It was decided that we would cut two records, meaning four sides. We quickly agreed on three of the songs: "He's a Chubby Little Fellow," "Santa, Santa, Santa," and one I especially liked, "If It Doesn't Snow on Christmas." But we had no prospects for the fourth side.

Meanwhile, a young New York songwriter named Johnny Marks had mailed me a home recording of a number called "Rudolph the Red-nosed Reindeer." I played it at home that night for my wife. It not only struck me as silly but I took the position that there were already too many reindeer flying around.

"Hell," I said to Ina, "how many kids can get past Dancer and Prancer right now?"

But to my surprise, Ina loved it. There was a line in the song about the other reindeer not letting Rudolph join in any reindeer games, and she was touched by it.

"Oh, Gene," she said, "it reminds me of the story of the Ugly Duckling. I think you ought to give it a try. The kids will love it."

With time running out, I reluctantly gave the demo record of "Rudolph" to Carl Cotner, and told him to work up an arrangement. "After all," I said, with a shrug, "we still have to do four songs."

The recording session did not go placidly. There was an argument with the A&R man over a point that no longer matters, if it did at the time, and everything seemed to drag. The job of the A&R man—the initials stand for artist and repertoire—is to look for songs and artists and fit the two together. In those days he also acted as the producer—if you let him. We finished the first three numbers and Carl Cotner said, "Gene, we have less than ten minutes left. What do you want to do?"

I looked at the clock. The union allowed you four numbers and three hours of recording time. I said, "It's only that 'Rudolph' thing. Throw it in and let's go."

Up to that moment I wasn't certain I'd even use it. Neither was anyone else. But "Rudolph the Red-nosed Reindeer" was an only take, which was unheard of, even in those days. This was before tape, meaning that you couldn't edit out your mistakes.

When we hit the last note the engineer's voice boomed over the studio speaker: "That's it! Wrap it up. No overtime today."

I always prided myself on the quickness with which I admit I was wrong, especially when it turned out as well as "Rudolph." America fell in love with the red-nosed reindeer. I introduced the song that winter in Madison Square Garden, at the annual rodeo we did there. We had a guy dressed in a reindeer costume with a big bulb of a nose, and when I got to the second verse of the song they threw a blue light on him and he danced. We did a class act.

"Rudolph" sold two and a half million records that first year and they are still counting. By the end of 1977, my record had passed the ten-million mark in sales. In all versions, by nearly four hundred artists world wide, in almost every language including Chinese, it had sold well over a hundred million copies. It is the second biggest seller, after Bing Crosby's recording of "White Christmas," of all time. It wasn't until years later that I learned, from Johnny Marks, that he had sent out demo records to Dinah Shore, Bing Crosby, and a half dozen other major artists, none of whom showed any interest. He added my name to the list as an afterthought. And, in the end, I recorded it to please my wife. All "Rudolph" did was move me out of the country class and onto the top pop charts for the first time.

The most famous reindeer of all is still going strong today. The song appeared on a new album by John Denver. "They all sound alike to me," Johnny Marks told an interviewer, "but I still like the Gene Autry version best."

Every Christmas since 1949, Johnny calls. We chat about the latest sales figures for "Rudolph," and he wishes Ina and me the best of holiday greetings. He talks about "Rudolph" as though he were real, and to Johnny he is, as our creations often tend to be. Somewhere in my home is a platinum record, which stands for the five-millionth copy sold. Not many singers ever got one of those. Old "Rudolph" is pretty real to me, too.

How that matched up with my cowboy image, I can't say. But as if "Rudolph" wasn't enough, we put our brand on the Easter bunny with a song called "Peter Cottontail." That one sold a million, too.

Gene Autry and Smiley Burnette in On Top of Old Smoky *(1952), Columbia.*

LAUREN BACALL

Lauren Bacall, Marcel Dalio and Humphrey Bogart in To Have and Have Not *(1945), Warner Bros.*

Borne Bette Joan Perske on September 16, 1924 in New York City . . . Fell in love with Humphrey Bogart during film debut, *To Have and Have Not* (1945) . . . Married Bogie 1945 . . . Widowed 1957 . . . Married Jason Robards, Jr. 1961 . . . Divorced 1969 . . . Favorite female movie star: Bette Davis . . . Credits include: *The Big Sleep* (1946) . . . *How to Marry a Millionaire* (1953) . . . *Murder on the Orient Express* (1974) . . . Bogart: "She's a real Joe."

"You Know How to Whistle . . ."

J ust after Christmas I was called to the studio by Howard [Hawks] and he gave me the only present I wanted from life. It was a scene from *To Have and Have Not*. He was going to make the movie—he had Bogart—it would start in February 1944, and he wanted me to test for it right after the first of the year. I read the scene—it was the "whistle" scene. I was to do the test with John Ridgely, an actor under contract to Warner Bros. whom Howard had used before and liked. I couldn't believe it. Was it really true I might actually get a part—go to work? I was on cloud ten—a very high, comfortable cloud, far from reality. He had mentioned the possibility of using me to Humphrey Bogart and it was fine with him—he'd been shown my first test, of course, and would be shown the second. Bogart was in Casablanca entertaining the troops and would not return before mid-January. Howard said he'd rehearse Ridgely and me every day, but nothing was definite—a lot depended on the quality of the test and Jack Warner's approval. It was very generous of John Ridgely to test with an unknown—he was getting good parts at Warners and was offering his time with nothing to gain but goodwill. Another example of an actor's generosity to another actor.

Not a word was to be said to anyone until a decision had been made. Charlie [Feldman, Hawks' partner] knew, of course, and when I called him, hysterical with joy, he laughed and said, "See, I told you something would happen when Howard was ready." In response to questions I dared not ask Howard (I could ask Charlie anything), he told me he thought my chance of getting the part was good—that Howard would not be making the test unless he thought so too.

I stopped everything but study from that moment on. The character's name was Marie, but the man, Harry, called her Slim. It was a good scene, very adult, sexy—much better than anything I had ever hoped for, with a great tag line about whistling. I'd do the best I could and Howard would guide me—I trusted him completely.

After that we rehearsed every day in Howard's office—Sundays, New Year's Eve, New Year's Day. John Ridgely would sit in a chair opposite Howard's desk, and I had to sit on his lap and kiss him. I was self-conscious and very nervous. Howard told me how to sit and where—made me do the whole thing while he watched. Kissing is fairly intimate—to do it with a man you hardly know and with your mentor watching and your future hanging in the balance is enough to put fear into the heart of a fairly experienced actor—to a novice like myself it was utterly terrifying. And I desperately wanted to be good for Howard—I couldn't bear to have him feel he'd signed a dud.

Howard took me to wardrobe, chose a dark skirt and jacket, put a beret on my head, and told me the test would be the next Tuesday. He drummed into my head that he wanted me to be insolent with the man—that I was being the forward one, but with humor—and told me about yet more scenes he had directed other actresses in to give me examples of the attitude he wanted. I hung on his every word, trying to figure out how the hell a girl who was totally without sexual experience could convey experience, worldliness, and knowledge of men.

On the day of the test I was my usual spastic self. Rose at 6:00 a.m., got to make-up before seven. Over-anxious. Hair and make-up done, with no alterations suggested this time. On the set before nine. Howard looked at my make-up and hair—called Sid Hickox, the cameraman, over. Howard knew how he wanted the scene photographed—*me* photographed. He wanted a mood created photographically. The molding was beginning for real. Who knew what kind of Frankenstein's monster he was creating?

I got into my costume. John Ridgely was ready, and we started to rehearse the opening of the scene on the set. We worked quietly, with Howard watching and the crew very much in the background. The day went well. It was a marvelous scene— Hickox was terrific—and Howard gave me such care. He was kind, affectionate (for him that would mean a smile, a hand on my shoulder, nothing too overt). He made me feel secure. At day's end I felt good about it. So did Howard. All that remained was to see the scene on film and get the verdict. More waiting, more anxiety.

The remainder of the week crawled by. I was on the phone to Charlie daily for news: When would Howard see the test? I drove that man crazy.

On Monday Howard saw the test and Charlie was present. Each of them called to tell me he thought it was good. Howard would show it to me on Wednesday. Another crucial Wednesday in my life! I drove to the studio with my heart in my mouth. In Howard's office I met Jules Furthman, a writer (he didn't look like a writer) who was writing the screenplay of *To Have and Have Not*. Howard took me to the projection room and as I slid low in my seat he ran my test. I was no judge then, nor would I ever be, of myself on the screen. Every fault—and there were many—was magnified, every move, look, the way I read a line—it all made me want to hide. But when the lights came on, Howard turned to me with a smile and said, "You should be pleased. Jack Warner saw this yesterday and liked it, so things look pretty good." I was afraid to believe it might happen. I'd know in a few days—if I could last that long.

Finally I got the call. Would I come to the studio for lunch with Howard? And then he told me—the part was mine. He and Charlie would have to sell half my contract to Warners or they wouldn't give me the part. But it was a great break, and to work with Bogart, a big star and good actor, could not be luckier for me. Actors of his stature were not often willing to have a complete unknown playing opposite them.

But I must say nothing yet about the part or the picture. Howard had plans. He wanted to find a good first name to go with my last one. Was there a name in my family that might be good—what was my grandmother's name? Sophie? No! He'd think of something.

He wanted me to continue working on my singing—continue reading aloud for my voice training—practice shouting, keeping my register low. He thought the picture would start at the beginning of February. After those months of waiting, it was finally happening. I was bursting with joy.

Mother was so happy for me—she knew how lucky I was. She had met Charlie several times, Howard once or twice, felt I was in good hands. She wanted to go back to New York, and as I was going to be working constantly from then on, it seemed a perfect time. She wanted to see the family. She missed her friends. Lee [Bacall's future stepfather]. So off she went, leaving me to my new life and my total preoccupation with it.

At lunch in the green room one day Howard told me he had thought of a name: Lauren. He wanted me to tell everyone when the interviews began that it was an old family name—had been my great-grandmother's. What invention! He wanted me to talk very little—be mysterious. That would be a departure. If there was one thing I had never been, it was mysterious, and if there was one thing I had never done, it was not talk. I had a lot to work on.

There was another woman's role in the picture and Warners had insisted that if they were to give me the lead, Howard had to use a girl they had under contract and had hopes for: Dolores Moran. Howard acquiesced. He was also going to use Hoagy Carmichael. Hoagy had never acted in his life, but Howard had the perfect part for him—Cricket, a piano player in the nightclub of the hotel in Cuba where most of the action took place. He'd play while I'd sing. (While I'd *what?*) They were good friends and Hoagy loved the idea. Howard had thought everything out very carefully indeed. He was tailoring everything to complement what he wanted me to be, and out of that would come his dream realized, his invention—emerging perfectly out of his mold after the proper baking time of all the right ingredients.

One day a couple of weeks before the picture was to start, I was about to walk into Howard's office when Humphrey Bogart came walking out. He said, "I just saw your test. We'll have a lot of fun together." Howard told me Bogart had truly liked the test and would be very helpful to me. . . .

The picture didn't begin until the following Tuesday. I had tested the wardrobe—hair—make-up. Sid Hickox had photographed them with Howard present, experimenting as he went, as Howard wanted me to look in the movie.

Walter Brennan had been cast in a large part, Marcel Dalio, Walter Surovy (Risë Stevens' husband), Sheldon Leonard, Dan Seymour—of course Hoagy. I went into the set the first day of shooting to see Howard and Bogart—I would not be working until the second day. Bogart's wife, Mayo Methot, was there—he introduced us. I talked to Howard, watched for a while, and went home to prepare for my own first day.

It came and I was ready for a straitjacket. Howard had planned to do a single scene that day—my first in the picture. I walked to the door of Bogart's room, said, "Anybody got a match?," leaned against the door, and Bogart threw me a small box of matches. I lit my cigarette, looking at him, said "Thanks," threw the matches back to him, and left. Well—we rehearsed it. My hand was shaking—my head was shaking—the cigarette was shaking. I was mortified. The harder I tried to stop, the more I shook. What must Howard be thinking? What must Bogart be thinking? What must the crew be thinking? Oh God, make it stop! I was in such pain.

Bogart tried to joke me out of it—he was quite aware that I was a new young thing who knew from nothing and was scared to death. Finally Howard thought we could try a take. Silence on the set. The bell rang. "Quiet—we're rolling," said the sound man. "Action," said Howard. This was for posterity, I thought—for real theatres, for real people to see. I came around the corner, said my first line, and Howard said, "Cut." He had broken the scene up—the first shot ended after the first line. The second set-up was the rest of it—then he'd move in for close-ups. By the end of the third or fourth take, I realized that one way to hold my trembling head still was to keep it down, chin low, almost to my chest, and eyes up at Bogart. It worked, and turned out to be the beginning of "The Look."

I found out very quickly that day what a terrific man Bogart was. He did everything possible to put me at ease. He was on my side. I felt safe—I still shook, but I shook less. He was not even remotely a flirt. I was, but I didn't flirt with him. There was much kidding around—our senses of humor went well together. Bogie's idea, of course, was that to make me laugh would relax me. He was right to a point, but nothing on earth would have relaxed me completely!

The crew were wonderful—fun and easy. It was a very happy atmosphere. I would often go to lunch with Howard. One day he told me he was very happy with the way I was working, but that I must remain somewhat aloof from the crew. Barbara Stanwyck, whom he thought very highly of—he'd made *Ball of Fire* with her, a terrific movie—was always fooling around with the crew, and he thought it a bad idea. "They don't like you any better for it. When you finish a scene, go back to your dressing room. Don't hang around the set—don't give it all away—save it for the scenes." He wanted me in a cocoon, only to emerge for work. Bogart could fool around to his heart's content—he was a star and a man—"though you notice he doesn't do too much of it."

One day at lunch when Howard was mesmerizing me with himself and his plans for me, he said, "Do you notice how noisy it is in here suddenly? That's because Leo Forbstein just walked in—Jews always make more noise." I felt that I was turning white, but I said nothing. I was afraid to—a side of myself I have never liked or been proud of—a side that was always there. Howard didn't dwell on it ever, but clearly he had very definite ideas about Jews—none too favorable, though he did business with them. They paid him—they were good for that. I would have to tell him about myself eventually or he'd find out through someone else. When the time came, what would happen would happen, but I had no intention of pushing it.

Howard started to line up special interviews for me. Nothing big would be released until just before the picture, and everything would be chosen with the greatest care. *Life, Look,* Kyle Crichton for *Collier's, Pic, Saturday Evening Post.* Only very special fan magazines. Newspapers. I probably had more concentrated coverage than any beginning young actress had ever had—due to Hawks, not me.

Hoagy Carmichael had written a song called "Baltimore Oriole." Howard was going to use it as my theme music in the movie—every time I appeared on screen there were to be strains of that song. He thought it would be marvelous if I could be always identified with it—appear on Bing Crosby's or Bob Hope's radio show, have the melody played, have me sing it, finally have me known as the "Baltimore Oriole." What a fantastic fantasy life Howard must have had! His was a glamorous, mysterious, tantalizing vision—but it wasn't me.

On days I didn't have lunch with Howard, I would eat with another actor or the publicity man or have a sandwich in my room or in the music department during a voice lesson. I could not sit at a table alone. Bogie used to lunch at the Lakeside Golf Club, which was directly across the road from the studio.

One afternoon I walked into Howard's bungalow and found a small, gray-haired, mustached, and attractive man stretched out on the couch with a book in his hand and a pipe in his mouth. That man was William Faulkner. He was contributing to the screenplay. Howard loved Faulkner—they had known each other a long time, had hunted together. Faulkner never had much money and Howard would always hire him for a movie when he could. He seldom came to the set—he was very shy—he liked it better in Howard's office. . . .

I don't know how it happened—it was almost imperceptible. It was about three weeks into the picture—the end of the day—I had one more shot, was sitting at the dressing table in the portable dressing room combing my hair. Bogie came in to bid me good night. He was standing behind me—we were joking as usual—when suddenly he leaned over, put his hand under my chin, and kissed me. It was impulsive—he was a bit shy—no lunging wolf tactics. He took a worn package of matches out of his pocket and asked me to put my phone number on the back. I did. I don't know why I did, except it was kind of part of our game. Bogie was meticulous about not being too personal, was known for never fooling around with women at work or anywhere else. He was not that kind of man, and also he was married to a woman who was a notorious drinker and fighter. A tough lady who would hit you with an ashtray, lamp, anything, as soon as not.

I analyzed nothing then—I was much too happy—I was having the time of my life. All that mattered to me was getting to the studio and working—my hours of sleep just got in the way! From the start of the movie, as Bogie and I got to know each other better—as the joking got more so—as we had more fun together—so the scenes changed little by little, our relationship strengthened on screen and involved us without our even knowing it. *I* certainly didn't know it. Gradually my focus began to shift away from Howard, more toward Bogie. Oh, I still paid full attention to Howard, but I think I depended more on Bogie. The construction of the scenes made that easy. I'm sure Howard became aware fairly early on that there was something between us and used it in the film.

At the end of the day of the phone number, I went home as usual to my routine: after eating something, I looked at my lines for the next day and got into bed. Around eleven o'clock the phone rang. It was Bogie. He'd had a few drinks, was away from his house, just wanted to see how I was. He called me Slim—I called him Steve, as in the movie. We joked back and forth—he finally said good night, he'd see me on the set. That was all, but from that moment on our relationship changed. He invited me to lunch at Lakeside a few times—or we'd sit in my dressing room or his with the door open, finding out more about one another. If he had a chess game going on the set—he was a first-rate chess player—I'd stand and watch, stand close to him. Physical proximity became more and more important. But still we joked.

Hedda Hopper came on the set one day and said, "Better be careful. You might have a lamp dropped on you one day." There was a column squib in the *Hollywood Reporter*: "You can have your B&B at lunch any day at Lakeside."

Bogie took to calling me more often. He had two friends named Pat and Zelma O'Moore. She had sung "Button Up Your Overcoat" in a Broadway show, but had since retired. Pat O'Moore was an Irish actor whom Bogie had befriended—he worked in Bogie's films and others when there was a part. They had a small boat which they kept in Newport in the slip next to Bogie's. They lived in a small trailer camp in town. Bogie took me there one night and we all had dinner together, but he couldn't do that often. Other nights he'd call very late—sometimes one or two in the morning—and come over to my apartment. It was an unusual role for Bogie. He was not by instinct or practice a cheat or a liar. He told me about his marriage—how he had more or less fallen into it. He'd been married twice before. When he was in his twenties, he'd been married to a famous Broadway actress, Helen Menken. Always his wives had been actresses—always wanting to continue their careers, always putting that first.

After Helen, he married an actress called Mary Philips. When they'd been married for seven or eight years he accepted an offer to come to California, and he wanted her to come with him. He didn't believe in separations and he also didn't believe in following women around. But she insisted on following her career on the stage and he said, "Okay, but don't stay away too long." She did. He met Mayo—fell into something with her (drink and bed, I should think), warned Mary to come out, then went to Chicago, where she was in a play with Roland Young. He got there, found that they were having an affair, and that was the end of that marriage. He felt he had to marry Mayo—he was a marrying man, she expected it, it was the gentlemanly thing to do, so he did it. And it got worse and worse. They were known as the Battling Bogarts—almost every evening wound up with her throwing something at Bogie, trying to hit him and succeeding most of the time. She'd stabbed him in the back with a knife on one occasion and he had the scar to prove it. He said he had to drink—it was the only way he could live with her. She was jealous—always accused him of having affairs with his leading ladies—always knocked him as an actor, making sarcastic references about the "big star." She'd sung "More Than You Know" in a Vincent Youmans musical, had been successful and was a good actress—but drink took over and the minute there was a third person present, she'd start on Bogie. He wasn't crying the blues to me—he accepted it. He didn't like it, but that's the way it was and he couldn't do anything about it.

I said nothing to anyone about seeing Bogie outside the studio. But anyone with half an eye could see that there was more between us than the scenes we played. I'd listen for his arrival in make-up in the morning. He'd get there about 8:30—he wore no make-up, just had his hair blacked in a bit in front where it was getting thin, but he'd come to see me having my hair combed out. Sometimes we'd go to the set together. I'd always leave my dressing-room door open so as not to miss him if he passed by. There was never enough time for me to be with him. In the picture I wore a black satin dress with a bare midriff that was held together with a black plastic ring. One day I cut out a picture of Bogie and fitted it into the ring—walked over to him casually on the set until he noticed it and laughed. Our jokes were total corn: "What did the ceiling say to the wall?" "Hold me up, I'm plastered." . . . "Do your eyes bother you?" "No." "They bother me." . . . And I'd make my gorilla face, which consisted of putting my tongue under my upper lip and dropping my jaw. All silly but marvelous. And he taught me constantly in scenes. We had one scene in which I had been teasing him—he was to take me out the door because he wanted to have a bath—stop and kiss me before being interrupted. He told Howard he'd seen the Lunts do something in a play scene once which he felt would work for us. After the kiss I was to run the back of my hand up the side of his face, which needed a shave, then give him a short, quick slap. It was a most suggestive and intimate bit of business. Much more so than writhing around on the floor would have been. And in rehearsals of other scenes he'd sometimes add something—a word or a bit of business—that would throw me. He'd say, "Just to make sure you're listening." He taught me to stay on my toes at all times.

By now Howard of course knew something was going on and he didn't like it. As we neared the end of the picture, he summoned me out to his house one night. I was petrified. Just he and his wife, Slim, were there. He sat me down and began. "When you started to work you were marvelous—paying attention, working hard. I thought, 'This girl is really something.' Then you started fooling around with Bogart. For one thing, it means nothing to him—this sort of thing happens all the time, he's not serious about you. When the picture's over, he'll forget all about it—that's the last you'll ever see of him. You're throwing away a chance anyone would give their right arm for. I'm not going to put up with it. I tell you I'll just send you to Monogram [the

studio that made the lowest form of pictures at that time]. I'll wash my hands of you."
Of course I burst into tears—tried to control myself, which only made it worse. Slim
said, "But what do you do, Howard, if you're stuck on a guy? How do you handle it?"
She was trying to help me. Howard would have none of it. "You just play the scenes,
do your work. You can laugh and have a good time, but just remember that when the
picture's over, *it* will be over." I told him I didn't want to disappoint him, I was trying
hard, I loved the work. Bogie had been wonderful to me and we had so much fun
together, but I'd try to be better—"Honestly, Howard."

I was so upset when I left—in such a state. I was sure he'd send me to
Monogram—that my career was over before it had begun. And didn't Bogie mean
anything he had ever said to me—was it all just for the picture—just empty talk—
did he really not care about me? I cried all night. The next morning I was a mess—
eyes all puffy and red. I had to put ice on my face at 6:00 a.m. and again when I got
to the studio—I didn't want anyone to see that I'd been crying. I was determined to
behave differently. Howard had almost convinced me. After all, Bogie was a married
man, he had nothing to lose by flirting with me, it was all frivolous. Only Bogie was
not a frivolous man—I knew he wasn't—and he wasn't cheap. I was confused,
terribly upset, and scared. Bogie greeted me as usual, only I was different and tried
not to be. But he knew instantly. "What's wrong?" "Nothing," said I. "C'mon—has
Howard been talking to you?" I nodded—"I'll tell you later."

Later that day when it would be least obtrusive I went into Bogie's dressing room
and told him what Howard had said to me. He stroked my hair and my face and said,
"No, Baby, he won't send you to Monogram—don't you worry, you're too valuable to
him. He just can't stand to see your attention diverted from him, that's all—he's
jealous. And I do mean what I say to you. We just must be very careful—I don't want
you to be hurt. And if Madam [his name for Mayo] finds out, you *could* be hurt, and I
couldn't stand that. But don't worry about Howard—his nose is out of joint, that's
all." And of course he was right—Howard was losing control and he didn't like that.
And I owed him a great deal—he'd done everything for me, and though I was afraid
of him, I did like him and respect him. But I'd have to be more careful of my
demeanor.

A few days after that we were to shoot me singing "How Little We Know." That was
to be a full day of me, Hoagy, a lot of extras, and no Bogie. I had prerecorded the
song and was to sing the playback, which is not easy, particularly for a novice.
Howard was satisfied with the recording, though he thought one or two notes might
have to be dubbed later on. Bogie and I planned to have dinner together that night,
with me cooking. The menu would be hamburgers, baked potato, and a salad. A
cook I wasn't. He called me on the set in the afternoon—he'd call me at home later to
make sure I'd returned.

At the end of that long day, Howard put his arm around me and said, "You did a
really good day's work, Betty, I'm proud of you." That's the only true compliment he

ever paid me. It was hard for him. I was pleased that he was satisfied—I thanked him—but he didn't know who I was on my way to as I left the studio.

How do you know when you're in love? I had no basis for comparison. Every emotional involvement I'd had before—like Kirk [Douglas]—I'd thought was love, but it wasn't. I was almost sure I loved Bogie—and more than that, that he was in love with me. We shared so much—understood so much about each other.

We started to drive home together, leaving the studio with Bogie in the lead in his car, me following in mine. We drove over Highland Avenue, turned right on Hollywood Boulevard to Franklin, then another right onto Selma Avenue, a small street that was curved and very residential—almost no traffic would pass through.

We'd pull over to the side and he'd come over to my car. There we would sit, holding hands, looking into each other's eyes, saying all the things we couldn't say at the studio. We'd sit on our street for fifteen or twenty minutes, dreading the moment of parting, then he'd get into his car and off we'd go, making the turn at Laurel Canyon Boulevard to Sunset Boulevard, continuing on until we reached Horn Avenue, where Bogie lived. As he made the turn, he'd wave his hand out the window—I'd do the same and go on to Beverly Hills. It was romantic—it was fun—it was exciting—it was all-encompassing. . . .

INGRID BERGMAN

Claude Rains (second from left), Paul Henreid, Humphrey Bogart and Ingrid Bergman in Casablanca *(1942), Warner Bros.–First National.*

**Born on August 29, 1915 in Stockholm, Sweden . . . Orphaned in infancy
. . . Married Peter Lindstrom, a dentist, in 1937 . . . Affair with Roberto Rossellini in 1949 put her career on the skids . . . Sent agent a telegram: "Sue anyone who says I'm pregnant" . . . Followed by: "Don't sue anyone" . . . Denounced in U.S. Senate as "Hollywood's apostle of degradation" and "free-love cultist"
. . . Married Rossellini 1950 . . . First American movie: *Intermezzo*
(1939) . . . *Casablanca* (1943) . . . *For Whom the Bell Tolls* (1943) . . . *Gaslight*
(1944) . . . *Notorious* (1946) . . . Won three Academy Awards . . . Disliked make-up . . . Loved to chew Black-Jack gum . . . "Hemingway said I was the greatest actress in the world."**

Casablanca's Other Ending

I n *Casablanca* I fell right back to where I'd come from. David O. Selznick liked it because at last I was going to wear lovely gowns and clothes and look pretty. Oh, it was so difficult in Hollywood to play against what Hollywood made you. As I have said, they typecast everyone. All the actors—Gary Cooper, James Stewart, Cary Grant, Humphrey Bogart—they were always playing themselves. But I came from Sweden where acting meant the certainty of change. You played old people, young people, nasty people, good people, but you rarely played what *you* looked like or what you were. You got inside somebody else's skin.

Now Michael Curtiz, the Hungarian director of *Casablanca* and a very experienced and talented director, picked up the same old theme: "Ingrid, you're so wrong, that's not what they do in America. America is type-casting. The audience wants it at the box office. They pay their money to see Gary Cooper being Gary Cooper, not the hunchback of Notre Dame. So you are going to ruin your career by trying to change and do different things. From now on you should simply be Ingrid Bergman; do the same, play the same sort of role all the time, and you develop this one attractive side that the audience will love."

I said, "No, I'm not going to do that. I'm going to change. I'm going to change as much as I can."

I liked Michael Curtiz. He was a good director but *Casablanca* started off disastrously and it was not his fault at all. From the very start Hal Wallis, the producer, was arguing with the writers, the Epstein brothers and Howard Koch, and every lunchtime Mike Curtiz argued with Hal Wallis. There had to be all sorts of changes in the script. So every day we were shooting off the cuff: every day they were handing out the dialogue and we were trying to make some sense of it. No one knew where the picture was going and no one knew how it was going to end, which didn't help any of us with our characterizations. Every morning we said, "Well, who are we? What are we doing here?" And Michael Curtiz would say, "We're not quite sure, but let's get through this scene today and we'll let you know tomorrow."

It was ridiculous. Just awful. Michael Curtiz didn't know what he was doing because he didn't know the story either. Humphrey Bogart was mad because he didn't know what was going on, so he retired to his trailer.

And all the time I wanted to know who I was supposed to be in love with, Paul Henreid or Humphrey Bogart?

"We don't know yet—just play it well . . . in-between."

I didn't dare to look at Humphrey Bogart with love because then I had to look at Paul Henreid with something that was not love.

They were going to shoot two endings because they couldn't work out whether I should fly off by airplane with my husband or stay with Humphrey Bogart. So the first ending we shot was that I say good-bye to Humphrey Bogart and fly off with Paul Henreid. Then if you remember, Claude Rains and Bogie walk off into the fog, saying that famous phrase, "Louis, I think this is the beginning of a beautiful friendship." And everybody said, "Hold it! That's it! We don't have to shoot the other ending. That's just perfect, a wonderful closing line."

But they hadn't known it was the closing line until they heard it. And they certainly didn't know it was going to turn out to be a classic and win an Oscar.

They were a wonderful group of actors, but because of the difficulties of the script we'd all been a bit on edge and I'd hardly got to know Humphrey Bogart at all. Oh, I'd kissed him, but I didn't know him.

He was polite naturally, but I always felt there was a distance; he was behind a wall. I was intimidated by him. *The Maltese Falcon* was playing in Hollywood at the time and I used to go and see it quite often during the shooting of *Casablanca*, because I felt I got to know him a little better through that picture.

Paul Henreid, Ingrid Bergman and Humphrey Bogart in Casablanca.

DIRK BOGARDE

Dirk Bogarde in The Servant *(1963), British.*

Born Derek Van Den Bogaerde on March 28, 1920 in London . . . Son of a Dutch art editor . . . Film Debut: extra in *Come On George* (1939) . . . Published poetry in literary magazines . . . Played a suspected homosexual in *Victim* (1961) . . . Other credits include: *Tale of Two Cities* (1958) . . . *The Servant* (1963) . . . *Darling* (1965) . . . *The Damned* (1970) . . . *Death in Venice* (1971) . . . *The Night Porter* (1974).

A Date With Judy Garland

J udy had been in a cinematic limbo, so to speak, since *A Star Is Born* which she made in 1954 with George Cukor. Apart from a small role in *Judgement at Nuremberg*, and the recent film with [Stanley] Kramer, she had not faced a camera for seven years. Now, with her shining new life, the stresses and strains were once more appearing like cracks in a patched-up wall. She was finding life difficult to handle and telephoned three or four times a week from New York, always about four or five in the morning my time. She couldn't sleep, and feared the dark; she wanted, and often got, constant reassurance, although I can't believe I ever made a great deal of sense blurred with sleep as I was. Sometimes she was on form and happy, but mostly she was depressed, worried, or planning wild All-Star-Concerts for the Kennedys, whom she much admired, or earthquake victims in Peru or Persia; these problems were harder to deal with at four in the morning.

"What time is it with you?" her voice careful, worried.

"Five a.m., you beastly woman."

"Oh! I waked you!"

"Doesn't matter . . . I have to get up soon anyway, it's a Studio day."

"Have you ever heard about a script called *The Lonely Stage?*"

"No . . . why?"

"Well there is one and they want me to do it; in London."

"I heard rumours, didn't know the title. So?"

"It stinks."

"Well, say 'no' then."

"But it's a good idea. The idea is good. The dialogue is just yuccky."

"What's it about if it's so good?"

There was a pause, she laughed ruefully.

"This big, big Star goes to London to do a concert at the Palladium and finds the man who got away . . . It's about me; I guess someone has read my lyrics."

"Well, get a new writer and see how you feel then."

"Would you do it with me?"

"Play the one who got away?"

"Sure."

"Of course I would. You know that. But I know they want an American star."

"Why for chrissakes! He's supposed to be British."

"Box Office."

"Don't give me that. I'll do it if you say yes. Yes?"

"Yes."

There was a pause again, crackle noises: "I love you very much," she said. And hung up.

She got to work pretty quickly, for a very few days later I was asked if I would care to do a film with Miss Garland. Although there was no script ready yet, would I take it on trust? I agreed, providing that it did not interfere with a film I was discussing with [director Basil] Dearden for July, *The Mind Benders*. The spokesman assured me warmly that the Garland film would commence in early May and that I would be well finished by June, since my role was not long. Miss Garland was the star. I would have plenty of time. Little did he know.

We all embarked, unwittingly, on a brakeless roller-coaster which, reaching its final peak, roared down ricketing and racketing, exploding us all into smithereens at the end.

Although the script, when it arrived finally, was a professional workmanlike job, well constructed and not quite as bad as Judy had led me to believe, I knew from her present state of depression and indecision (for she now telephoned me nightly, filled with doubts and fears and an unreasoning dislike of her part as written) that something would have to be done quickly or we would all be in for a very bumpy ride. I implored the producers not to show it to her when she arrived in England.

"But we have made a number of changes according to her wishes."

"If you show her that she'll turn right around and go back to the States. I know Judy, and I know her present mood."

"Well, what do we do? This is the script she agreed."

"I think she agreed only the story line. If you let me have a day or two I could try and re-write some of the stuff she has to say; but don't show it to her until I have talked with her."

They agreed, worriedly. Her present mood was frantic. Panicked by marital trouble in New York, she was in terror that the children, Liza, Lorna and Joe, would be forcibly moved from her, so she shoved them on to a flight in such haste that Liza arrived in London in slacks and a shirt with a bundle of odd garments clutched in her arms and Judy immediately sought to have them all made wards of the British Court. It was not the calmest way to start a very difficult assignment. To compound the problems which she had to face she was hurried to a foul little house in Sunningdale which the Company had rented for her for the duration of the film, adjacent to the golf course, because they thought she liked to play golf. This was a grave error and only served to make her feel that they were amateur idiots, since her affection for golf at a time like this was nil to say the least.

"Who do they think they've hired? Babe Zaharias?"

She eventually found a house in Hyde Park Gardens and moved in just before we started to work. She was tired, frightened, and quite alone. Now at the top of her career again, after years in a limbo of illness and despair, and box office failure, she was unsure and unequipped to handle things for herself; [theatrical agent Dennis] van Thal willingly took over her domestic problems which were many, while I tried to assist her with the professional ones. The script was the first. Someone, idiotically, had already shown it to her and it caused immense distress. She was trusting no one from now on in. The storm was in the wind.

The first day at the Studio, make-up tests only, was not so bad. The crew, handpicked for such an august Star, were delighted and proud to be working with her. She was charming, funny, easy, and almost gay. It all seemed, on the surface, as if things would settle down. In her dressing room, later, massed with flowers and crates of Blue Nun, cards of good wishes and boxes of Bendicks chocolates, she shut the door firmly and announced that she was leaving . . . immediately . . . and slammed into the bathroom.

"You can't leave. You have a contract, darling. We're in."

"I'm not in . . . it won't be the first contract I've broken. I can't play this crap. They promised changes: they failed."

She was sitting on the closed lavatory seat, always her place of refuge in moments of shattering panic, a glass of Blue Nun clinking in her hands, her face pale, drawn, body shaking, looking small, ill and hopeless. For an hour I sat on the edge of the bath and reasoned with her; she wouldn't budge. Just shook her head slowly at every suggestion, at every gentle argument I brought forward. Finally, in desperation, I read her the first scene which we were to play and which I had entirely re-written. She stopped her head-shaking and sat listening; then reached out and took the pages and started to read them aloud with me. She laughed a couple of times, put down the Blue Nun; we went over it two or three times . . . she was suddenly, immediately, worryingly, happy.

"Hey! It's good . . . did you do all this?"

"Yes."

"It's really funny . . . don't you think Atlantic City would be funnier than Wilmette? They're both *awful*, but Atlantic City . . . I can make that funny . . . let's do it again. With Atlantic City instead."

We started shooting a day later at the Palladium. She was happy, in marvellous voice, nervous, excited; it was her first big number in the film, "Hello, Blue Bird". I had given her a blue bird brooch in sapphires; she was in her familiar dressing room, surrounded by an adoring company of Make-Up and Hair people; she was literally, at eight in the morning, bubbling with pleasure. She held the brooch tightly in a small closed fist.

"We'll be a new team, you and I. Won't it be great!" She was sparkling.

"Gaynor and Farrell!"

"MacDonald and Eddy!"

"I don't sing . . ."

"The Lunts!"

We held each other laughing, promising each other our futures.

At twelve-thirty she was on her way to hospital in an urgently clanging ambulance. We had started as we had, obviously, intended to go on.

"But why? Why, darling? What did you do it for . . . it was such a good beginning."

"It was a lousy beginning." Unrepentant, unashamed, pale, two days later.

"What went wrong? Was it me? Something I did?"

"No . . ." She twisted a spit-curl into place in the mirror and stuck it to her cheek. "Something *he* didn't do."

"Who?"

"Neame, our so darling director. He didn't even say 'thank you' when I finished the number, he didn't say anything. Just 'Marvellous, Judy, darling'." She mocked a very British accent. " 'Marvellous, Judy darling'. Christ!"

"That's not so. He was thrilled by what you did, we all were, everyone was, you must know that, you must have felt it?"

"I don't 'feel' things. I need to be told; OK? Confidence. Who the hell does he think I am, Dorothy Adorable? I'm a goddamned star . . . I need help."

"Darling, you'll have to get used to the way we all work here. It's not the same as the States, we don't use the exaggerations, great, greatest, the best. It's all a bit cooler. If you don't understand that you'll get hurt; we don't get hysterical very often."

She shrugged and pulled on a shoe angrily. "That damned British understatement, the stiff upper lip . . . well, it won't do for Frances Gumm."

"Who the hell's that?"

For a moment she looked at me in the mirror with a face of white stone. Then it cracked, and she started to smile a little, she reached out her hand and took mine. Not facing me directly. Ashamed suddenly, aware of bad behaviour. In the wrong. I pressed her hand hard. She lowered her head.

"It's me. Frances Ethel. Isn't it awful?"

"Well, Frances Ethel, just remember that Neame had one hell of a day . . . he had to clear the Palladium by four-thirty for the evening show there . . . he was under pressure and first days shooting are frightening for everyone."

She withdrew her hand gently. "Just you tell Neame he'd better watch out for me. *I* get scared, he think he's the only one? I need help and trust. I don't trust him. I want him off the production."

She didn't have him off; but she never trusted him again and the first serious crack was opened, never to be more than very temporarily repaired. It was a very uncomfortable situation for Ronnie Neame, and he behaved impeccably with the patience and care of a saint. He was helpful, enthusiastic, and agreeable to all the re-writes I did for our scenes together. He did everything possible to make her happy and secure and lavished her with praise, justified always, but she never quite bent towards him again, even though after our first few scenes together she was patently thrilled by her work and was giving a quite superb performance. For a little time we settled down; writing every evening and every week-end. Sometimes she came down to Nore [Bogarde's home] and made brilliant suggestions, funny, real, moving, and although she never wrote a word herself, she sat in my office all the time, smoking, sleeping, keeping close, awaiting each page as it came off the machine, reading it aloud, rejecting some words or phrases, offering better alternatives. It was a marvellous, happy combination. We honed and polished and rehearsed continually, avidly, so that when we eventually got to the take it was smooth and precise, spinning along on ball bearings. Spirits everywhere rose; her work was proving to be the best she had ever done, and she knew it.

"I'm good, aren't I?" She was humble, happy, sure.

"Gooder than you've ever been."

"You didn't see *A Star Is Born* . . . not really, they hacked it to bits, George Cukor and I have never ever seen it . . . do you know that? They mutilated it. Do you remember the scene I did in the dressing room with [Charles] Bickford, about a ten-minute monologue? Remember? Well . . . could you write me something like that for the end of this thing? A long scene, all about . . . all about . . ." she fished slowly in the air seeking words, "all about what it means to be Jenny Bowman." Her name in the film.

"I'm not sure that I know all about what it means to be Jenny Bowman."

"Sure you do . . . she's me. You know that, don't you? She's really me. And you know me all right, Buster. That line you wrote that you say to the kid . . . remember? 'Jenny gives more love than anyone but takes more love than anyone can possibly give.' Remember that?" she chuckled happily, wickedly. "I reckon you know; and I'll always help you out with a real Garland-line when you get stuck. I'm full of goodies!"

But the good times grew fewer and fewer as Judy got later and later, or sometimes didn't even arrive at all for work. We used to sit about from eight-thirty, in dull, depressed heaps; the crew played cards and drank endless cups of tea; the guts were slipping out of the production. We were losing so many work days that I realised that the film I wanted so much to make with Dearden, and to which I had wholeheartedly committed myself, was in jeopardy. I would never, at this rate, make the Start Date and they would probably have to recast.

"Judy . . . you know I have to start another film in July?"

"So?"

"Well with all these delays . . ."

"Don't you start blaming me! I've been sick . . ."

"I know, but just remember that I only have seven weeks' work on this . . . you have ten, if I can't finish my part in that time I'll just have to leave."

"You can't."

"I have a contract with the other people. Signed."

"Break it."

"I don't want to. I want to do the film, desperately."

She turned from the mirror, we always seemed to have these discussions in her portable dressing room on the set, and looked me straight in the eye.

"When you leave, lover, I leave. Finish. Right?"

"But you can't . . . for God's sake . . ."

"Don't tell me what I can't do! Everyone tells me what I can and can't do . . . I do what I want to do . . . and I don't want to shoot one bloody frame on this stinking mess after you have gone. When you leave for your oh-so-marvellous movie, I leave on the first flight for L.A. . . . don't you forget it!"

"I've always promised I'd never ever lie to you, right?"

"Right."

"But I'm leaving at the end of my seven weeks."

"Then we won't have a movie, will we?" She pulled off her ear-rings slowly and put each one carefully on the tray before her.

"You won't have a movie. This is your movie, no one else's. We've got the big scene to do; you want to do it, you know that, so far this is the best work you have ever done, better perhaps than *Star*. It's your time, your career; I promise you I'll never fail you, but you must promise me to not fail yourself . . . please? Darling, be a good girl and come back again . . . please."

"Don't you good girl me, for godssake! They hate me out there. Have you seen those loving Cockney faces full of 'good girl'; they hate me. I feel the hate."

"They don't, they don't; they're working for you all the way . . . you know that."

She swivelled round on her chair and took my hands suddenly. "You really, really want to do this damned movie of yours?"

"I do."

"What's it about?"

"Deprivation of the senses."

"In English?"

"Brainwashing. It's a new, terrible weapon."

"Someone used it on me."

"They used it on the American troops in Korea. No one knows much about it yet."

"I do, all about it. I invented it; Louis B. Mayer invented it. My loving damn agents 'Frick' and 'Frack' invented it. There is nothing I don't know about it, do you hear? Nothing I don't know about your terrible new weapon. *I've* been so brainwashed I'm Persil White all through." She burst into tears and I held her very tightly. Above her shoulder I saw my own face reflect in the mirror; it was Persil White as well.

At Canterbury; a one-day location at the cathedral started well. She met the Red Dean and made him laugh, posed for the Press. At the lunch break an ashen faced wardrobe-mistress hurried from her caravan, her costume bundled in one arm, shoes in the other. "She's not working any more; you never heard such language." Grim-faced producers, the director, a covey of assistants; one or two blazered choir-boys hoping for an autograph. Despair wafting like smoke from a dying bonfire.

In her caravan, curtains drawn, light filtered, a litter of clothes, papers, a fallen vase of carnations, water dripping on the cheap linoleum. Judy hunched at her dressing table in a green silk kimono; hair a ruin, make-up wiped roughly off a white, anguished face. In front of her a tin tray with a wrecked salmon mayonnaise.

"What's wrong, pussy cat?"

"Get out . . . get right out."

"You were so happy this morning."

"Now I'm not."

"My fault?"

"You know damned well . . ."

"I don't . . . what is it?"

"I wanted you to stay tonight in Folkestone . . . I booked you a room; Liza, Lorna, Joey, all of us together. Just one night, one happy, lovely night . . ."

"I can't, darling, I told you. I have to get back by eight."

"You told me. The only thing I have ever asked of you." She started to weep silently. "Tonight, there's a full moon, did you know? A full moon, we could have all gone along the beach together, along the shore, in the moonlight, peaceful, calm, I need calm. The kids want to go. I want to go. Just one time and you refuse."

"I told you why."

"They were all looking forward to it . . ." she suddenly took her knife from the tray and stabbed me in the arm. I grabbed her wrist and we fell, in a sprawling heap together among the sodden carnations and the tumbled tray of salmon mayonnaise. "I hate you! I hate you!" She struggled and heaved, the knife still tight in her fist, I twisted her wrist and she cried out suddenly. Somewhere the knife clattered. I was across her, heavy; she fought for breath.

"Say you hate me . . . say you hate me."

"I don't." I still held her twisted wrist firmly. She moved under me, her free hand scrabbling in the debris. A fork suddenly thrust against my cheek, under the right eye.

She stared up in the gloom. "This can do as much damage. Say you hate me, I know you hate me, they all do, hate me . . ."

Gently I leant down and kissed her face; she crumpled, sobbing uncontrollably, her arms around me, clutching like a drowning child. I helped her up and we stood in the ruins of her lunch and the water from the fallen flowers, standing together until the pain had eased, then I gently put her from me, smoothing her straggling hair, wiping her nose with my finger.

"You are all snotty . . . disgusting."

She half laughed, pushed the hair from her face, her eyes wide, streaming, filled with pain.

"How long will it take to make you presentable; an hour?" She wiped her mouth with the back of a hand, shrugged the kimono over her shoulders. "About; wheel them in."

Outside the sun was so brilliant that I could just see the anxious huddle, a few discreet paces from the caravan; Neame was twisting and untwisting a white plastic spoon.

"She'll work," I said. I suddenly realised that I was still wearing my hat, that there was a splatter of mayonnaise on my tie. Wisely they stood aside and no one followed me, blindly I walked into a tree; and knocked myself out.

We had one week, one final week which she did for me, of complete, unforgettable magic. She was on time every day, her work was brilliant, we tore into the scenes and she blasted off the screen. My final day was our big scene. We started together rehearsing in her dressing room at eight-thirty. No one came near us. She had wanted to play it sitting down, not to move; I wrote it so that she had sprained an ankle and was carted, drunk, to St George's Hospital. She sat in a chair, I knelt at her feet. We rehearsed for six hours, with half an hour for a sandwich, in the cramped little caravan. At four-thirty we went on to the floor and shot the entire scene just once. It lasted eight minutes and was one of the most perfect moments of supreme screen-acting I have ever witnessed. I shall never see its like again. She never put a foot wrong, not an effect was missed, the overlaps, the stumbling, the range, above all the brilliance of her range. The range was amazing; from black farce right through to black tragedy, a cadenza of pain and suffering, of bald, unvarnished truth. It had taken us three days to write; she passed every line as I set it down, "warts," she said, "and all"; it took six hours to rehearse, eight minutes to shoot, and when it was over one of the crew walking across from the stage was stopped by one of his fellows.

"What," said the man, "happened on your stage today?"

"A miracle," said Bob.

A miracle it was indeed; in that last week of June, we shot twenty minutes of screen time and, more or less, finished off the main bulk of our work together. Judy was quite aware of what she was doing. She gave me the week in order that I could go off to do my "damned movie" as she called it, knowing full well that she would then be on her own to finish off the film which she so detested. The following week only a few seconds were shot, and she behaved unkindly and uncontrolledly, falling, in one instance, in a bathroom, cracking her head badly, necessitating, yet again, hospital treatment. Once more she tried to fire the patient, unhappy Neame, and finally, on Black Friday the 13th of July she walked off the film and that was that. I still had one or two small pick-up shots to do with her, and was forced to do them with a double, wigged, and dressed in her clothes. The miracle, though gigantic, was finally over. With my completion of the seven weeks' work, in my acceptance of the film with Dearden to which I had been fully committed, I could no longer stay at her side and she felt completely rejected. In a hostile atmosphere, untrusting and by now quite unloved, she was unable to contain her terror and her unhappiness; her private life lay about her like a pillaged room, there were court cases, and a bitter struggle to retain her children whom she adored above all things, but I could no longer heed the urgent summonses by telephone, nor could I make her understand that my duty, if one dared use such a word, now lay with Dearden and a new, extremely involving film.

"You are walking away from me," she cried in anguish, "you are walking away, like they all do . . . walking away backwards, smiling."

Useless to try to explain; there was no way now that I knew to help her. All I did know was that being with her, working with her, loving her as I did, had made me the most privileged of men.

LOUISE BROOKS

Louise Brooks in Diary of a Lost Girl *(1930), German.*

Born November 14, 1906 in Cherryvale, Kansas . . . Started dancing professionally at 15 . . . Appearances in Ziegfield Follies led to movie career in 1925 . . . Sporting dramatically bobbed hair, played in *American Venus* (1926) and *Rolled Stockings* (1927) . . . In 1928 starred in *A Girl in Every Port* and *Beggars of Life* . . . Major success in Germany as nymphomaniac Lulu in G. W. Pabst's classic, *Pandora's Box* (1929) . . . Quit films in 1931 . . . Comeback in 1936 with roles in B Westerns . . . *Empty Saddles* (1936) . . . *Overland Stage Raiders* (1938) . . . Worked as a salesgirl in the 1940s . . . A recluse since late 1940s, she wrote more acutely about film than any other star . . . Died 1985.

Humphrey and Bogey

Humphrey Bogart spent the last twenty-one years of his life laboriously converting the established character of a middle-aged man from that of a conventional, well-bred theatre actor named Humphrey to one that complemented his film roles—a rebellious tough known as Bogey. In the years since his death, in 1957, biographers catering to the Bogey Cult have transformed him into a cinematic saint—St. Bogart—in whom I can find scarcely a trace of the Humphrey I first knew in 1924 or the Bogey I last saw in 1943. The earliest strokes in the biographers' portraits are those that paint him as a "loner," a man of "self-determination," who makes "all his own decisions," with regard for nothing beyond immediate satisfaction. Such a description will not do for a twentieth-century film star in Hollywood. Being myself a born loner, who was temporarily deflected from the hermit's path by a career in the theatre and films, I can state categorically that in Bogart's time there was no other occupation in the world that so closely resembled enslavement as the career of a film star. He had self-determination only in this: he might or he might not sign a film contract. If he signed the contract, he became subject to those who paid his salary and released his films. If he did not sign the contract, he was no film star. I, for example, when I was under contract to Paramount in 1928, complained about being forced to hang around Hollywood waiting to make some film. "That's what we are paying you for—your time" was the harsh comment of the front office. "You mean my life," I said to myself. When the coming of talkies made the cutting of actors' salaries practicable and I was the only one on the Paramount lot who refused to take a cut, thereby losing my contract, I doubted whether such "independent" decisions would lengthen my career. When I was the only one of the cast who refused to return to make the talkie version of *The Canary Murder Case,* my last silent film there, the studio doused me with ugly publicity and made my doubts a certainty. I was blacklisted. No major studio would hire me to make a film. In later years, whenever Bogart, at Warner Brothers, followed the lead of James Cagney and Errol Flynn by going on strike and demanding better films and more money, the studio would make a pleasant game of it. The actors were allowed a triumphant interval in which to feel like lords of the lot; the publicity stirred up by these mock battles was free and beneficial; and a great deal of money was saved while the actors' salaries were suspended. Studio contracts were always a joke, as far as actors were concerned. Studios could break them at will; the actors were bound by their fear of impoverishing lawsuits and permanent unemployment.

As a loner, I count as my two most precious rights those that allow me to choose the periods of my aloneness and allow me to choose the people with whom I will spend the periods of my not-aloneness. To a film star, on the other hand, to be let alone for an instant is terrifying. It is the first signpost on the road to oblivion. Obviously, an actor cannot choose the people with whom he will work, or when or how he will work with them. He goes to work at a time specified by the studio. He spends his working day under the control not only of his director but also of the scriptwriter, the cameraman, the wardrobe department, and the publicity office. Since publicity is the lifeblood of stardom, without which a star will die, it is equally obvious that he must keep it flowing through his private life, which feeds the envy and curiosity that bring many people into theatres. Bogart, having rightly ascribed much of his previous failure in the theatre and films to a lack of publicity value, determined that from the moment he settled at Warner Brothers, in 1936, all his time not spent before the camera would be spent with journalists and columnists, who would invent for him the private character of Bogey. They carved him into the desired peg upon which they could hang their favorite ancient gags and barroom fables. A small part of Bogey's character was founded on his film roles; the greater part was founded on the pranks of those gangsters idolized by the film producer Mark Hellinger, who was an ex-columnist. During the last ten years of his life, Bogart allowed himself to be presented to the world by journalists as a coarse and drunken bully, and as a puppet Iago who fomented evil without a motive. He was neither.

In 1924, my first impression of Humphrey Bogart was of a slim boy with charming manners, who was unusually quiet for an actor. His handsome face was made extraordinary by a most beautiful mouth. It was very full, rosy, and perfectly modeled—perfectly, that is, except that, to make it completely fascinating, at one corner of his upper lip a scarred, quilted piece hung down in a tiny scallop. When Humphrey went into films, a surgeon sewed up the scallop, and only a small scar remained. Photographically, it was an improvement, but I missed this endearing disfigurement. The scar on his lip has since become a symbol of his heroism. In those early years, it was taken for granted that he got punched in the mouth at some speakeasy. When Humphrey drank, he became exhausted and occasionally fell asleep (as in *Casablanca*) with his head in his arms on the table. If he was abruptly shaken awake, he would say something rude and sometimes get socked for it. On one occasion, he purposely did not get his split lip sewed up, because he both loved and hated his beautiful mouth. America in the twenties was exclusively Anglo-Saxon in its ideas of beauty, and vulgar people made fun of Humphrey's "nigger lips." The lip wound gave him no speech impediment, either before or after it was mended. But when he at last made a hit in films, observing how much an unusual feature, such as Clark Gable's prominent ears, added to the publicity value of a star, he decided to exploit his mouth. Over the years, Bogey practiced all kinds of lip gymnastics, accompanied by nasal tones, snarls, lisps, and slurs. His painful wince, his leer, his fiendish grin were the most accomplished ever seen on film. Only Erich von Stroheim was his superior in lip-twitching. But in 1924 Humphrey, in New York, was speaking his lines with a well-projected baritone and good diction in a small part in a play called *Nerves*. Mary Philips also had a small part in *Nerves*. Kenneth MacKenna played a leading role. The play's nerves would have been a good deal shakier if the cast had known that after Humphrey married and was divorced by Helen Menken he would marry Mary Philips, and that after Kenneth married and was divorced by Kay Francis he would marry Mary Philips, who by then had divorced Humphrey.

In respect to future entanglements, the Broadways theatrical season of 1925–26 was even more arresting. James Cagney, who was to become Humphrey's redheaded bête noire at Warner Brothers, was playing in *Outside Looking In*; Leslie Howard, who was to put Humphrey in a position to rival Cagney, was playing in *The Green Hat*; Helen Menken was in *Makropoulos Secret*; Mary Philips was in *The Wisdom Tooth*; and Bogart's Wife Number 3, Mayo Methot, was in *Alias the Deacon*. In *The Cradle Snatchers*, Humphrey was playing a college boy being snatched by middle-aged Mary Boland, while offstage in the Bronx the year-old Lauren Bacall lay in her cradle waiting for Bogey to snatch her twenty years later as Wife Number 4.

From the 1921–22 season, when Humphrey first appeared on Broadway—with Alice Brady, in *Drifting*—through the 1929–30 season, when he got his first Hollywood contract, 2,044 plays were produced in New York. Out of perhaps two thousand young American dramatic actors working in those plays, only four besides Bogart became major film stars—Cagney, Spencer Tracy, Fredric March, and Clark Gable. Moreover, whether or not it is generally admitted as frankly as it once was by Barbra Streisand—she said, "To me being really famous is being a movie star"—that is the goal of all actors in the theatre.

In 1930, Humphrey's failure in Hollywood was as predictable as Cagney's success. Cagney's character was already a gaudy perfection in the theatre. In *Penny Arcade*, the play that won him his first film contract with Warner Brothers, Cagney appeared as the same little hoodlum killer that made him famous in films. Bogart was selected out of *It's a Wise Child*, in which he played a gentlemanly young cad, and so had only his good looks to recommend him to Hollywood producers, who didn't know how to transform him into Bogey. Bogart used to refer to a review by Alexander Woollcott as his favorite among the reviews he had received while on the stage: it described his performance in *Swifty* as "inadequate." To be mentioned at all in any review amounted to praise for Bogart. On the stage, he was as formless as an impression lost through lack of meditation, as blurred as a name inked on blotting paper.

In the twenties, under the supervision of old producers like David Belasco, stage direction dated back to the feverish technique of the English theatre before the plays of Ibsen, Chekhov, and Bernard Shaw revolutionized it, introducing what Lytton Strachey called "a new quiet and subtle style of acting—a prose style." In New York, we began to realize how bad our directors and actors were when the new young English stars began to appear on Broadway. There was Lynn Fontanne in *Pygmalion*, Roland Young in *The Last of Mrs. Cheyney*, Leslie Howard in *Berkeley Square*, and Gertrude Lawrence and Noel Coward in *Private Lives*. These marvelous actors of realism spoke their lines as if they had just thought of them. They moved about the stage with ease. And they actually paid attention to—they actually *heard*—what other actors were saying. The conventional Broadway technique of that period exposed more showing off then acting, more of a fight than a play. Every actor's aim was to kill the other actors' lines—especially if the lines provoked laughter. Ina Claire was celebrated for waving a large chiffon handkerchief on other actors' lines and forcing them to work with their backs to the audience. Far from being criticized, she was envied for such tricks.

After thirteen years of conditioning by this kind of "stage" acting, when Bogart got a job in Robert Sherwood's *The Petrified Forest*—starring Leslie Howard and directed by Arthur Hopkins—which opened in January, 1935, nothing but searching ambition could have enabled him to see in Leslie Howard's quiet, natural acting technique a style he could adapt to his own personality, a style that would prepare him for *The African Queen*. In that film he developed his character with his voice alone. Nothing but inflexible willpower could have enabled him to tear down his ingrained acting habits in order to submit all over again to the self-conscious agony of learning to act. Working with Leslie gave him command of the Duke Mantee part in the play and, later, in the film; but the films of the following five years reveal the terrible struggle for supremacy between the new Bogey technique and the old theatrical habits of Humphrey. With a poor director, Frank McDonald, in *Isle of Fury*, he was Humphrey again, reciting his memorized lines, striking attitudes while he waited for the other actors to get done with theirs. In *Dark Victory*, working with a great director, Edmund Goulding, who was also a great clown, and acting with the emotional Bette Davis, who could fire up on the word "camera," he was stricken with grotesque, amateur embarrassment. Unlike most technical actors, Humphrey was extremely sensitive to his director. But, like most actors from the theatre, he was slow in building a mood and grimly serious about maintaining it. Cagney, in *The Roaring Twenties*, threw him into confusion, splitting him between Bogey and Humphrey. Cagney's swift dialogue and his swift movements, which had the glitter and precision of a meat slicer, were impossible to anticipate or counterattack. Humphrey was at his best working with less inspired and more technical actors, such as Walter Huston. He was also at his best playing an inarticulate, uncomplicated character, like the punk in *San Quentin*. His senseless pursuit of death became pathetic, even noble, because it came out of his own indomitable perseverance in pursuing stardom. In *The Maltese Falcon* his part was uncomplicated, but too much dialogue betrayed the fact that his miserable theatrical training had left him permanently afraid of words. In short speeches, he cleverly masked his fear with his tricks of mouth and voice, but when, in this film, he was allotted part of the burden of exposition, his eyes glazed and invisible comic-strip balloons circled his dialogue. Even more unfortunate were his efforts at repartee with Mary Astor in *Across the Pacific*. In his last films, it was not the theatre Humphrey who overcame Bogey—it was the real man, Humphrey Bogart, whose fundamental inertia had always menaced his career. As a dead soul waiting for release in death in *The Desperate Hours*, he was incomparable until, unaccountably, a sentimental heart began to beat, and he handed over the film to Fredric March. However, before inertia set in, he played one fascinatingly complex character, craftily directed by Nicholas Ray, in a film whose title perfectly defined Bogart's own isolation among people. That film was *In a Lonely Place*. It gave him a role that he could play with complexity, because the film character's pride in his art, his selfishness, his drunkenness, his lack of energy stabbed with lightning strokes of violence were shared by the real Bogart. In his preface to *The Doctor's Dilemma*, Shaw wrote,

> No man who is occupied in doing a very difficult thing, and doing it very well, ever loses his self-respect. . . . The common man may have to found his self-respect on sobriety, honesty, and industry; but . . . an artist needs no such props for his sense of dignity. . . . The truth is, hardly any of us have ethical energy enough for more than one really inflexible point of honor. . . . An actor, a painter, a composer, an author, may be as selfish as he likes without reproach from the public if only his art is superb; and he cannot fulfil this condition without sufficient effort and sacrifice to make him feel noble and martyred in spite of his selfishness.

Superficially, Humphrey's character and way of life so little resembled those of the secure and temperate Leslie Howard that what induced Leslie to become his guide and champion is not immediately apparent, but Leslie did become both. I would never have known the reason for his sympathetic attitude toward Humphrey if I had not met Leslie in New York in November, 1931, when he was rehearsing his new play, *The Animal Kingdom*.

On the afternoon of my twenty-fifth birthday, my friend George Marshall announced that he was going to celebrate the event by taking me to dinner at the Casino in the Park with Leslie Howard and his wife. I was surprised and pleased, not only because George had been mad at me for turning down an offer to work for RKO in Hollywood but also because he so little liked spending unnecessary money on me. (The last time I spoke to him on the phone, in 1960, he was still wondering why he had given me a mink coat in 1928.)

Conversationally, the dinner party was not well balanced. When I was with George, I said little, fearing that I might give him material for an inquiry into how I spent my time when he was away in Washington. Leslie, who had evidently accepted the invitation because he enjoyed George's social performances, said nothing. Mrs. Howard, a large Englishwoman who looked more like Leslie's mother than his wife, tried to inject gracious remarks here and there into the stream of George's witty stories, but his loud voice was as hard on them as it was on Eddie Duchin's orchestra, playing in the background. George was a tall, physical man of thirty-five.

At the end of each story, he would let out a self-appreciative haw-haw-haw and then clap Leslie on the back with such enthusiasm that Leslie crumpled over the table like a paper angel.

Dinner ended, George asked Mrs. Howard to dance, and Leslie and I were left alone at the table, regarding each other.

I opened the conversation: "I hate my dress. Bernard Newman at Bergdorf Goodman talked me into buying it, but it's much too young for me."

Leslie studied the dress—a lettuce-green organza evening gown, with a full skirt, short sleeves, and baby collar. I turned in my chair to show him a bow in back. "What do you usually wear?" he asked.

"Oh, something white and glittery, with no back and cut down to here in front."

He thought about this for a moment, and then we both laughed and had another glass of champagne. He had become suddenly, brilliantly alive. His famous watchful eyes began to sparkle mischievously as we compared our impressions of Hollywood. As much as I, he detested having to sit most of the day in the studio waiting for sets and lights to be changed. After that, he talked about the theatre—how he dreaded having to study a new part, how slow he was at learning his lines.

I laughed in disbelief. "You're kidding me!"

"No, it's perfectly true," he said. "I wasn't cut out to be an actor. I haven't the energy for acting—it's too exhausting."

When Mrs. Howard and George returned from their dance and observed our happy intimacy, they decided to take us home. In the cab, Mrs. Howard and I sat on the back seat, facing George and Leslie, on the jumpseats. My knees touched Leslie's, and we smiled at each other. But I knew when we said good night that I would not see him again. It would be too exhausting.

It was the recognition of this same threatening exhaustion in Humphrey, I think, that touched Leslie's heart, leading him to force Jack Warner to give Humphrey the Duke Mantee part when *The Petrified Forest* was filmed. Furthermore, whereas from the beginning of his career Leslie had confessed his lack of energy and let it work for him in the creation of the quiet, natural actor, he saw that Humphrey fought his weakness, trying ineffectually to emulate the dynamic style of most successful actors. The futility of this he conveyed to Humphrey in the direction of the play. And once Humphrey grasped the idea that he, too, might achieve success with some version of natural acting, he went about contriving it with the cunning of a lover. For all actors know that truly natural acting is rejected by the audience. Although people are better equipped to judge acting than any other art, the hypocrisy of "sincerity" prevents them from admitting that they, too, are always acting some role of their own invention. To be a successful actor, then, it is necessary to add eccentricities and mystery to naturalness, so that the audience can admire and puzzle over something different from itself. Leslie's eccentricities were his fondness for his pipe and for English tweed. Bogart's eccentricities were the use of his mouth and speech. As for mystery, Leslie would have become less if he had revealed himself; Bogart did reveal himself and became more.

Humphrey, according to his biographers, had an amazing number of "recreations." He played golf, tennis, bridge, chess. He sailed. He read *books!* Except on one occasion, the only thing I ever saw him do was sit drinking and talking with people. That one occasion was an evening in New York when he and I, Blyth Daly, and the actress Alice Brady played what Alice innocently called bridge, in her apartment on East Fifty-seventh Street. For one thing, Alice never stopped talking. Then, as soon as the cards were dealt, she would get up to mix drinks. After the bidding, she would get up to empty ashtrays. When she was dummy, she would go to the piano to play and sing in French—her mother's tongue. At any time at all, she would jump up, with all her bracelets jingling, to fly at one of her four yapping wire-haired fox terriers. We were relieved when her doorbell rang and Elsie Ferguson, with her handsome actor husband, came in for a nightcap after the theatre. The bridge game was over. Sipping a brandy across the room from me, Elsie was as beautiful in 1930 as she had been in films in 1918. And it was with the old film charm that she said good night a few minutes later, leaving Alice sitting on her husband's lap.

"How long have Alice and Elsie's husband known each other?" I asked Humphrey as we left the apartment building.

He looked at me blankly.

It was Blyth who answered, "You idiot, they just met!"

That blank look of Humphrey's was the key to his attitude toward sex. He was so contemptuous of other men's needs to publicize their amorous triumphs that he refused to notice them. Being supremely confident of his own attractiveness to women, he scorned every form of demonstrativeness. When a woman appealed to him, he waited for her the way the flame waits for the moth. "Man survives earthquakes, epidemics, the horrors of war, and all the agonies of the soul," wrote Tolstoy, "but the tragedy that has always tormented him, and always will, is the tragedy of the bedroom." It was security in sex that preserved Humphrey's ego until his eventual success after he had endured the bitterest humiliation, ridicule, and failure. Certainly no other actor could have read those two speeches in *Across the Pacific* with his peculiar emphasis. When Sidney Greenstreet showed him his gun, Bogey produced his and said, "My gun is bigger than your gun." And again, later, when he pulled his gun on Greenstreet, he said, "I told you—mine is bigger than yours."

Each of Humphrey's wives was fittingly chosen to accord with the progress of his career. When he began to act and had so much to learn about the theatre, he married Helen Menken, the star of *Seventh Heaven*. Helen's white, thin face was always ecstatically lifted up to her vision of the Drama. I never heard her talk about anything except the art of the theatre. They were divorced in 1927, after Helen had become a sensation in *The Captive*, which was closed by the District Attorney on its one hundred sixtieth performance because of its lesbian theme. Humphrey worked that year in the twelve pitiful performances of a comedy called *Baby Mine*, in which Roscoe "Fatty" Arbuckle tried to erase the scandal that had driven him from Hollywood. Except for a two-week revival of Maxwell Anderson's *Saturday's Children*, in 1928, Humphrey did not work again on Broadway until 1929, when, with his new wife, Mary Philips, he appeared in *Skyrocket*, which closed after eleven performances. "The art of the theatre" having become a sore subject, Mary was exactly right for him during that time, when he required comfort more than inspiration.

Except for Leslie Howard, no one contributed so much to Humphrey's success as his third wife, Mayo Methot. He found her at a time of lethargy and loneliness, when he might have gone on playing secondary gangster parts at Warner Brothers for a year and then been out. But he met Mayo and she set fire to him. Those passions—envy, hatred, and violence, which were essential to the Bogey character, which had been simmering beneath his failure for so many years—she brought to a boil, blowing the lid off all his inhibitions forever. Part of her mission was accomplished under my direct observation.

In October, 1935, I left my ballroom dance act with Dario Borzani at the Persian Room in New York to make a test for the Republic Studio in Hollywood for a film called *Dancing Feet*. On the day after the test was completed and seen, the studio gave the part I had tested for to a girl who couldn't dance. Having little money and no more faith in myself, I stayed on in Hollywood for lack of a better plan. I was living at the Ronda Apartments. One day, I strolled down the street to Robert Benchley's cottage at the Garden of Allah, and there was Humphrey sitting on the floor, leaning against a sofa, with a glass of Scotch-and-soda in his hand. He had little to say about his part in *The Petrified Forest*, which was in production at Warner Brothers. Two unsuccessful experiences in Hollywood did not allow him to feel optimistic. Not feeling optimistic, either, was a boy from the M-G-M Studio who had been sent to pick up a script that Benchley had not yet begun to write, for one of his comedy short subjects. The boy watched Bob prepare for the typewriter with a glass of straight Scotch. It was almost impossible for anyone working on a Benchley film to stay sober, because he demanded that they keep pace with his drinking. The following evening, I received a phone call from the theatrical agent Mary Huntoon, who was an old friend of mine and a niece of Dwight Deere Wiman, the producer of *The Little Shows*, with songs by Rodgers and Hart. She said that Humphrey and she were having a drink at her house (she had just become his agent), and that Humphrey would like me to join them. Coming from anyone else, the invitation would have meant that two bored people wanted company. Coming from Humphrey, it was nothing less than a declaration of love. Full of curiosity, I hastened to the scene. It was not a happy one. Humphrey was so intuitive about women that, after a glowing welcome, he retreated slowly into gloom and silence and Scotch, leaving the conversation to Mary and me. Riding home in the cab, I thought about how different Humphrey and I were. He could love only a woman he had known a long time or—what amounted to the same thing—one who was flung at him in the intimacy of a play or film. To me, love was an adventure into the unknown.

By the time I next saw Humphrey, *The Petrified Forest* had been released and he had made a solid hit in it. It was early in 1936, at the Beverly Hills home of Eric Hatch, who had written the film *My Man Godfrey*. When I went into the dining room, Eric and his wife, Mischa Auer and his wife, and Humphrey were sitting at the table. Mrs. Hatch got up to pour me a cup of coffee. As I drank it, I watched Humphrey, whom I had never seen in such an emotional state. Everyone else was watching him, too. Then the doorbell rang, and, as if on cue, we all got up and went downstairs into the vaulted living room to meet Mayo Methot, who was entering from the hall, clad in a sheath of peacock-blue silk. That night, instead of having our usual talk and laughter, we became an audience galvanized by a scene of the most passionate love played out between Mayo and Humphrey without so much as a touch of hands. Drinks were mixed and seats were taken as Mayo moved restlessly to the phonograph and put on an old Argentine tango, "Adios Muchachos." She got up and danced with Mischa. The dance began as a burlesque, with him throwing her about and glaring lustfully into her eyes. Gradually, however, her exquisitely persuasive body began to rule his movements, and they danced in the falling arcs, the slow recoveries, and the voluptuous pauses of the true tango. The spell was broken by a maid, who announced that Mayo's husband had telephoned to say he was on his way to the house. Humphrey sprang from the sofa to whisk her away. But wait! She had taken off her slippers to dance, and now one of them could not be found. Everyone searched for it except me, and that must have aroused Humphrey's suspicions, because quite suddenly he lunged at me with the most hideous face, rasping, "God damn you, Louise, tell us where you hid Mayo's slipper!" I was too stunned by this strange and violent Humphrey to speak. Fortunately, at this moment Mischa stretched up to an oak beam, which no one else was tall enough to reach, and brought down the slipper. The lovers fled through the back door as the front doorbell rang.

It was in December of 1943, in New York, that I saw Humphrey for the last time. I was dining at the "21" Club with screenwriter Townsend Martin. Between the dinner and the supper hour, when the bar was empty, Mayo and Humphrey came in and stood briefly at our table to say hello and tell us that they were on their way to Africa to entertain the troops. I was shocked to see how dreadfully Humphrey's face had aged. The effects of the war he had waged against his inertia—work and whiskey without sleep and food—were visible at last. Mayo looked as though she had just got out of bed with her clothes on. Her suit was rumpled, her hair not combed, her face not made up. They sat at a table in a far corner of the room as if they wanted to be alone, yet they neither spoke nor looked at each other till their drinks were brought to the table. Then Mayo turned to speak fiercely to Humphrey, as if she were continuing some argument that could never be resolved. Slumped against the banquette, unmoved, he stared at his hand slowly turning his glass round and round on the table. It was plain that the team of "The Battling Bogarts" was soon to break up. He was Bogey now, his character firmly set, capable of battling alone. With the release of *Casablanca*, Humphrey Bogart had become big business. It was time for Lauren Bacall to make her entrance—she who was also to become his perfect screen partner, as seductive as Eve, as cool as the serpent.

My most vivid remembrance of the real Humphrey Bogart is of a night in New York at Tony's Bar on Fifty-second Street. I went in at about one o'clock in the morning and sat at a table near Humphrey, who was sitting in a booth with the actor Thomas Mitchell. It was a few weeks before the Broadway version of *The Petrified Forest* would close, in June, 1935. Humphrey had nothing to look forward to except summer stock in Skowhegan, Maine. Presently, Mitchell paid his bill and went out, leaving Humphrey alone, drinking steadily, with weary determination. His head drooped lower and lower. When I left, he had fallen into his exhausted sleep, with his head sunk in his arms on the table. "Poor Humphrey," I said to Tony. "He's finally licked."

My most vivid remembrance of the screen Humphrey Bogart is of a scene in John Huston's *The Treasure of the Sierra Madre*. He lies in the dirt, about to drag himself to the waterhole. He has endured everything to get his gold—and now must he give it up? Wide open, the tragic eyes are raised to heaven in a terrible, beseeching look. In the agony of that beautiful face I see the face of my St. Bogart.

Louise Brooks, John Wayne and others in Overland Stage Raiders *(1938), Republic.*

RICHARD BURTON

Richard Burton and Elizabeth Taylor in Cleopatra *(1963), 20th Century-Fox.*

Born Richard Walter Jenkins, Jr. on November 10, 1925 in South Wales . . .
Twelfth of thirteen children of Welsh coal-miner . . . Scholarship to Oxford
. . . Took last name of prep school teacher and mentor . . . First film: *The Last
Days of Dolwyn* (1948) . . . First American film: *My Cousin Rachel*
(1952) . . . Married Sybil Williams 1949 . . . Divorced 1963 . . . Married
Elizabeth Taylor 1964 . . . Divorced 1974 . . . Remarried 1975 . . . Redivorced
1976 . . . Credits include: *Cleopatra* (1963) . . . *Becket* (1964) . . . *The Night of
the Iguana* (1964) . . . *Who's Afraid of Virginia Woolf?* (1966) . . . *Equus*
(1977) . . . Averaged one million dollars per movie with Liz . . . Died 1984.

Liz at First Sight

The house in California—it was in the Bel Air district of Los Angeles, I think—looked as if it had been flung by a giant hand against the side of a hill and had stuck.

From the main living room, master bedroom, guest bedrooms, dining room, kitchen level, the house jutted and dropped one floor to a "playroom."

The "playroom" was not for children.

It was complete with bar and barman, hot-dog simmerer, king-sized double-doored two-toned refrigerator, drugstore hotplates, big-game trophies on the walls (the host was a big-game hunter who acted in his spare time), and huge, deep, low divans and easy chairs—villainously uncomfortable for men, but marvellously made for cute little women who could tuck their cute little legs away and blazingly efface their cute little pouting little personalities in niches of the vast furniture and make like cute little pussycats.

Below the "playroom" the house again jutted and dropped to the swimming pool, the showers, and the changing rooms.

It was my first time in California and my first visit to a swank house. There were quite a lot of people in and around the pool, all suntanned and all drinking the Sunday morning liveners—Bloddy Marys, boilermakers, highballs, iced beer. I knew some of the people and was introduced to the others. Wet brown arms reached out of the pool and shook my hand. The people were all friendly, and they called me Dick immediately. I asked if they would please call me Richard—Dick, I said, made me feel like a symbol of some kind. They laughed, some of them. It was, of course, Sunday morning and I was nervous.

I was enjoying this small social triumph, but then a girl sitting on the other side of the pool lowered her book, took off her sunglasses and looked at me. She was so extraordinarily beautiful that I nearly laughed out loud. I didn't, of course, which was just as well. The girl was not, and, quite clearly, was not going to be laughing back. I had an idea that, finding nothing of interest, she was looking right through me and was examining the texture of the wall behind. If there was a flaw in the sandstone, I knew she'd find it and probe it right to the pith. I fancied that if she chose so, the house would eventually collapse.

I smiled at her and, after a long moment, just as I felt my own smile turning into a cross-eyed grimace, she started slightly and smiled back. There was little friendliness in the smile. A new ice cube formed of its own accord in my Scotch-on-the-rocks.

She sipped some beer and went back to her book. I affected to become social with the others but out of the corner of my mind—while I played for the others the part of a poor miner's son who was puzzled, but delighted by the attention these lovely people paid to him—I had her under close observation. She was, I decided, the most astonishingly self-contained, pulchritudinous, remote, removed, inaccessible woman I had ever seen. She spoke to no one. She looked at no one. She steadily kept on reading her book. Was she merely sullen? I wondered. I thought not. There was no trace of sulkiness in the divine face. She was a Mona Lisa type, I thought. In my business everyone is a type. She is older than the deck chair on which she sits, I thought headily, and she is famine, fire, destruction, and plague, she is the Dark Lady of the Sonnets, the onlie true begetter. She is a secret wrapped in an enigma inside a mystery, I thought, with a mental man-to-man nod to Churchill. Her breasts were apocalyptic, they would topple empires down before they withered. Indeed, her body was a miracle of construction and the work of an engineer of genius. It needed nothing except itself. It was true art, I thought, executed in terms of itself. It was smitten by its own passion. I used to think things like that. I was not long down from Oxford and Walter Pater was still talked of and I read the art reviews in the quality weeklies without much caring about the art itself, and it was a Sunday morning in Bel Air, and I was nervous, and there was the Scotch-on-the-rocks.

Like Miniver Cheevy I kept on drinking and, in the heady flow of the attention I was getting, told story after story as the afternoon boozed slowly on. I went in swimming once or twice. So did she, but, lamentably, always after I'd come out. She swam easily and gracefully as an Englishwoman would and not with the masculine drive and kick of most American girls. She was unquestionably gorgeous. I can think of no other word to describe a combination of plenitude, frugality, abundance, tightness. She was lavish. She was a dark unyielding largesse. She was, in short, too bloody much, and not only that, she was totally ignoring me. I became frustrated almost to screaming when I had finished a well-received and humorous story about the death of my grandfather and found that she was turned away in deep conversation with another woman. I think I tried to eavesdrop but was stayed by words like—Tony and Janet and Marlon and Sammy. She was not, obviously, talking about me.

Eventually, with half-seas-ed cunning and with all the nonchalance of a traffic ham, I worked my way to her side of the pool. She was describing—in words not normally written—what she thought of a producer at M.G.M. This was my first encounter with freedom of speech in the U.S.A., and it took my breath away. My brain throbbed; I almost sobered up. I was profoundly shocked. It was ripe stuff. I checked her again. There was no question about it. She was female. In America the women apparently had not only got the vote—they'd got the words to go with it.

I was also somewhat puzzled and disturbed by the half-look she gave me as she uttered the enormities. Was she deliberately trying to shock me? Those huge violet-blue eyes (the biggest I've ever seen, outside those who have glandular trouble—thyroid, et cetera) had an odd glint in them. You couldn't describe it as a twinkle. . . . Searchlights can not twinkle, they turn on and off and probe the heavens and so on.

Still I couldn't be left out. I had to join in and say something. I didn't reckon on the Scotch though. I didn't reckon that it had warped my judgment and my sense of timing, my choice of occasion. With all the studied frenzy of Dutch courage I waded into the depths of those perilous eyes.

In my best chiffon-and-cut-glass Oxford accent I said:

"You have a remarkable command of Olde Englishe."

There was a pause in which I realized with brilliant clarity the relativity of time. Aeons passed, civilizations came and went, brave men and cowards died in battles not yet fought, while those cosmic headlights examined my flawed personality. Every pockmark on my face became a crater of the moon. I reached up with a casual hand to cover up the right-cheeked evidence of my acne'd youth. Halfway up I realized my hand was just as ugly as my face and decided to leave the bloody thing and die instead. But while contemplating the various ways of suicide and having sensibly decided, since I had a good start, to drink myself to death, I was saved by her voice which said, "Don't you use words like that at the Old Vic?"

"They do," I said, "but *I* don't. I come from a family and an attitude that believe such words are an indication of weakness in vocabulary and emptiness of mind. . . . Despite Jones's writing that in times of acute shared agony and fear, as in trench warfare, obscenities repeated in certain patterns can at times become almost liturgical, almost poetic. . . . " I ran out of gas.

There was another pause; more empires fell. Captains and kings and counsellors arrived and departed. She said three four-letter words. These were, I think, "Well! Well! Well!"

Somebody laughed uneasily. The girl had turned away. I had been dismissed. I felt as lonely as a muezzin, as a reluctant piano lesson on a Saturday afternoon, as the Last Post played on a cracked bugle.

I went home and somebody asked, when I told them where I'd been, what she was like. "Dark. Dark. Dark. Dark. She probably," I said, "shaves." To nobody in particular I observed that the human body is eighty percent water.

It wasn't until five years later that I saw her again, across a restaurant—I can't remember which restaurant or indeed which country or continent. I think she waved at me. I think I scowled back—particularly at her new husband. She had the impertinence to look happy, even radiant. I had liked him a great deal, but now he'd married this girl I write of, and he hadn't even had the grace to ask me to be in *Around the World in Eighty Days*. I was the only actor in the world who hadn't been asked—with a promise of a small Cézanne—to act in that film. I still liked him and though I bitterly resented her obvious happiness and though I muttered mysteriously to myself words like "bucolic" and "bovine content," I believe that I forced a smile at them through my clenched teeth as I left.

*   *   *

The years have gone by—seven or eight. It's Sunday in Paris in early winter. There is a persistent drizzle of cold grey rain. This pleases us. It means we can walk to Fouquet's and not ride in the car because the poor little notorious couple will not be bothered by paparazzi. Their cameras do not like rain. She is excited at the thought of this tiny expedition—Fouquet's is one block away from our hotel. She glows. I am excited too. I glow. "Is the dress all right?" she asks.

"Whenas in silks my Julia goes," I say. "Then, then, methinks, how sweetly flows the liquefaction of her clothes!"

"Richard," she says, "I'll methink you right across the liquefaction of your face if you don't give me a straight answer. Is it all right?"

"Lovely," I say. "And don't shout and bawl at me like that," I say, "or you'll be a partner to the shortest marriage since my Great-Aunt Mary Jane Loughor dropped just as she was signing the marriage certificate in the chapel vestry."

We went down in the elevator. I tipped the concierge a wink—the only kind of tip I really enjoy giving. We walked along the Rue de Berri to the Champs Élysées. We turned right, towards the Arc de Triomphe—the cold rain had swept the great street empty of people. Almost. There was a man and a greyhound. A Fiat car squelched through the wet. We were alone in a street in a city where all but us and the man with the greyhound and the man in the Fiat had died in a vast silent painless war that had come in the night.

"Alone, alone, all, all alone," I sang, "alone on a wide, wide sea! And never a saint. . . ." The Fiat screamed into a U-turn. The man parked it ahead of us. He leaped out of his car and started towards us. He was thirty-five years old; his hairline receded; he was wearing a short raincoat and pointed shoes and three cameras. And I had known him all, already known him all. I'd known him in Rome and London and Paris and Geneva. Had known him at airports and railway stations—I'd known him shout insults in Italian and French and English and German. I had not liked him. He was running towards us. He was unique because he was alone. I'd known him before only in numbers, running with the pack, elbowing, screaming, frantic. I'd known him, with old-fashioned gallantry, call my wife a whore and me a gigolo and my friends pimps. I had not liked him.

"When," I said, "when the world is over, when the oceans and the graves deliver up their dead and this planet has gone screaming back to seething gas and we stand alone in an endless multitude for the final severe searching before the Supreme Judge, the last thing we'll see," I said, warming to my speech, "is one of these blokes trying to take a photograph of it all and asking the Great Mathematician to cheat his look a little to the left."

"Now, Richard, don't start that rubbish, don't say things like that," she said. "Don't get into one of your death moods, we'll have it for the rest of the day. Trouble with the Welsh is," she said, "that they think everybody's Welsh, even Death."

We had stopped.

"Why not? He's a local man," I said. "He's a very distinguished feller. We must be prepared for him and courteous when he comes."

"Don't," she said quickly. "Don't make fun. You can't talk your way out of the fear of death."

"You want a bet?"

"Don't, please don't talk about it."

"Good God. It's the most absorbing subject and has been since the first man died."

"And don't you die on me," she said. "I couldn't bear it again."

"Don't you die on me either." We stared at each other.

Her brilliant eyes had dimmed. The violet in them had turned dark—almost to blackness. They looked like water over coal, like black macadam in the rain under street lamps at night.

An emotion compounded of—who knows what?—of fear and love and pride and beauty and self-pity seized us both by the throat and shook us like a dog. The man crouched three feet away from us, backing as we walked, clicking and clicking. I feinted a kick at the photographer's left knee. As he dropped his camera I backhanded him across the face. He was off balance and fell quickly onto his back. Equally quickly he was up and clicking and clicking and cursing in a sweet courteous stream in three languages. I cursed back in four. The Welsh language is little known to paparazzi.

We entered Fouquet's, My wife was silent and bright with fury. I ordered a drink. "Why did you do that? Why do you have to spoil the day?"

"I had to do something." I said. "I was terrified that I was going to cry and I can't abide weeping in a man."

"Go back and apologize." she said.

I went downstairs.

I came back.

"Did you?" she asked.

"Yes."

"How did he take it?"

"Like a proper little gentleman," I said. "He belted me right across the chops."

She laughed.

I licked the tender, slightly shredded flesh beside my molars, and I cursed some more.

"Stop that!"

"What's the matter," I said, "didn't you use words like that in Culver City?"

Her lower jaw hideously receding, her upper front teeth vilely bucking, and in a very highfaluting, nauseous English accent, she said:

"Yes, of course, *they* did but *I* didn't—I come from a race and family that believe the use of such words to be an indication of weakness in vocabulary and intellectual emptiness. . . ."

She smiled at me and patted my hand. I made a plaintive woofing noise and she smiled again.

The ice cubes in my Scotch-on-the-rocks melted and sank without trace.

Elizabeth Taylor and Richard Burton in Who's Afraid of Virginia Woolf? *(1966), Warner Bros.*

JAMES CAGNEY

James Cagney and Mae Clarke in The Public Enemy *(1931), Warner Bros.*

Born James Francis Cagney Jr. on July 1, 1899 in New York City . . . Father a saloon-keeper . . . Educated at Columbia University . . . Poet and sailor . . . First acting job was as a female impersonator in vaudeville . . . First film: *Sinner's Holiday* (1930) . . . Followed by: *The Public Enemy* (1931) . . . *Angels with Dirty Faces* (1938) . . . *Yankee Doodle Dandy* (1942; his only Oscar) . . . *West Point Story* (1950) . . . *Mr. Roberts* (1955) . . . Retired from movies 1961 . . . Married to Francis Willard Vernon for over fifty years . . . Gained instant fame when he ground half a grapefruit into Mae Clarke's pretty face in *Public Enemy*.

I *Never* Said "You Dirty Rat"

In *The Millionaire*, my only picture with George Arliss, I played a fast-talking insurance man who has to sell a policy and warn Mr. Arliss that he is getting nothing out of life in his retirement. That was my only scene with this great star, and it lasted just two minutes. I wanted it to be good. In the scene, he sits with a shawl about his shoulders, and during the rehearsal, I said, "Mr. Arliss, may I adjust your shawl if it falls down off your shoulders?" He said, "Young man, you do anything you like. I trust your judgment implicitly." Which I thought was awfully nice coming from a grand old trouper to a young guy just beginning to get warm in the business.

Then came *The Public Enemy*. The story was about street pals—one soft-spoken, the other a really tough little article. For some incredible reason, I was cast as the quiet one; and Eddie Woods, a fine actor but a boy of gentle background, well-spoken and well-educated, became the tough guy. Fortunately, Bill Wellman, the director, had seen *Doorway to Hell*, and he quickly became aware of the obvious casting error. He knew at once that I could project that direct gutter quality, so Eddie and I switched roles after Wellman made an issue of it with Darryl Zanuck.

The picture had its hazards, among them real bullets. This was before the special-effects boys learned how to make "exploding" bullets safe as cap guns. At the time Warner's employed a man named Bailey who had been a machine gunner in World War I, and this boy knew how to make that instrument perform. He sat with the machine gun on a platform above as I skittered along and then ducked down the street behind a "stone" wall. Seconds after I did this, Bailey opened up on the edge of the wall. It crumbled to sawdust, and so would I, had I been there two seconds before.

Another little uncomfortable moment came when that good actor, Donald Cook, who was my brother in the film, had to display his war-shattered nerves by hauling off and hitting me in the mouth. I think he had some coaching. I've always suspected that Bill Wellman said to him, "Go ahead, let him have it. He can take it," because when Donald belted me, he didn't pull a thing. Instead of faking it as one always does, he just punched me straight in the mouth, broke a tooth, and knocked me galley west.

Public Enemy had a fine cast: Eddie, Donald, Mae Clarke, and the unforgettable Jean Harlow. Borrowed just for that picture, she was a very, very distinct type of gal. Brand new in the business, she didn't much know the acting end, but she certainly was a personality and very pleasant to work with. I never saw her after *Public Enemy*, but I was saddened at her death, a needless death as I understand it, because she neglected a serious gall bladder condition.

When Mae Clarke and I played the grapefruit scene, we had no idea that it would create such a stir. This bit of business derived from a real incident in Chicago when a hoodlum named Hymie Weiss was listening to his girl friend endlessly yakking away at breakfast one morning. He didn't like it, so he took an omelet she had just prepared and shoved it in her face. Repeating this on the screen would have been a shade too messy, so we used the grapefruit half. I was not to hear the end of that little episode for years. Invariably whenever I went into a restaurant, there was always some wag having the waiter bring me a tray of grapefruit. It got to be awfully tiresome, although it never stopped me from eating it in the proper amount at the proper time.

A little-known sidelight to the grapefruit scene is that Mae was then married to Monte Brice, Fanny's brother. Mae and Monte had divorced, and apparently with a little rancor, because every time I'd push the grapefruit into Mae's face at the Strand Theatre, there was a guaranteed audience of one—Monte. He would come in just before the scene was shown, gloat over it, then leave.

Public Enemy was one of the first low-budget million-dollar grossers in the business. I'm usually not too much concerned with business details, but in this instance I know just how much the film cost because Bill Wellman told me. The whole thing came in for $151,000, and it took up just twenty-six days to make.

After *Public Enemy* was released, Warner's gave me star billing, which was pleasant enough but hardly compensation for the lack of compensation. I kept grinding the pictures out, working at a swift tempo, and seeing everywhere about me the rough-handed treatment of actors by management. Actors were considered to be expendable material, just like props or makeup. I watched this, and I was to remember. . . .

Next on the agenda was *Angels with Dirty Faces*, which got some attention at the time but, like so many of the catch-as-catch-can pictures we made then, it had an insubstantial script that the actors patched up here and there by improvising right on the set. In *Angels*, for instance, one of the first scenes has Pat O'Brien as the priest in the confessional, and I as Rocky the hood on the other side of the covered window. In the script as written, the priest slides back the latticed opening and says, "What can I do for you, my son?" Then I am supposed to say, "What did you do with those fountain pens we stole out of the freight car fifteen years ago?" The priest says, "Rocky!" and we shake hands. This was ludicrous. Pat and I, raised in the Church, knew the ceremonial forms, and very well did we know them. As it happened, on this picture the director, the producer and the writer were all Jewish, so how could they be expected to know? I said to the director, Mike Curtiz, "Mike, you can't do the scene as written." He asked why and I said, "There is a certain ritual to confession, and the ritual must be observed. The priest doesn't say, 'What can I do for you, my son?' First, the penitent says, 'Bless me, father, for I have sinned. I confess to Almighty God and to you, father. My last confession was thus-and-so many weeks ago, et cetera, et cetera.' That's just for *openers*. Then after it's all over, the priest gives the penitent some penance. And there's no hand-shaking, believe me!" Mike said, "Well, couldn't they walk *outside* and shake hands?" So Pat and I fashioned the scene as it needed to be.

By this time in my career, what with my experiences in the other pictures featuring gunfire going slightly awry, one would think I'd learned my lesson. But here I was in *Angels with Dirty Faces* facing the real thing again. I was up at a window firing down at the police, and one shot called for me to be right at the opening as machine-gun bullets took the window out around my head. Then, whatever it was—common sense or a hunch—something made me cautious, and I said to Mike Curtiz, "Do it in process." (That was basically a superimposition.)

"Jim, this man will not hurt you."

"Do it in process, Mike. I will not be there." I got out of the scene, and Burke, the professional machine gunner, fired the shots. One of the bullets hit the steel edge of the window, was deflected, and went right through the wall where my head had been. That convinced me, need I say it, that flirting this way with real bullets was ridiculous.

The character I played in the picture, Rocky Sullivan, was in part modeled on a fella I used to see when I was a kid. He was a hophead and a pimp, with four girls in his string. He worked out of a Hungarian rathskeller on First Avenue between Seventy-seventh and Seventy-eighth Streets—a tall dude with an expensive straw hat and an electric-blue suit. All day long he would stand on that corner, hitch up his trousers, twist his neck and move his necktie, lift his shoulders, snap his fingers, then bring his hands together in a soft smack. His invariable greeting was "Whadda ya hear? Whadda ya say?" The capacity for observation is something every actor must have to some degree, so I recalled this fella and his mannerisms, and gave them to Rocky Sullivan just to bring some modicum of difference to this roughneck. I did that gesturing maybe six times in the picture—that was over thirty years ago—and the impressionists are still doing me doing *him*.

The Cagney mimics I've seen lately, however, don't hitch the trousers so much as just put their hands out in front and kind of wag their heads a bit, and I think they've lost something. One item a number of them do get right is the one of holding my arms in front of my thighs instead of at the side, as most people do. This is my natural stance, due to my having done a great deal of weight lifting from boyhood on. Indeed, I have done so much lifting and hard work through the years that I can't straighten my arms. My tendons have actually shortened. I don't try to hold my arms in any particular way, they just hang there in front, completely relaxed.

Most of my imitators also say, "All right, you guys!" which I don't remember ever saying. I think some of these modifications of Rocky came from the Bowery Boys grabbing some of those mannerisms and altering them slightly when they made their own series. Their constant repetition of those altered mannerisms might have influenced the professional imitators because, for instance, "All right, you guys!" sounds like a Bowery Boys' line to me. Moreover, I *never* said, "You dirty rat!"

The Bowery Boys, known as the Dead End Kids when we made *Angels with Dirty Faces* in 1938, had been throwing their weight around quite a bit with directors and other actors at the time. It developed that I was to have a little off-screen encounter with them. Our opening scene in the picture takes place in the basement of a deserted building. I am fresh out of Sing Sing, and the kids have just rolled me for my wallet. I walk in, tell them to hand over, and with a little emphatic coercion force them to get up the wallet. According to the script my next line was "Come here, suckers," and I lead them over to the door on which is carved "Rocky Sullivan," put there when I was a kid. The kids must look at this with respectful awe because of my rough reputation and say, *"You're* Rocky Sullivan?"

We shot the scene, but just before I said, "Come here, suckers," Leo Gorcey said, "He's psychic!" thereby throwing the rhythm of the scene right out the window, souring the whole thing very nicely. So in the next take just before I said, "Come here, suckers," I gave Leo Gorcey a stiff arm right above the nose—bang! His head went back, hitting the kid behind him, stunning them both momentarily. Then I said, "Now listen here, we've got some work to do, so let's have none of this goddamned nonsense. When we get on, we're pros—we're doing the job we're asked to do. Understood?"

"Yeah," they said. One of the kids turned to Gorcey and said, "Who the hell you think you got there—Bogart?" I learned later that Bogie had incurred their disfavor on a film they'd done together, and they expressed their displeasure by taking his pants off. But in our picture, once they had learned that their jumping me would be troublesome for them, we got along fine.

The leading lady of *Angels with Dirty Faces* was that lovely, talented gal, Ann Sheridan. So much to offer—and a three-pack-a-day smoker. She just didn't eat because cigarettes killed her appetite. One day a well-known doctor came on the *Angels* set, and after we got talking a bit, I asked him to lunch, inviting Annie to join us. At the table she lit a cigarette immediately. She ordered ham and eggs, took one little bit of the ham, then lit another cigarette. The doctor asked her if she smoked a great deal and she said, "Oh, yes." He said, "And you don't eat." Annie said she just didn't feel like eating at the moment. The doctor said, "You know, time was when coronary thrombosis was a great new thing among women. Whenever it happened, it went up and down the land, doctor to doctor—'a female coronary!' Not lately. Cigarettes have done it." Annie said, "Oh, really?" and went right on smoking. Years later when lung cancer hit, she didn't have much of a chance, and what a powerful shame that was. A mighty nice gal, Annie.

The ending of *Angels with Dirty Faces* has prompted a continually asked question over the years: did Rocky turn yellow as he walked to the electric chair, or did he just pretend to? For those who haven't seen the picture, I must explain that Rocky becomes the idol of the street kids in his old neighborhood, and when he is ultimately brought to justice and condemned to die, these youngsters still hold him up as a model to emulate. Rocky's childhood pal, now a priest, comes to him in the death house and pleads with him to kill the kids' unhealthy admiration of him by turning yellow at the last minute, by pretending cowardice as he is being led to the electric chair. Rocky scorns the request.

The execution scene is this: cheekily contemptuous of my escorts, I am being led along the last mile when suddenly without warning, I go into a seizure of fear, twisting and turning in the clutch of the guards as I try to prevent them from leading me into the death chamber. Or *is* it a seizure of fear? Am I not instead doing a favor for my priest pal and the kids by pretending to be yellow, thereby discouraging the youngsters from following in my convict footsteps? Through the years I have actually had little kids come up to me on the street and ask, "Didya do it for the father, huh?" I think in looking at the film it is virtually impossible to say which course Rocky took—which is just the way I wanted it. I played it with deliberate ambiguity so that the spectator can take his choice. It seems to me it works out fine in either case. You have to decide.

It was this picture and others like it, of course, that guaranteed me a tough-guy image, an image that I am bound to say has sometimes proved mighty wearisome to me off the screen. People who don't know me have asked friends if I was really a tough character, and upon receiving assurance that I was just doing a job when portraying a hood, have perhaps not always been convinced. One fella at Warner's with a very real ability to inject himself into any conversation, had a question for me one time. "Off-screen," had said, "you're very quiet and unassuming, but when you get on there, you're a pretty boisterous fella." I admitted this. His memorable comeback was, "Now, when are you acting—on screen, or off?"

CHARLES CHAPLIN

Charles Chaplin in The Tramp *(1915), Essanay.*

Born Charles Spencer Chaplin, Jr. on April 16, 1889 in London . . . Parents music-hall entertainers . . . Mother institutionalized . . . Placed in orphanage for destitute children . . . Professional performer by the age of eight . . . Played in opening performance of *Peter Pan* 1904 . . . Met Mack Sennett during U.S. tour 1914 . . . Began starring in Keystone Films . . . Improvised world-famous "tramp" costume in *Kid Auto Races at Venice* (1914) . . . Other credits: *The Tramp* (1915) . . . *Easy Street* (1917) . . . *The Immigrant* (1917) . . . Earning $10,000 per week . . . One of the founders of United Artists in 1919 . . . First full-length film: *The Kid* (1921) . . . Followed by: *The Gold Rush* (1925) . . . *City Lights* (1931) . . . *Modern Times* (1936) . . . *The Great Dictator* (1940) . . . In 1918, Chaplin, 29, married 16-year-old actress . . . In 1924, Chaplin, 35, married 16-year-old actress . . . In 1936, Chaplin, 47, married 19-year-old Paulette Goddard . . . In 1943, Chaplin, 54, married 18-year-old Oona O'Neill (Eugene's daughter) . . . Knighted 1975 . . . Died 1977.

The Tramp

Eager and anxious, I arrived in Los Angeles and took a room at a small hotel, the Great Northern. The first evening, I took a busman's holiday and saw the second show at the Empress, where the Karno Company had worked. The attendant recognized me and came a few moments later to tell me that Mr. Sennett and Miss Mabel Normand were sitting two rows back and had asked if I would join them. I was thrilled, and after a hurried, whispered introduction we all watched the show together. When it was over, we walked a few paces down Main Street, and went to a rathskeller for a light supper and a drink. Mr. Sennett was shocked to see how young I looked. "I thought you were a much older man," he said. I could detect a tinge of concern, which made me anxious, remembering that all Sennett's comedians were oldish-looking men. Fred Mace was over fifty and Ford Sterling in his forties. "I can make up as old as you like," I answered. Mabel Normand, however, was more reassuring. Whatever her reservations were about me, she did not reveal them. Mr. Sennett said that I would not start immediately, but should come to the studio in Edendale and get acquainted with the people. When we left the café, we bundled into Mr. Sennett's glamorous racing car and I was driven to my hotel.

The following morning I boarded a streetcar for Edendale, a suburb of Los Angeles. It was an anomalous-looking place that could not make up its mind whether to be a humble residential district or a semi-industrial one. It had small lumberyards and junkyards, and abandoned-looking small farms on which were built one or two shacky wooden stores that fronted the road. After many inquiries I found myself opposite the Keystone Studio. It was a dilapidated affair with a green fence round it, one hundred and fifty feet square. The entrance to it was up a garden path through an old bungalow—the whole place looked just as anomalous as Edendale itself. I stood gazing at it from the opposite side of the road, debating whether to go in or not.

It was lunchtime and I watched the men and women in their make-up come pouring out of the bungalow, including the Keystone Cops. They crossed the road to a small general store and came out eating sandwiches and hot dogs. Some called after each other in loud, raucous voices: "Hey, Hank, come on!" "Tell Slim to hurry!"

Suddenly I was seized with shyness and walked quickly to the corner at a safe distance, looking to see if Mr. Sennett or Miss Normand would come out of the bungalow, but they did not appear. For half an hour I stood there, then decided to go back to the hotel. The problem of entering the studio and facing all those people became an insuperable one. For two days I arrived outside the studio, but I had not the courage to go in. The third day Mr. Sennett telephoned and wanted to know why I had not shown up. I made some sort of excuse. "Come down right away, we'll be waiting for you," he said. So I went down and boldly marched into the bungalow and asked for Mr. Sennett.

He was pleased to see me and took me immediately into the studio. I was enthralled. A soft, even light pervaded the whole stage. It came from broad streams of white linen that diffused the sun and gave an ethereal quality to everything. This diffusion was for photographing in daylight.

After being introduced to one or two actors, I became interested in what was going on. There were three sets side by side, and three comedy companies were at work in them. It was like viewing something at the World's Fair. In one set Mabel Normand was banging on a door, shouting, "Let me in!" Then the camera stopped and that was it—I had no idea films were made piecemeal in this fashion.

On another set was the great Ford Sterling, whom I was to replace. Mr. Sennett introduced me to him. Ford was leaving Keystone to form his own company with Universal. He was immensely popular with the public and with everyone in the studio. They surrounded his set and were laughing eagerly at him.

Sennett took me aside and explained their method of working. "We have no scenario—we get an idea, then follow the natural sequence of events until it leads up to a chase, which is the essence of our comedy."

This method was edifying, but personally I hated a chase. It dissipates one's personality; little as I knew about movies, I knew that nothing transcended personality.

That day I went from set to set watching the companies at work. They all seemed to be imitating Ford Sterling. This worried me, because his style did not suit me. He played a harassed Dutchman, ad-libbing through the scene with a Dutch accent, which was funny but was lost in silent pictures. I wondered what Sennett expected of me. He had seen my work and must have known that I was not suitable to play Ford's type of comedy; my style was just the opposite. Yet every story and situation conceived in the studio was consciously or unconsciously made for Sterling; even Roscoe [Fatty] Arbuckle was imitating Sterling.

The studio had evidently been a farm. Mabel Normand's dressing room was situated in an old bungalow and adjoining it was another room where the ladies of the stock company dressed. Across from the bungalow was what had evidently been a barn, the main dressing room for minor members of the stock company and the Keystone Cops, the majority of whom were ex-circus clowns and prize fighters. I was allotted the star dressing room used by Mack Sennett, Ford Sterling and Roscoe Arbuckle. It was another barnlike structure, which might have been the harness room. Besides Mabel Normand, there were several other beautiful girls. It was a strange and unique atmosphere of beauty and beast.

For days I wandered around the studio, wondering when I would start work. Occasionally I would meet Sennett crossing the stage, but he would look through me, preoccupied. I had an uncomfortable feeling that he thought he had made a mistake in engaging me which did little to ameliorate my nervous tension.

Each day my peace of mind depended on Sennett. If perchance he saw me and smiled, my hopes would rise. The rest of the company had a wait-and-see attitude, but some, I felt, considered me a doubtful substitute for Ford Sterling.

When Saturday came, Sennett was most amiable. Said he, "Go to the front office and get your check." I told him I was more anxious to get to work. I wanted to talk about imitating Ford Sterling, but he dismissed me with the remark, "Don't worry, we'll get around to that."

Nine days of inactivity had passed and the tension was excruciating. Ford, however, would console me, and after work he would occasionally give me a lift downtown, where we would stop in at the Alexandria Bar for a drink and meet several of his friends. One of them, a Mr. Elmer Ellsworth, whom I disliked at first and thought rather crass, would jokingly taunt me: "I understand you're taking Ford's place. Well, are you funny?"

"Modesty forbids," I said squirmishly. This sort of ribbing was most embarrassing, especially in the presence of Ford. But he graciously took me off the hook with the remark, "Didn't you catch him at the Empress playing the drunk? Very funny."

"Well, he hasn't made me laugh yet," said Ellsworth.

He was a big, cumbersome man, and looked glandular, with a melancholy, hangdog expression, hairless face, sad eyes, a loose mouth and a smile that showed two missing front teeth. Ford whispered inpressively that he was a great authority on literature, finance and politics, one of the best-informed men in the country, and that he had a great sense of humor. However, I did not appreciate it and decided I would try to avoid him. But one night at the Alexandria Bar, he said, "Hasn't this limey got started yet?"

"Not yet." I laughed uncomfortably.

"Well, you'd better be funny."

Having taken a great deal from the gentleman, I gave him back some of his own medicine: "Well, if I'm half as funny as you look, I'll do all right."

"Blimey! A sarcastic wit, eh? I'll buy him a drink after that."

At last the moment came. Sennett was away on location with Mabel Normand as well as the Ford Sterling Company, so there was hardly anyone left in the studio. Mr. Henry Lehrman, Keystone's top director after Sennett, was to start a new picture and wanted me to play a newspaper reporter. Lehrman was a vain man and very conscious of the fact that he had made some successful comedies of a mechanical nature; he used to say that he didn't need personalities, that he got all his laughs from mechanical effects and film cutting.

We had no story. It was to be a documentary about the printing press done with a few comedy touches. I wore a light frock coat, a top hat and a handlebar mustache. When we started I could see that Lehrman was groping for ideas. And of course, being a newcomer at Keystone, I was anxious to make suggestions. This was where I created antagonism with Lehrman. In a scene in which I had an interview with an editor of a newspaper I crammed in every conceivable gag I could think of, even to suggesting business for others in the cast. Although the picture was completed in three days, I thought we contrived some very funny gags. But when I saw the finished film it broke my heart, for the cutter had butchered it beyond recognition, cutting into the middle of all my funny business. I was bewildered, and wondered why they had done this. Henry Lehrman confessed years later that he had deliberately done it, because, as he put it, he thought I knew too much.

The day after I finished with Lehrman, Sennett returned from location. Ford Sterling was on one set, Arbuckle on another; the whole stage was crowded with three companies at work. I was in my street clothes and had nothing to do, so I stood where Sennett could see me. He was standing with Mabel, looking into a hotel lobby set, biting the end of a cigar. "We need some gags here," he said, then turned to me. "Put on a comedy made-up. Anything will do."

I had no idea what make-up to put on. I did not like my getup as the press reporter. However, on the way to the wardrobe I thought I would dress in baggy pants, big shoes, a cane and a derby hat. I wanted everything a contradiction: the pants baggy, the coat tight, the hat small and the shoes large. I was undecided whether to look old or young, but remembering Sennett had expected me to be a much older man, I added a small mustache, which, I reasoned, would add age without hiding my expression.

I had no idea of the character. But the moment I was dressed, the clothes and the make-up made me feel the person he was. I began to know him, and by the time I walked onto the stage he was fully born. When I confronted Sennett I assumed the character and strutted about, swinging my cane and parading before him. Gags and comedy ideas went racing through my mind.

The secret of Mack Sennett's success was his enthusiasm. He was a great audience and laughed genuinely at what he thought funny. He stood and giggled until his body began to shake. This encouraged me and I began to explain the character: "You know this fellow is many-sided, a tramp, a gentleman, a poet, a dreamer, a lonely fellow, always hopeful of romance and adventure. He would have you believe he is a scientist, a musician, a duke, a polo player. However, he is not above picking up cigarette butts or robbing a baby of its candy. And, of course, if the occasion warrants it, he will kick a lady in the rear—but only in extreme anger!"

I carried on this way for ten minutes or more, keeping Sennett in continuous chuckles. "All right," said he, "get on the set and see what you can do there." As with the Lehrman film, I knew little of what the story was about, other than that Mabel Normand gets involved with her husband and a lover.

In all comedy business an attitude is most important, but it is not always easy to find an attitude. However, in the hotel lobby I felt I was an impostor posing as one of the guests, but in reality I was a tramp just wanting a little shelter. I entered and stumbled over the foot of a lady. I turned and raised my hat apologetically, then turned and stumbled over a cuspidor, then turned and raised my hat to the cuspidor. Behind the camera they began to laugh.

Quite a crowd had gathered there, not only the players of the other companies who left their sets to watch us, but also the stagehands, the carpenters and the wardrobe department. That indeed was a compliment. And by the time we had finished rehearsing we had quite a large audience laughing. Very soon I saw Ford Sterling peering over the shoulders of others. When it was over I knew I had made good.

At the end of the day when I went to the dressing room, Ford Sterling and Roscoe Arbuckle were taking off their make-up. Very little was said, but the atmosphere was charged with crosscurrents. Both Ford and Roscoe liked me, but I frankly felt they were undergoing some inner conflict.

It was a long scene that ran seventy-five feet. Later Mr. Sennett and Mr. Lehrman debated whether to let it run its full length, as the average comedy scene rarely ran over ten. "If it's funny," I said, "does length really matter?" They decided to let the scene run its full seventy-five feet. As the clothes had imbued me with the character, I then and there decided I would keep to this costume, whatever happened.

That evening I went home on the streetcar with one of the small bit players. Said he, "Boy, you've started something; nobody ever got those kind of laughs on the set before, not even Ford Sterling—and you should have seen his face watching you, it was a study!"

"Let's hope they'll laugh the same way in the theatre," I said, by way of suppressing my elation.

A few days later, at the Alexandria Bar, I overheard Ford giving his description of my character to our mutual friend Elmer Ellsworth: "The guy has baggy pants, flat feet, the most miserable, bedraggled-looking little bastard you ever saw; makes itchy gestures as though he's got crabs under his arms—but he's funny."

My character was different and unfamiliar to the American, and even unfamiliar to myself. But with the clothes on I felt he was a reality, a living person. In fact he ignited all sorts of crazy ideas that I would never have dreamt of, until I was dressed and made up as the Tramp.

I became quite friendly with a small-bit player, and each night going home on the streetcar he would give me a bulletin of the studio's reactions that day and talk of my comedy ideas. "That was a wonderful gag, dipping your fingers in the finger bowl, then wiping them on the old man's whiskers—they've never seen that kind of stuff around there." And so he would carry on, having me stepping on air.

Under Sennett's direction I felt comfortable, because everything was spontaneously worked out on the set. As no one was positive or sure of himself (not even the director), I concluded that I knew as much as the other fellow. This gave me confidence; I began to offer suggestions which Sennett readily accepted. Thus grew a belief in myself that I was creative and could write my own stories. Sennett indeed had inspired this belief. But although I had pleased Sennett I had yet to please the public.

In the next picture I was assigned to Lehrman again. He was leaving Sennett to join Sterling and to oblige Sennett was staying on two weeks longer than his contract called for. I still had abundant suggestions when I started working with him. He would listen and smile but would not accept any of them. "That may be funny in the theatre," he would say, "but in pictures we have no time for it. We must be on the go—comedy is an excuse for a chase."

I did not agree with this generality. "Humor is humor," I argued, "whether in films or on the stage." But he insisted on the same rigmarole, doing what Keystone had always done. All action had to be fast—which meant running and climbing on top of the roofs of houses and streetcars, jumping into rivers and diving off piers. In spite of his comedy theories I happened to get in one or two bits of individual funny business, but, as before, he managed to have them mutilated in the cutting room.

I do not think Lehrman gave a very promising report to Sennett about me. After Lehrman, I was assigned to another director, Mr. Nichols, an oldish man in his late fifties who had been in motion pictures since their inception. I had the same trouble with him. He had but one gag, which was to take the comedian by the neck and bounce him from one scene to another. I tried to suggest subtler business, but he too would not listen. "We have no time, no time!" he would cry. All he wanted was an imitation of Ford Sterling. Although I only mildly rebelled, it appears that he went to Sennett saying that I was a son of a bitch to work with.

About this time the picture which Sennett had directed, *Mabel's Strange Predicament*, was shown downtown. With fear and trepidation, I saw it with an audience. With Ford Sterling's appearance there was always a stir of enthusiasm and laughter, but I was received in cold silence. All the funny stuff I had done in the hotel lobby hardly got a smile. But as the picture progressed, the audience began to titter, then laugh, and toward the end of the picture there were one or two big laughs. At that showing I discovered that the audience was not partial to a newcomer.

I doubt whether this first effort came up to Sennett's expectations. I believe he was disappointed. He came to me a day or so later: "Listen, they say you're difficult to work with." I tried to explain that I was conscientious and was working only for the good of the picture. "Well," said Sennett, coldly, "just do what you're told and we'll be satisfied." But the following day I had another altercation with Nichols, and I blew up. "Any three-dollar-a-day extra can do what you want me to do," I declared. "I want to do something with merit, not just be bounced around and fall off streetcars. I'm not getting a hundred and fifty dollars a week just for that."

Poor old "Pop" Nichols, as we called him, was in a terrible state. "I've been in this business over ten years," he said. "What the hell do you know about it?" I tried to reason with him, but to no avail. I tried to reason with members of the cast, but they also were against me. "Oh, he knows, he knows, he's been in the business much longer than you have," said an old actor.

I made about five pictures and in some of them I had managed to put over one or two bits of comedy business of my own, in spite of the butchers in the cutting room. Familiar with their method of cutting films, I would contrive business and gags just for entering and exiting from a scene, knowing that they would have difficulty in cutting them out. I took every opportunity I could to learn the business. I was in and out of the developing plant and cutting room, watching the cutter piece the films together.

Now I was anxious to write and direct my own comedies, so I talked to Sennett about it. But he would not hear of it; instead he assigned me to Mabel Normand, who had just started directing her own pictures. This nettled me, for, charming as Mabel was, I doubted her competence as a director; so the first day there came the inevitable blowup. We were on location in the suburbs of Los Angeles, and in one scene Mabel wanted me to stand with a hose and water down the road so that the villain's car would skid over it. I suggested standing on the hose so that the water can't come out, and when I look down the nozzle I unconsciously step off the hose and the water squirts in my face. But she shut me up quickly: "We have no time! We have no time! Do what you're told."

That was enough, I could not take it—and from such a pretty girl. "I'm sorry, Miss Normand, I will not do what I'm told. I don't think you are competent to tell me what to do."

The scene was in the center of the road, and I left it and sat down on the curb. Sweet Mabel—at that time she was only twenty, pretty and charming, everybody's favorite; everybody loved her. Now she sat by the camera bewildered; nobody had ever spoken to her so directly before. I also was susceptible to her charm and beauty and secretly had a soft spot in my heart for her, but this was my work. Immediately the staff and the cast surrounded Mabel and went into conference. One or two extras, Mabel told me afterwards, wanted to slug me, but she stopped them from doing so. Then she sent the assistant over to find out if I was going to continue working. I crossed the road to where she was sitting. "I'm sorry," I said apologetically, "I just don't think it's funny or amusing. But if you'll allow me to offer a few comedy suggestions . . ."

She did not argue. "Very well," she said. "If you won't do what you're told, we'll go back to the studio." Although the situation was desperate, I was resigned, so I shrugged. We had not lost much of the day's work, for we had been shooting since nine in the morning. It was now past five in the afternoon and the sun was sinking fast.

At the studio, while I was taking off my grease paint, Sennett came bursting into the dressing room. "What the hell's the idea?" he said.

I tried to explain. "The story needs gagging up," I said, "but Miss Normand will not listen to any suggestions."

"You'll do what you're told or get out, contract or no contract," he said.

I was very calm. "Mr. Sennett," I answered, "I earned my bread and cheese before

I came here, and if I'm fired—well, I'm fired. But I'm conscientious and just as keen to make a good picture as you are."

Without saying anything further he slammed the door.

That night, going home on the streetcar with my friend, I told him what had happened.

"Too bad. You were going great there for a while," he said.

"Do you think they'll fire me?" I said cheerfully, in order to hide my anxiety.

"I wouldn't be at all surprised. When I saw him leaving your dressing room he looked pretty mad."

"Well, it's O.K. with me. I've gotten fifteen hundred dollars in my belt and that will more than pay my fare back to England. However, I'll show up tomorrow and if they don't want me—*c'est la vie.*"

There was an eight o'clock call the following morning and I was not sure what to do, so I sat in the dressing room without making up. About ten minutes to eight Sennett poked his head in the door. "Charlie, I want to talk to you. Let's go into Mabel's dressing room." His tone was surprisingly friendly.

"Yes, Mr. Sennett," I said, following him.

Mabel was not there. She was in the projection room looking at rushes.

"Listen," said Mack, "Mabel's very fond of you, we all are fond of you and think you're a fine artist."

I was surprised at this sudden change and I immediately began to melt. "I certainly have the greatest respect and admiration for Miss Normand," I said, "but I don't think she is competent to direct—after all, she's very young."

"Whatever you think, just swallow your pride and help out," said Sennett, patting me on the shoulder.

"That's precisely what I've been trying to do."

"Well, do your best to get along with her."

"Listen, if you'll let me direct myself, you'll have no trouble," I said.

Mack paused a moment. "Who's going to pay for the film if we can't release it?"

"I will," I answered. "I'll deposit fifteen hundred dollars in any bank and if you can't release the picture you can keep the money."

Mack thought a moment. "Have you a story?"

"Of course, as many as you want."

"All right," said Mack. "Finish the picture with Mabel, then I'll see." We shook hands in a most friendly manner. Later I went to Mabel and apologized, and that evening Sennett took us both out to dinner. The next day Mabel could not have been sweeter. She even came to me for suggestions and ideas. Thus, to the bewilderment of the camera crew and the rest of the cast, we happily completed the picture. Sennett's sudden change of attitude baffled me. It was months later, however, that I found out the reason: it appears that Sennett intended firing me at the end of the week, but the morning after I had quarreled with Mabel, Mack received a telegram from the New York office telling him to hurry up with more Chaplin pictures as there was a terrific demand for them.

The average number of prints for a Keystone Comedy release was twenty. Thirty was considered quite successful. The last picture, which was the fourth one, reached forty-five copies, and demands for further copies were increasing. Hence Mack's friendliness after the telegram.

The mechanics of directing were simple in those days. I had only to know my left from my right for entrances and exits. If one exited right from a scene, one came in left in the next scene; if one exited towards the camera, one entered with one's back to the camera in the next scene. These, of course, were primary rules.

But with more experience I found that the placing of a camera was not only psychological but articulated a scene; in fact, it was the basis of cinematic style. If the camera is a little too near, or too far, it can enhance or spoil an effect. Because economy of movement is important you don't want an actor to walk any unnecessary distance unless there is a special reason, for walking is not dramatic. Therefore placement of camera should effect composition and a graceful entrance for the actor. Placement of camera is cinematic inflection. There is no set rule that a close-up gives more emphasis than a long shot. A close-up is a question of feeling; in some instances a long shot can effect greater emphasis.

An example of this is in one of my early comedies, *Skating*. The tramp enters the rink and skates with one foot up, gliding and twirling, tripping and bumping into people and getting into all sorts of mischief, eventually leaving everyone piled up on their backs in the foreground of the camera, while he skates to the rear of the rink, becoming a very small figure in the background, and sits among the spectators innocently reviewing the havoc he has just created. Yet the small figure of the tramp in the distance was funnier than he would have been in a close-up.

When I started directing my first picture, I was not as confident as I thought I would be; in fact, I had a slight attack of panic. But after Sennett saw the first day's work I was reassured. The picture was called *Caught in the Rain*. It was not a world-beater, but it was funny and quite a success. When I finished it, I was anxious to know Sennett's reaction. I waited for him as he came out of the projection room. "Well, are you ready to start another?" he said. From then on I wrote and directed all my own comedies. As an inducement, Sennett gave me a twenty-five-dollar bonus for each picture.

He now practically adopted me, and took me to dinner every night. He would discuss stories for the other companies with me and I would suggest crazy ideas which I felt were too personal to be understood by the public. But Sennett would laugh and accept them.

Now, when I saw my films with an audience, their reaction was different. The stir and excitement at the announcement of a Keystone Comedy, those joyful little screams that my first appearance evoked even before I had done anything, were most gratifying. I was a great favorite with the audience: if I could just continue this way of life I could be satisfied. With my bonus I was making two hundred dollars a week.

Since I was engrossed in work I had little time for the Alexandria Bar or my sarcastic friend, Elmer Ellsworth. I met him, however, weeks later, on the street. "Say, listen," said he, "I've been seeing your pictures lately, and, by God, you're good! You have a quality entirely different from all the rest. And I'm not kidding. You're funny! Why the hell didn't you say so in the first place?" Of course, we became very good friends after that.

There was a lot Keystone taught me and a lot I taught Keystone. In those days they knew little about technique, stagecraft or movement, which I brought to them from the theatre. They also knew little about natural pantomime. In blocking a scene, a director would have three or four actors blatantly stand in a straight line facing the camera, and, with the broadest gestures, one would pantomime "I-want-to-marry-your-daughter" by pointing to himself, then to his ring finger, then to the girl. Their miming dealt little with subtlety or effectiveness, so I stood out in contrast. In those early movies, I knew I had many advantages, and that, like a geologist, I was entering a rich, unexplored field. I suppose that was the most exciting period of my career, for I was on the threshold of something wonderful.

Success makes one endearing and I became the familiar friend of everyone in the studio. I was "Charlie" to the extras, to the stagehands, the wardrobe department, and the cameramen. Although I am not a fraternizer, this pleased me indeed, for I knew that this familiarity meant I was a success.

Now I had confidence in my ideas, and I can thank Sennett for that, for although unlettered like myself, he had belief in his own taste, and such belief he instilled in me. His manner of working had given me confidence; it seemed right. His remark that first day at the studio: "We have no scenario—we get an idea then follow the natural sequence of events . . ." had stimulated my imagination.

The Tramp.

JACKIE COOPER

Wallace Beery and Jackie Cooper in The Champ *(1931), MGM.*

Born John Cooper, Jr. on September 15, 1921 in Los Angeles . . . Nephew of director Norman Taurog . . . Began appearing in film comedies at age of 3 . . . Early fame with *Our Gang* . . . *The Champ* (1931) . . . *The Bowery* (1933) . . . *Treasure Island* (1934) . . . *Peck's Bad Boy* (1934) . . . *The Devil Is a Sissy* (1936) . . . Innocent romance with Judy Garland . . . Not so innocent with Joan Crawford . . . Career declined in 1940s . . . Attempted comeback in such B movies as *Stork Bites Man* (1947) . . . TV series: *The People's Choice* in 1955 . . . *Hennessey* in 1959 . . . Directed many episodes of *The Rockford Files*, *Trapper John, M.D.*, and *Quincy* . . . In 1978, replaced an ailing Keenan Wynn as *Daily Planet* editor Perry White in *Superman* films.

Coming of Age
in Hollywood

F or a boy like me, with very normal urges, Hollywood and the movie studios were a spectacular place to grow up. For example, when I was sixteen, and at Paramount, one of us kids discovered the Paulette Goddard scenic view. Pretty soon we all knew about it. Somebody had noticed that there was a vantage point with a direct, unimpeded, and total view into her dressing room. Furthermore—and this was the juicy part—Miss Goddard liked to loll around her dressing room topless.

You can imagine what sport a bunch of young teenage boys would have with that knowledge. Paulette Goddard was a lady of fantastic construction. I cannot vouch for my contemporaries, for Mickey Rooney and Jackie Searle and the others, but I know that I would find many excuses to take myself to that particular vantage point and just hope that she was there and in her usual state of astounding undress.

On any lot, too, there was a constant parade of chorus girls and dress (or undress) extras, for the lavish musicals and spectacular costume dramas that were being filmed there. Just a stroll around the lot, and an enterprising young lad could gawk at dozens of gorgeous girls, and since this particular enterprising young lad was well known, they gawked back. I was no longer in the cute and precious stage, so they had no excuse to fondle me, but I was a star, and they were almost always ambitious, so they would talk to me, and I quickly learned how to converse with girls.

I remember one day when I was eleven or twelve, on the MGM lot, watching with tremendous interest the progress of Jean Harlow down a street. She was wearing a gown so sheer that it was possible—indeed, probable—that everything she had was in almost plain view. And she had plenty. My mother was with me, and she noticed my interest, and she laughed. She didn't reprimand me for gawking, and she wasn't embarrassed or shocked by it. She thought it was normal and an indication that I was normal and, also, growing up.

I knew the facts of life. My mother was a very progressive and intelligent lady, and she had answered all my childhood and adolescent questions fully and without embarrassment. If she was, for example, talking to a friend about "labor" when I was nine or ten, and I would ask her what she meant, she would tell me. No hesitation and no detours. Yet she would never give me too much information. Some parents I know, in their desire to be forward-thinking, will answer a child's innocent question with an hour-long dissertation complete with slides. At that age, if I saw a pregnant lady and I asked my mother why she had such a fat tummy, my mother would say,

"She's carrying a baby in her stomach." I would say, "Oh," and that would be that. No more, no less. My curiosity would be amply satisfied, but I would not be burdened with information which I did not need and could not, for that matter, understand yet.

My mother answered all my questions, and she would always give another bit of helpful information. She would caution me not to talk to the other kids about such matters. I guess she felt that they would give me the wrong dope—kids often having been given wrong ideas by other kids—which would only confuse me. I never did ask the other kids.

In my era the human body was pretty much a hidden commodity. Until Paulette Goddard's time I really had only seen one body—mine. There were no centerfolds in magazines for kids to moon over. The bikini hadn't been invented yet. There were no nude scenes in movies. And so girls, to me as I entered those exciting teenage years, were still a mystery. What was it they had, under all those clothes, which somehow stirred me? I knew, of course, and yet I didn't know. I knew intellectually, but I had yet to see for myself.

There had been one small experience when I was very young. It had been when I was so young, in fact, that it served only to disturb me, rather than excite me.

When I was seven or eight, we rented a beach house. This particular beach house had an outdoor shower. My aunt Julie—a year or so younger than my mother and the one with the family reputation of being the beauty—would get in the shower with me. It was an enclosed shower, so nobody else could see or even knew. We were both naked. I remembered looking at her. I remember being bothered by it. Nothing happened in the shower, but it was, to me, an unpleasant experience.

I was twelve or so when I went to some parties when we lived in Ocean Park. There was a little girl across the street whose name, if my memory isn't playing tricks on me, was Farrell Minick. She was the first girl of twelve or thirteen—the first *big* girl—who paid any attention to me, the kind of attention a boy realizes comes because he is liked, not because he has a worm in his pocket. There were parties, and we went, and we played spin the bottle. My first real kiss was from Farrell Minick after the bottle had spun in her direction. . . .

I had known Judy Garland around MGM, but not well. Then we did a radio show together—it was hosted by Wally Beery—and our mothers thought we looked good together. What's more, since we were both in the business and understood what it was like to be in the business, we had that in common. So Mabel Cooper and Ethel Gumm decided that Jackie Cooper and Judy Garland would be okay to go out a little. They both recognized the fact that their children were growing up and needed to consort with people of the other sex, and they felt that this would be a good thing. Judy was about nine months older than I was, but I was taller, so that was okay.

I cannot speak for Judy, but I was pleased by the prospect of seeing more of her.

We had things in common besides acting at MGM. Music, mostly. I had begun playing the drums, and so we had a lot to talk about.

I was invited over to her house for a Sunday dinner. The dinner itself was a bore—too many adults, and I didn't know them—but afterward, in Judy's room, we played Benny Goodman records, and we held hands.

We had to reciprocate and have Judy over to our house for dinner. I learned that it may be okay for a girl to ask a boy up to her room, but the reverse is considered sinful. So Judy and I walked on the beach, and she said, "Can I kiss you?" and so I was in love. She said she was, too.

I hadn't yet reached my fourteenth birthday, and I couldn't drive, so when I asked her out on a date, I had to prevail on my mother to hire a driver. We went to a movie—holding sweating hands—and then somewhere for an ice cream soda. We had other dates, and I discovered the joys of necking in the back seat of a car, with a discreet driver who turned up the rearview mirror. And we talked, by the hour, on the telephone. She told me how mean L. B. Mayer was to her, how he continually picked on her appearance (when I directed the television movie *Rainbow* about her, I had the writers add a scene about Mayer and Judy, drawing on information she herself had given me). She told me about her family problems. I am sure I told her mine, although what I had to tell—mostly, I suppose, about my grandmother—paled when compared to Judy's accounts of her parents and their actions toward her.

Judy put an end to our relationship a few months after it began. She did it very nicely. It hardly hurt. She had fallen for an older man, Billy Halop, who was sixteen or so and just recently imported from New York. We remained good friends, although I seldom saw her after that. She did ask me to do her a favor once, a couple of years later. She had fallen—as many other women had—for Artie Shaw. But she knew he was forbidden fruit, too old, too experienced, so she could never let him pick her up. Instead, would I pick her up? I was still okay. Then I was to take her to wherever she was meeting Artie and just sort of hang around someplace else for a few hours, then pick her up and take her home. You know how it is with us shnooks. I said sure. I did that a few times. They weren't the greatest nights in my life, but I felt I had been a good friend.

I had also had a brief on-the-set fling with Deanna Durbin, when we did a picture together. It is an old Hollywood custom for leading men and leading lady to fall for each other. In *That Certain Age* I kissed her on screen, and I gave her a few off-screen kisses, too. We had problems finding privacy on the bustling movie set and finally took to a tactic which I imagine has stood romantically inclined couples on movie sets in good stead for many years. We would duck behind the backdrops and find a few precious—although musty—moments of quiet and togetherness. Then, when the call came for the first team to report back, she would go one way and I would go the other way. And we probably fooled nobody, with our smeared makeup and our perspiring bodies.

I was seventeen, and I began to go over to Joan Crawford's house to play badminton. She was a friend of my mother's and, over the years, had offered me the use of her court. She didn't have room for a tennis court, so had put in a badminton court, and I had learned to enjoy playing that game.

The court was right off the pool house, and one day, sweaty from an hour of exertion, I went into the pool house with Joan. I was thirsty, and she poured me a Coke. As she bent over, I looked down her dress.

"You're growing up, aren't you?" she said.

I was brash, fresh from some romantic triumph, I suppose, and I made some remark which I assumed was sophisticated, witty, and very sexually provocative.

"You had better get out of here, young man," she said.

But I didn't go. Instead, I made a move toward her, and she stood up, looked at me appraisingly, and then closed all the drapes. And I made love to Joan Crawford. Or, rather, she made love to me.

Over the next six months or so the performance was repeated eight or nine times. After the first time, however, it was always late at night. I would set a date with her, then manage to sneak out of the house after my mother and stepfather had gone to sleep. I would roll my car down the street until I was far enough away so I could start the engine without waking them. And I would drive to Joan's house.

She was a very erudite professor of love. At the time I suppose she was in her early thirties. I was seventeen. She was a wild woman. She would bathe me, powder me, cologne me. Then she would do it over again. She would put on high heels, a garter belt, and a large hat and pose in front of the mirror, turning this way and that way.

"Look," she would say. I was already looking. But that sort of thing didn't particularly excite me. I kept thinking: The lady is crazy.

But I recognized that she was an extraordinary performer, that I was learning things that most men don't learn until they are much older—if at all. There was never any drinking or drugs with her. It was all business. She was very organized. When I left, she would put me on her calendar for the next visit. I could hardly wait.

One night, after one of our sessions, she said that was the last time. She said I should never call her again.

"And put it all out of your mind," she said. "It never happened."

And then she gave me one last kiss and added, "But we'll always be friends."

I was floating during that period. Fortunately I had enough sense not to blab my conquest all over town, but it was a magnificent secret to have. My friends might brag about some pimply-faced teenager or gawky sixteen-year-old they had had, and I would nod my congratulations. And I would think to myself: But I have been with one of the Love Goddesses of the Screen. Maybe I didn't say anything because I had enough sense not to. But maybe it was because I knew they wouldn't have believed me.

The last time I saw Joan Crawford was when I was doing a guest shot in Peter

Falk's *Columbo* series. She was on the Universal lot at the same time, doing something, and the studio was buzzing with the news that Crawford was around. By accident, I happened to run into her, and she took my hand, looked in my eyes, and, I think, remembered.

Christopher Reeve, Margot Kidder and Jackie Cooper in Superman *(1978), Warner Bros.*

BING CROSBY

Kitty Carlisle and Bing Crosby in She Loves Me Not *(1934), Paramount.*

Born Harry Lillis Crosby on May 2, 1901 in Tacoma, Washington . . . Educated at Gonzaga U. . . . Took nickname from favorite comic strip "The Bingville Bugle" . . . Crooning with Paul Whiteman band in 1926 . . . Married Dixie Lee 1930 . . . Widowed 1952 . . . Theme song: "When the Blue of the Night" . . . First film: *King of Jazz* (1930) . . . Went "on the road" with Bob Hope in 1940 in *Road to Singapore* . . . Academy Award for *Going My Way* (1944) . . . *White Christmas* (1954) . . . *High Society* (1956) . . . *Bing Crosby Show* on TV in 1964 . . . Invested wisely: fortune at one time estimated between 200 million and 400 million dollars . . . Died of heart attack on golf course in 1977.

"The Ears Are Wingy"

It was in the 1934 film, *She Loves Me Not*, that I made my brave stand against having my ears glued back to increase my beauty. This nuisance had its beginning in the time when I was courting Dixie and was having my trouble with Abe Frank [nightclub impresario]. I played a lot of golf then with a Broadway actor, Dick Keene. Dick was working at Fox, and it was his notion that I'd be a good bet for picture work. He took me to see Jim Ryan, the casting director at Fox's Western Avenue studio. Ryan had me sing a couple of songs and read a few lines, and he seemed to like the way I did them. But after looking me over for a while, he said, "I'm afraid there's no future for you in pictures."

"Why not?" I asked.

"They could never photograph you," he said. "The ears are wingy."

I thought he said, "The years are winging," meaning that I was acquiring mileage. I wasn't very old and I flipped.

"I don't mean your age," he said. "Your ears protrude. They stick out too far. A camera pointed straight at you would make you look like a taxi with both doors open. They'd have to photograph you three-quarter-face or profile, and that would put too much of a limit on the cameraman. I'm sorry."

Dick and I went out feeling pretty crestfallen.

Seven or eight years later I became a parishioner of the Chruch of the Good Shepherd in Beverly Hills. Jim Ryan is a member of the congregation and we sit near each other. I always get up and go out before he does, and I never fail to bat my ears significantly at him as I go by. We both grin.

When I went to work in *The Big Broadcast*, Paramount shared Ryan's views of my ears as a photographic problem and they insisted on gluing them back against my head with spirit gum. I must admit that I was surprised at what the gluing did to my appearance. I looked streamlined, like a whippet dashing after a mechanical bunny. I put up with the spirit gum for a long time. Then they tried adhesive; then they went back to spirit gum. George Raft's ears were batty, too, but he'd had a muscle cut behind his ears which made them fall back against his noggin without having to be pushed by a make-up man. I wouldn't go for such an operation. I liked my ears the way they were—at least for everyday use. However, I was resigned to pinning them back for screen purposes, although both the glue and the adhesive were disagreeable. Then, too, no matter how firmly they were pinned back, they kept popping out all the time, much to the annoyance of Paramount's make-up department.

One of the scenes from *She Loves Me Not* had to be heavily lighted and the heat kept loosening the stickum until my ears popped out eight or ten times. The tenth time I said, "This time they're going to stay out."

"I've got orders not to shoot you that way," the cameraman told me.

"They're out and they're going to stay out," I said. "I'll be at the Lakeside Golf Club. If the studio changes its mind, tell them to call me there."

The first tee at Lakeside is my refuge when the studio is obdurate about what seems to me a reasonable request. If I'm convinced that they are being bull-headed or are pulling rank on me, I retire there to await developments. Finally a man at the studio called. "We'll shoot them sticking out if you feel so strongly about it," he said. So *She Loves me Not* was shot partly with them out and partly with them in. In the first part I looked like a whippet in full flight. In the second part I looked like Dumbo. They've been out ever since.

But though I won a victory over stickum back of my ears, I capitulated to another nuisance—cake make-up. This nuisance was wished on me by Harry Ray, a make-up man. He was never around when we needed him, so we called him Mile-Away Ray or The Seldom-Seen Kid. He'd make me up in the morning, and disappear, and my face would grow shiny. We spent a lot of time figuring where he vanished to. There was one theory that he hid in a restaurant several blocks away called, with obvious inaccuracy, the Health Center. An alternate theory was that he flitted around the lot visiting other sets, playing Run, Sheep, Run and Prisoner's Base with the scouts and posses we sent to look for him.

When he was on deck, we engaged in a running debate because I refused to wear cake make-up. I'd used the professional kind in my vaudeville days, but my skin was dry, and it had made my face itch. After it had dried and I'd had it on a while it seemed to grow flaky and I'd go around all day screwing my face up like a man with a tic. I'd developed quite a hatred for it. In the end, the Seldom-Seen Kid played on my college loyalty. Gonzaga was coming to town to play Loyola, and Mile-Away Ray lured me into a bet on the game. The bet was that if Loyola won I'd wear the make-up he wanted me to wear. Loyola won and I wore it.

Robert Hope, of the non-classic profile and the unlissome mid-section, is sometimes goaded by a knowledge of his own lack of physical charms into referring to me as "skin head." I don't have to specify what he means. It's generally known that for screen purposes I wear a device the trade calls a "scalp doily," a "mucket" or "a divot." The technical name for it is a hair piece.

I hate to put it on, and I'm always trying to have interior scenes photographed out-of-doors, so I can wear a hat. Before he died, Buddy DeSylva, former head of production at Paramount, promised me that if I would do a favor for him—I forget just what it was now—he'd buy a story for me in which I could play a rabbi and wear a hat all the time.

Each morning when I get a script, I look through it to see if there's any way I can get through the day without donning a mucket. Not that it's such a chore to put on, but the glue in it makes my forehead itch and I can't scratch the itching places without pulling it off. I'm always plotting ways to do a love scene wearing a hat. In one scene I was to meet a girl at a railway station and greet her with a big embrace and a kiss. "You'll have to take your hat off for this one," the director said firmly.

If he thought I'd give up that easily, he'd misjudged me. "Not me," I said. "This fellow's so excited at seeing his girl he doesn't remember to take his hat off. He's deeply in love with her and hasn't seen her for a long time, so he has no time to think about the social amenities when she arrives. He just grabs her, and after that he's too busy to take his hat off."

In the *Road to Morocco*, I tried to wear a hat in bed, but Dave Butler, the director, was obdurate. I finally talked him into a night cap with a tassel.

Speaking of muckets, Wally Westmore of the fabulous Westmore family, identified with the make-up end of the picture business almost since its inception, has kept me in pictures years longer than I would ordinarily have lasted. It was he and his brothers, the "Marryin' Westmores," who developed the "bowser," as it's sometimes called, which has saved many an actor whose thinning thatch would otherwise have doomed him to an early theatrical demise. Who but Wally could have been taken on a trip to Paris for exterior location shots on my last picture, *Little Boy Lost*, on the unlikely possibility that I might be induced to doff my chapeau and need a hair piece? It was Wally's first trip to Paris and some mornings, following expansive evenings, he got it on backwards, sideways, or tipped rakishly.

Another prop for my manly beauty was forced upon me in a 1935 movie called *Mississippi*. It's fairer to say that I forced it upon myself, for I'd let my weight creep up to one hundred and ninety pounds. I was eating a lot and getting lots of sleep, and it had been a long time between pictures, so I'd blown up to an unfashionable one-nine-o. *Mississippi* was a period picture—Civil War—and the pants I had to wear in it were so tight that my extra suet was conspicuous. As a result, I had to be strapped up, and I soon found out why women are so anxious to get out of their girdles.

SAMMY DAVIS, JR.

Joey Bishop (third from left), Sammy Davis, Jr., Frank Sinatra, Peter Lawford, Dean Martin and others in Ocean's 11 *(1960), Warner Bros.*

Born December 8, 1925 in New York City . . . Started singing and dancing at age 3 with the Will Mastin (his uncle) Trio . . . Lost left eye in car accident in 1954 . . . Appeared on Broadway in *Mr. Wonderful* (1956) . . . First film: *The Benny Goodman Story* (1959) . . . Followed by: *Porgy and Bess* (1959) . . . *Ocean's 11* (1960) . . . *Robin and the Seven Hoods* (1964) . . . Married Swedish actress May Britt in 1960 . . . Once described himself as a "one-eyed Jewish Negro."

The Rat Pack

The sign in front of The Sands was a classic, as marquees go, for nightclub shows:

FRANK SINATRA
DEAN MARTIN
SAMMY DAVIS, JR.
PETER LAWFORD
JOEY BISHOP

A few months before, when we'd made our plans to shoot *Ocean's 11* and play the hotel simultaneously, the newspapers had been filled with stories about Eisenhower, De Gaulle, and Khrushchev planning a Summit Conference, and Frank had joked, "We'll have our own little Summit meeting." One of the papers printed it, others picked it up, and it stuck.

Within a week after our "Summit" was announced there wasn't a room to be had in any hotel in town. People flew in from Chicago, Los Angeles, New York—from all over the country—weeks before we got there, to be sure their rooms weren't sold out from under them. We'd been in Vegas for a week, and still plane, train, and busloads of people were pouring into town, arriving without hotel reservations, sleeping in lobbies, cars, anywhere, hoping to get rooms.

All of Vegas was affected by it but The Sands was the hub and you could hardly push your way through the lobby and casino. Hundreds of people crowded the entrance to the Copa Room, fighting for tables with money, connections, or both.

I was in the middle of a dance when Peter wandered on-stage. I switched to a soft-shoe and motioned for him to join me. He fell in alongside me and grinned, "I'm not prejudiced, Sam. I'll dance with you." I smiled cynically, "But will you go to *school* with me?" Frank and Dean came on wheeling a room-service table loaded down with booze. They poured drinks and Dean did a few minutes of staggering—the only cold-sober lush in show business. Suddenly Frank turned to the band. "Cut!" He beckoned to me. "You! Over here."

I played it with nervous looks at Peter and Dean who shrugged like: You'd better do as he says. I crossed the stage and stood in front of him, head hanging, meek.

Frank folded his arms and looked at me like I was a worm. "Look at what Peter's wearing. Look at what Dean and I are wearing." They were all in dinner suits. "Now look at yourself." I made a whole thing out of inspecting my blazer, silk ascot, and gray flannels. I smiled a thin, Stan Laurel smile. Frank snapped, "Where do you get off coming on this stage in that little toy suit? Just where do you think you are? On your *yacht?*" I hung my head, taking it, playing my role of "the Kid." He glowered. "Now you go get yourself into a regular grown-up tuxedo like the rest of us. Go on. Get out of here. Get off this stage."

"*Hold it!*" I sneered, "What're you, *Esquire* magazine? You don't tell me what to do! Y'hear that, *Mister* Sinatra?" The audience egged me on: Yeah! Tell him Sam. Attababy! I poked him in the chest with my forefinger. "*Nobody* tells me what to do." I crossed my arms arrogantly. "What're you, some kind of a big deal? Not to *me!*" I strutted around the stage taking bows while the audience cheered. I stopped in front of Frank again, looked up at him, and flicked a piece of lint off his lapel. "I'll change my suit when I'm plenty good and ready!"

He spoke quietly. "When'll that be?" He was smiling, beady-eyed.

I did a sickly grin. "I'm ready, Frank."

After the shows we sat in the lounge while the crew set up cameras so we could begin shooting when daylight broke. Frank's presence in the hotel created its own atmosphere. Everybody was having a better time, looking for laughs, kicks, almost as though they felt they had to live up to his reputation. The hotel kept eight security guards around him to prevent the crowds from turning into a mob scene. Almost anyone else would be at his wit's end because of the money involved in the picture—his money—and all the details and aggravations plus the two shows a night. But he was doing jokes with me and the other guys, the same kind of bits we'd have done if he'd come down for a weekend just for laughs. I felt someone tapping me on the shoulder. A woman in her forties glanced timidly toward him. "Sammy, could you please get his autograph for me?"

She was about the eightieth person to ask me that week. "Darling, he's right here. Why don't you just ask him?"

She shrank back. "But I've heard . . ."

"Don't go by what you've heard. Go by what you see with your own eyes. He's not going to hurt you."

She tapped him on the shoulder so lightly he didn't feel it, then looked at me helplessly. I nodded reassuringly and she tried again. He looked around. "Hello honey."

Her hands sprang to her face. "You called me honey!"

He smiled and gave her his autograph and she tottered dazedly into the crowd.

The bad guy image which had grown so immense bore no resemblance to the man, but the legend of Frank Sinatra was uncontrollable and a wall of fear had been built around him. The day we arrived in Vegas there was a television show being filmed on the hotel grounds and somebody took it upon himself to say "No shooting today. Clear the hotel. Frank Sinatra's coming in." If Frank had known, he'd have been furious. Never would he stop a performer from working. But people are always hovering around, overprotecting him, biting their nails, fearful that he'll blow up and walk out. Certainly he wants the respect and attention due his stature in the business. Professionally he wants the best musicians, the best lighting and sound equipment; he's in a position to expect them and he has the temperament to refuse to be imposed upon: if a club owner hasn't provided the right microphones, Frank might very well refuse to go on and the story "Sinatra walked out" would get passed around, distorted, like "That's how he is all the time." Obviously, a man does not attain Frank's success and *keep it* by doing irrational flounce outs.

Never would he even desire a restaurant to be "cleared" because he's eating there. Wherever he plays he makes the whole town rich and if he wanted privacy he could say "I want a tunnel dug from my dressing room to my suite" and the bulldozers would be working in an hour. He could say "I'm in my room, send up Connecticut" and the management would try. But he's a warm guy who likes people and he loves to get out and sit in the lounge, have dinner in the dining room or go to a friend's restaurant and pay his respects. He never has been to Atlantic City without dropping into the bar where my mother works. Even if she's not there when he comes in, he'll stay and have a drink, knowing that within minutes the word will spread, the place will be jammed and my mother will get credit for it. Countless times a friend has been in trouble, or in a hospital, and the phone has rung and it's Frank from halfway across the world and he clowns with the guy to cheer him up, and the hospital tab gets picked up, quietly. Stories like this are legion but they aren't the ones which circulate.

We finished shooting around four every afternoon and the five of us met in the steam room at six when it was officially closed for the day. Frank came in one evening, carrying a bundle of newspaper clippings and we sat there passing around soggy clippings, from England, France, South America—everywhere, astounded by the incredible worldwide attention we were getting.

Peter said, "Listen to this one: 'The quintet of Sinatra, Martin, Davis, Lawford and Bishop moved into Las Vegas in the form of an attack force with Sinatra as the nominal leader of their clan.'"

"I don't want to be the leader. One of you guys be the leader."

Peter jabbed the paper with his finger, "Sorry, Frank, but it says here *you're* the leader."

"Hold it," I said. "I wanta go on record that I ain't belongin' to nothing that's called a *clan*."

Dean sighed, "I don't know, pally," he nodded toward Frank, "you'd better discuss that with the leader."

I shook my head. "Maybe he's *your* leader but *my* leader is Martin Luther King!"

The papers had been developing "The Clan" and "The Pack" image of us as five guys who buddy around, having laughs, and in their spare time make a movie and do shows at The Sands. We were amused by it but no one could understand better than we how silly it was. I never discussed it with Frank but he, being an astute showman, must have thought: Dean's good box-office, Sammy does great in clubs, Peter has a television following—why not make a picture utilizing the combined drawing power?

It was not unlike what was done years ago when Hollywood teamed stars like Katherine Hepburn and Spencer Tracy, Walter Pidgeon and Greer Garson, William Powell and Myrna Loy, Cagney and Raft; and although each had been tremendous on his own, when they came together in a picture it virtually exploded at the box office. In the last ten or fifteen years the studios had stopped doing it, but now Frank's idea had so captured the public's imagination that movie theaters all over the world were ordering a picture that wasn't even finished. Recognizing the potential in our combination he formulated what he called The Five Year Plan: assuming things continued as it seemed they would, we'd make five pictures together, one a year.

When we'd settled into our shooting schedule, I called May.

"Tell me."

I smiled at the already familiar greeting.

She said, "I hear it's fantastic there."

"How'd you like to come down for the weekend and see for yourself?"

"I'd love to. But do you think you can get me a hotel room?"

I played it like the King of France wandering through Paris in disguise—the classic scene in which the loyal, deserving subject whose wife is wrongfully imprisoned asks hopefully, "But do you think you can possibly get my case to the attention of His Majesty?" and the King smiles behind his disguise and chuckles "I believe I can manage it."

I was so delighted with myself it was practically incest.

She was the fifth person out of the plane. She paused at the top of the ramp and I couldn't decide if she was playing "Mary Moviestar Arriving in Las Vegas" or if she was looking for me. As she came through the gate she smiled and her face was like sunshine. She put out her hand. "Hello, there."

"Hello there, yourself." I took the make-up bag she was carrying. A lady was standing behind her and I had a sudden horrible moment of recognition: it was the same woman who'd walked into the movie theater with her in L.A. and there was a definite family resemblance.

"I'd like you to meet my mother, Mrs. Wilkens."

I did one of the great recoveries of my life with an eighteenth century bow that had all the flair of: Charmed, m'lady. "I'm so glad you could come, Mrs. Wilkens." For that statement alone, my nose should have grown twelve inches.

"My mother is going back to Sweden next week and I thought she'd enjoy seeing Las Vegas before she leaves."

They went to their rooms to relax and unpack, and I headed toward the health club. *Now* she brings her mother. To a party in a nightclub—*then* she doesn't bring her. No. She waits for a weekend in Vegas!

Frank was alone in the steam room. I sat down next to him. "Will you do me a favor?"

"Sure, what is it?"

"I invited May Britt down for the weekend. She's got her mother with her, but with all the press in town I want to be absolutely sure nobody connects us. I don't want to louse her up with her studio, so will you cover for me? Would you let it be known that she's your guest?" As I was asking I realized that I was imposing upon him, but he just looked at me with a penetrating curiosity.

"Sure, Charley, she's my guest."

I introduced May from the stage with the other celebrities, and her mother beamed with pride. I met them in the lounge after the second show, we gambled a little, had a bite to eat with Frank and the guys. I didn't have any scenes the next afternoon so I took them sightseeing, showing them downtown Vegas and everything I could think of that her mother might like to see. As we drove back across the desert from Lake Mead, May said, "My mother's a little tired. I think we'll have dinner in our room so she can go to sleep early. Can I come to see your second show alone?"

"Of course. I've got a permanent table. There'll be some of my friends there so you won't have to sit alone."

As soon as I got off I sent Murphy out front to escort her backstage.

"Hello, there. I liked your show." Murphy did a sneaky-foot out the door like one of the discreet men of all time, and we were alone.

She was wearing a bright yellow dress. She had a sunburn which highlighted her freckles, and her hair was hanging long and golden over her shoulders. We smiled wordlessly at each other.

"Would you like something to drink?"

"No. Thank you very much. But you have one if you like."

"No, thanks. I don't feel like one either."

"The club was really packed."

"Yeah . . . things sure are swinging. . . ."

The inane chitchat was coming out of our ears. I was desperate to make conversation, but I'd never really *talked* to a girl before. It was always laughs, jokes, and pow! into bed or not. She walked over to the TV set and stood there, her eyes glued to it. I stared at it, too.

It was impossible to believe. Here's a girl I could get drunk just from looking at, she's just seen me do the show of my life, she's in my dressing room, the door is closed—and we're standing like idiots watching a twenty-year-old movie. A minute later we were both pretending to be hung-up in the commercial.

I looked at her beautiful face. She glanced up as she sensed me staring at her. The haughty look she'd had in *The Blue Angel* and when we'd first met was completely gone, her cheeks were flushed, and she seemed self-conscious. I walked the two steps over to her, put my hands on her shoulders and kissed her.

She was a little tall. I asked, "Would you mind taking off your shoes?"

She laughed and kicked them off. I kissed her again.

Suddenly it was easy to talk. I remembered the closed door and opened it and as I turned I caught the trace of a smile of satisfaction on her face.

Front row: Sammy Davis, Jr., Frank Sinatra and Dean Martin in Robin and the Seven Hoods *(1964), Warner Bros.*

EDDIE FISHER

Elizabeth Taylor and Eddie Fisher in Butterfield 8 *(1960), MGM.*

Born Edwin Jack Fisher on August 10, 1928 in Philadelphia . . . Teen idol and crooner . . . Winner on *Arthur Godfrey's Talent Scouts* . . . First solo record "My Bolero" (1949) . . . First hit "Thinking of You" (1950) . . . Peaked in 1950s when he regularly starred on *Your Hit Parade* . . . Married Debbie Reynolds 1955 . . . Carrie Fisher born in 1956 . . . Divorced 1959 . . . Married Elizabeth Taylor 1959 . . . Known as "Mr. Elizabeth Taylor" . . . Divorced 1964 . . . Married Connie Stevens 1966 . . . Divorced 1969 . . . Movies: Bit part in *All About Eve* (1950) . . . *Bundle of Joy* (1956) . . . *Butterfield 8* (1960) . . . Voted worst actor of the year by *Harvard Lampoon* . . . Eddie: "The husband is always the last to know."

Lucky Liz

W hen Debbie gave birth to our son in February 1958, I got dizzy all over again, just as I had when Carrie was born. I was overjoyed to have a son, but even though I loved both my children, that didn't change the way I felt about our marriage. I began planning for a separation, and after selling the Beverly Hills mansion, I bought a furnished house in Holmby Hills that would be perfect for Debbie and the children. I didn't know where I would go, or when. There was no other woman in my life. I only knew I couldn't go on living with Debbie.

We named our son Todd Emmanuel to honor two of my dearest friends, Mike Todd and Mannie Sacks. Tragically, before my little boy was a year old, both men would be dead.

Mike and Elizabeth had spent the last several months globe-trotting to promote *Around the World.* Mike never did anything small. To celebrate the first anniversary of the premiere in New York, he threw a party at Madison Square Garden for eighteen thousand of his "intimate" friends. Then he took Elizabeth to Russia, where that personification of freewheeling capitalism and his glamorous movie star wife must have created quite a stir. For his travels around this country, Mike used a twin-engine Lockheed, which he christened the *Lucky Liz.* Like a kid with a new toy he loved to show off, he was always urging his friends to use it. I flew on the *Lucky Liz* only once, when Mike and Elizabeth invited Debbie and me to join them on a flight to Las Vegas to celebrate New Year's Eve.

Three months later, in March 1958, Mike was selected to receive an award as "Showman of the Year" from the Friars Club at a testimonial dinner at the Waldorf-Astoria in New York. I was invited to attend and asked Sammy Cahn to write a parody of "Around the World in 80 Days," which I would sing at the dinner.

Mike called me up. "Let's take the *Lucky Liz* to New York together," he said.

"Mike, I'd love to but I can't. I've got to go to North Carolina to film a Chesterfield commercial. I'll be flying to New York from there."

"Take my plane to North Carolina," Mike said.

"That doesn't make any sense," I told him. "How will you get to New York?"

Mike didn't like to take no for an answer. He called again and again, urging me to take his plane, but still I refused. I flew east on a commercial flight, and later on the night of March 21, in a torrential rainstorm, Mike took off for New York from the Burbank airport in the *Lucky Liz.*

Elizabeth was not with him. A couple of days before, she had been sent home from the set of *Cat on a Hot Tin Roof* with a high temperature and a severe case of bronchitis. She begged Mike to let her come, but the doctors advised against it and for once Mike didn't give in to her. They said their goodbyes and Mike promised to call her from Albuquerque when the plane landed to refuel. He never made it. In the early hours of the morning on March 22, the *Lucky Liz* went down in the mountains of western New Mexico.

I was in New York at the Essex House when I heard the news. Jim Mahoney, my press agent, and a couple of other friends were waiting for me in the living room that morning. "Eddie," Jim said, "Mike's dead. His plane crashed in New Mexico."

I just stood there staring at them, too stunned to speak. Then I turned and started back into the bedroom. My friends tried to follow me but Jim stopped them. "No," he said. "Let him be by himself."

I shut the door behind me. This was my first experience with the death of someone very close to me and it didn't make any sense. It can't be true, I thought; it can't have happened, not to Mike. I put my hands over my eyes, sat down on the bed, and cried.

There were guards at both the front and the back doors of their house in Beverly Hills. Reporters, photographers, and curiosity seekers were milling around outside. Inside, friends and relatives had gathered to do what they could for Elizabeth. I had taken the first available flight to Los Angeles and went directly to the house. I spoke briefly with Dick Hanley, Mike's secretary; Elizabeth's friend Sydney Guilaroff, the hairdresser; Arthur Loew, Jr.; Rex Kennamer, Elizabeth's doctor. Everyone was very worried about her.

Then Elizabeth appeared, dressed in a nightgown and obviously heavily sedated, wandering down the steps from the bedroom in a daze. She didn't speak to me. She looked right at me without the slightest sign of recognition and walked into the living room. Suddenly she started screaming, and just as suddenly stopped. One moment she would be talking rationally, and the next crying hysterically. Everyone urged her to go back to bed.

She recognized me as she began to climb the stairs. "Eddie," she said, "come back tomorrow and we can sit and talk."

I was deeply concerned about Elizabeth, afraid she would try to commit suicide or lose her mind completely. But the next day, when Debbie and I came to the house for dinner, she seemed to be in control of herself. There was a kind of unreal serenity about her, as if all her emotions had been drained. She asked me to stay after dinner. There were thousands of letters and telegrams in boxes by her bed, and she wanted me to come upstairs and read them to her.

We sat there for hours that night, as I read the letters and Elizabeth listened. They had been written by the famous and the unknown, they came from friends and even enemies, and not one of them said an unkind word about Mike. Both Elizabeth and I cried. Each new letter reminded me of the friend I had lost. For Elizabeth they seemed to have the opposite effect: it was a comfort to her to know that so many other people had loved Mike. We would repeat this scene several times in the weeks ahead, me reading and trying to forget, Elizabeth listening to keep the memory of Mike alive.

Elizabeth asked me to come to the funeral. Howard Hughes put a DC-7 at her disposal for the flight to Chicago, where Mike was to be buried. Hughes had once asked Elizabeth to come see him in Palm Springs. He said he had a proposition he wanted to discuss with her. Very reluctantly, she went with Greg Bautzer, Hughes's lawyer and confidant, and when she arrived, Hughes proposed, offering her a million dollars if she would marry him. She laughed and told him to go to hell. Hughes had no ulterior motives in offering the DC-7. He must have realized that Elizabeth could not have traveled any other way, and the offer was made to me impersonally, through his longtime business associate Noah Dietrich.

There were a lot of people on the plane: a couple of newspaper reporters, but mostly friends of Mike's. I sat in the back and didn't speak to Elizabeth at all until just before the funeral. We were staying at the Ambassador and she came to my room, sat on the bed, and began to talk. Still under sedation, still barely able to cope with her own grief, she knew how I felt about Mike and was trying to comfort me.

The cemetery looked like a county fair. Hundreds of people were sitting on the tombstones, eating ice cream cones and drinking soda pop, littering the ground with bottles and bags. They began screaming and shoving to get a better look when the hearse and limousines arrived. Police barricades had been erected to keep them at a distance, and a tent covered the grave site, but all through the brief service, we could hear their shouts: "Come on out, Liz! Come out so we can get a look at you!" Elizabeth held her emotions in check, with the exception of a flash of anger when one of Mike's relatives made a fuss about the seating arrangements around the coffin. Nothing was left of Mike; as far as I knew, the coffin was empty. The only thing that had been recovered from the crash, I was told, was a small piece of a pair of platinum cuff links I had given him.

Reporters later wrote that Elizabeth hurled herself hysterically over Mike's grave. It wasn't true. After the service, she asked us all to leave the tent and then spent a few moments there alone. When she emerged, the crowd surged through the barricades, surrounding her, shouting and snatching at her clothes, just like the funeral scene in *A Star Is Born*, only this was hideously real. Rex Kennamer, Mike Todd, Jr., and I tried to protect her, and pushing our way through the crowd, finally made it to the limousine. We couldn't drive away. People swarmed all over the car, rocking it back and forth and pounding on the windows, while Elizabeth sat huddled between Rex and me in the back seat, numb with horror.

I saw Elizabeth quite often during the next several weeks, although not as often as many of her other friends, and never alone unless she asked me to read more of the letters. I had grown to admire her, but the strongest bond between us had always been Mike, and now he was gone. She went back to work and then left the house she had shared with Mike to stay with Arthur Loew, Jr., the heir to a large Hollywood fortune. Loew was a friend and I liked him; he was a humorous man, but he had the reputation of being something of a playboy, and even though it was none of my business, I wondered why Elizabeth was staying at his house. What I didn't realize at the time was that she could never be alone.

In June, three months after Mike's death, I was due to begin a six-week engagement at the Tropicana in Las Vegas, and Elizabeth called to ask if she could come to the opening. I was very happy that she wanted to be there, and also a little worried; it would be the first time she had appeared in public since the funeral, and everyone was still concerned about her. But when I introduced her at the end of my act and the spotlight swung around to pick her out of the audience, she looked radiant. She had come with Loew, Mike Todd Jr., and other friends, and outwardly at least, she seemed to be recovering from Mike's death.

My dressing room was jammed with well-wishers after the show, including Elizabeth. Photographers took pictures of us, and it was later said that we were gazing at each other with love in our eyes. It wasn't so. At that moment there was nothing more than a warm friendship between us. Even though we had lost Mike, we wanted to keep that.

Later we were all sitting in the lounge and I heard Elizabeth complain that she wasn't able to sleep. Both Milton [Blackstone] and [Dr.] Max [Jacobson] were with us—Max had given me the usual injection before my performance—and after Elizabeth left, it occurred to me that he might have something to help her sleep. I called Elizabeth's room and she invited us both to come up. Max gave her a mild sedative and then left but I stayed a few minutes longer. We talked, and I realized then that Elizabeth was still deeply mourning Mike.

I didn't see her the next day; she went back to Los Angeles. But after my last show that night—it was about three in the morning—I got a call from Elizabeth. "When are you coming back?" she said. "I must see you."

There was both an urgency and a new intimacy in the tone of her voice, and I wondered why she wanted to see me. Was it just because of Mike, to keep his memory alive through me? Or did she want to tell me something she had been unable to say the night before? I was puzzled, but I intended to see her as soon as I got back. I wanted to stay close to Elizabeth, whatever else happened in our lives. It seemed like the most natural relationship in the world, a way to keep Mike's memory alive for me too.

I got back to Los Angeles just in time to celebrate my thirtieth birthday. Debbie gave a surprise party for me and about twenty-five of our friends at Romanoff's, and when we sat down at the table, the chair next to mine was empty—Elizabeth's. She hadn't shown up. I was hurt and disappointed, but thought to myself, Well, that's Elizabeth. She called right in the middle of the party: "Eddie, I'm so sorry. I've got my period and I feel terrible."

"Come on, Elizabeth," I joked. "The only thing you've got is a hangover."

She giggled. "Well, anyway, happy birthday. And can you come over and see me tomorrow? I want to give you something of Mike's."

I went to Loew's house the next day and found her dressed in a flesh-colored bathing suit, dangling her feet in the pool, with little Liza between her legs. Our eyes met and that was it. Not a word was spoken. I was in love with Elizabeth. And remembering the intimacy in her voice when she called me in Las Vegas, seeing the expression in her eyes now, I was certain she was in love with me.

She gave me little Liza to hold while she went into the house. She returned with a gold money clip that had belonged to Mike. I couldn't seem to catch my breath to thank her. My feelings were in such turmoil that I just wanted to get out of there. Cradling Liza in her arms, Elizabeth walked with me to the door. There, I turned to her and said, "Would you like to go for a drive tomorrow?"

She nodded yes.

I picked her up the following afternoon. She brought Liza and held her in one arm. I reached over and took her hand. We drove way out past Malibu, holding hands, again without saying a word. Finally, I said, "Elizabeth, I'm going to marry you."

She looked at me and said, "When?"

"I don't know. But I *am* going to marry you."

She smiled but didn't say anything, and we drove on until we found an isolated spot on the beach. We played with Liza on the sand for a while. Then we kissed. And at that moment we both knew we belonged to each other.

We began to see each other constantly. We went for long drives or had lunch together in some quiet, out-of-the-way restaurant, talking and holding hands under the table. We made up excuses to meet. Elizabeth would call the house, pretending she had some problem she wanted to talk to me about, and I would stop whatever I was doing and pick her up for another drive. One problem was real enough. Mike had left his affairs in a mess and Elizabeth was completely helpless about money. Like Debbie, she was under contract at MGM and had never earned more than a salary from her pictures. She wasn't poor, of course, but she and Mike had lived extravagantly, and with Mike's death the money just wasn't there anymore. She was even told by Herman Odell, one of the lawyers handling Mike's estate, that she would receive no further income from the share of *Around the World in 80 Days* that Mike had left her, now or in the foreseeable future. Elizabeth showed me the letter and we spread it out on the table in front of us in a restaurant, pretending to talk business when we were really talking about love.

I was hardly a financial wizard about handling my own affairs, and I was so overwhelmed by my feelings for Elizabeth that I wasn't sure I could make sense out of anything. But I did try to help her and spoke to Ed Weisl about the letter. He was chairman of the executive committee at Paramount; I had met him on a boat trip to Europe. He called back twenty-four hours later and said that Paramount would pay Elizabeth ten million dollars for her share of the picture. Perversely, Elizabeth said she didn't want to sell. So much for her financial problems. But we both knew there was no easy solution to the problems our love would create.

As Mike's best friend, it was quite natural for me to be seeing Elizabeth, and as time went on, we made no secret of our meetings. We spent many evenings with friends at La Scala or the Polo Lounge and more often than not Debbie was with us. We all went to a preview showing of *Cat on a Hot Tin Roof.* Our feelings for each other were the secret, and they were so intense, so necessary, that I was sure all who saw us, unless they were blind, saw love. I was afraid we couldn't hide it for long, afraid, too, of what people would say when they found out. But oddly, no one seemed to notice, not the usually sharp-eyed gossip columnists, not our friends, not even Debbie. At a party or a restaurant, the three of us would be sitting together and Elizabeth would reach for my hand under the table. When it was time for me to take Debbie home, she would beg me to stay. Elizabeth seldom bothered to conceal her feelings and she made it very difficult for me to conceal mine. But if Debbie suspected there was something going on between us, she didn't say a word.

We knew we would have to tell Debbie, but somehow I could never find the right moment. Is there ever a right moment to tell your wife you're in love with another woman? Elizabeth would have done anything I asked her to do, but neither of us was sure what was right and what was wrong. Was it too soon after Mike's death, were we doing a terrible thing to Debbie? Divorce, Elizabeth's children, mine—it all seemed hopelessly complicated. We were desperate, knowing the time had come when something had to be done. But what?

Finally Elizabeth decided to go to Europe. She had planned the trip as a vacation—and had spent a fortune on clothes—before we discovered how we felt about each other. I fabricated a meeting with my sponsors in New York to be with her for a few days before she sailed, and made reservations at the Essex House. Elizabeth had a suite at the Plaza. We met there when she arrived. The rooms were filled with flowers, and as soon as we were alone, Elizabeth said, "When are we going to make love?"

I stayed at the Plaza that night. It was the first time we had done anything more than kiss and hold hands. And then next day we walked to the zoo in Central Park and then took a ride in a horse-drawn hansom. Incredibly, nobody bothered us, nobody paid any attention, or if they did, we didn't notice. Our feelings for each other were even more intense than before, so fierce they were painful.

Back at the Plaza, Elizabeth got a call from Cary Grant and motioned to me to listen in on the extension. After a few moments of conversation, he asked her for a date. Giggling, she refused and my male ego soared. That night I stayed at the Plaza again and we sat up very late, talking about our future together. But before we could do anything else, we had to tell Debbie. I called California and when she was on the phone, I said, "Elizabeth and I are here together in New York and we're very much in love."

We were certain Debbie had already heard about us, but for a moment she seemed genuinely shocked. Then she said, "Well, we can't talk about it over the phone. We'll talk about it when you get home." She acted as if I had told her I had a toothache; nothing serious, nothing she had to worry about.

Elizabeth and I were puzzled by Debbie's reaction. Still it was a relief to us that she knew. We felt less guilty about our emotions, less anxious about being seen in public, and we began to go out together in New York. We saw a play and went to nightclubs and restaurants, always with friends so we wouldn't be alone. We wanted to avoid publicity, but people were beginning to notice, and once when a photographer tried to ambush us at the Blue Angel, I had to duck out the back door. The heat was on. We were being indiscreet.

Elizabeth canceled her trip to Europe; it was impossible for us to separate. But where could we go to be together? I took her to Grossinger's. We would be safe there; people would leave us alone. Jennie [Grossinger] couldn't have been more wonderful. She liked Debbie, but she loved Elizabeth on sight and we stayed at her house. Jennie knew we were sleeping together, of course, but she never once criticized us or made us feel uncomfortable in any way. She didn't have that in her. And in her wisdom, she probably knew that these were the last peaceful moments that Elizabeth and I would have together for a very long time.

We told reporters that I had come to Grossinger's to cut the ribbon on the new indoor swimming pool. I even went through the ceremony, but at least one reporter wasn't fooled. Earl Wilson write about Elizabeth and me in his column and the hue and cry began. It was the Labor Day weekend. Exactly nine years earlier Eddie Cantor had "discovered' me at Grossinger's and my whole life changed. Now I had been discovered again at Grossinger's, this time in the company of Elizabeth Taylor, and my life would take a new and totally different direction.

ERROL FLYNN

Errol Flynn and Alexis Smith in Gentleman Jim *(1942), Warner Bros.*

Born Australia (not in Antrim, Northern Ireland, as he liked it to be known) on June 20, 1909 . . . Expelled from most schools attended . . . First film: *In the Wake of the Bounty* (1933) . . . Arrived in Hollywood 1935 . . . In 1942 tried and acquitted on charges of statutory rape of two teenage girls aboard his yacht . . . Credits: *Captain Blood* (1935) . . . *The Charge of the Light Brigade* (1936) . . . *The Adventures of Robin Hood* (1938) . . . *Gentleman Jim* (1942) . . . *The Sun Also Rises* (1957) . . . *Cuban Rebel Girls* (1959) . . . Died of "hard living" 1959 . . . Jack Warner: "To the Walter Mittys of the world he was all the heroes in one magnificent, sexy, animal package."

"In Like Flynn"

O
n this particular night, late in 1942, I was alone in my Mulholland study.

My valet Alexandre came in, trembling like an autumn leaf. Two men were at the door, he said in French. They had shown him some official papers, also a policeman's badge.

"What do they want?"

"They say they must see you."

I laughed. "What the hell are you shaking for? They're not here to see you. Go on, let them in. . . ."

In came two dicks. They were in plain clothes, but I could have told, on the street, a hundred feet from them, they were police. Plain-clothes men usually look more like police than uniformed cops. You get to be able to make a fine distinction like that after you've had your share of contact with these necessary gentlemen. They were quite pleasant. "Come on in, gentlemen."

"Have a seat," I said. Did they want some coffee, or drinks perhaps? They said yes, they'd have coffee.

I didn't know then never to talk to *two* policemen if you are alone. I know it now. Two coppers will outweigh anything you have to say.

After a minute or two one of them said, "Mr Flynn, we have a very serious charge against you."

What had I done?

"Well, your accuser is in Juvenile Hall and we've come to take a statement from you."

"What's it all about?"

A pause. Then, "Statutory rape."

My smile disappeared in a hurry. Rape? I didn't know what statutory rape meant. I didn't know the difference between statutory rape and rape.

Rape to me meant picking up a chair and hitting some young lady over the head with it and having your wicked way. I hadn't done any of these things.

"I don't know what you're talking about."

"It concerns a Miss Betty Hansen—and we are holding you."

"I've never heard of her. Betty Hansen? Who is she?"

"She's a teen-ager and she's been picked up for vagrancy. Among her possessions we found your phone number, and she has claimed that you had sexual intercourse with her on a certain date."

"Where was this supposed to have happened?"

"We're not supposed to tell you, Mr Flynn, but it happened at the house rented by your friends, Stephen Raphael, Bruce Cabot and Freddie McEvoy."

This was a big rambling place, with a tennis court, owned by Colleen Moore, of silent films. The sporting crowd foregathered there to bet on tennis matches, to swim, play cards, ping-pong, poker—amusements practically always instigated by Freddie. It was a bachelor's house, rented by famous and/or moneyed bachelors, and it was a place I frequented. Usually it cost me a lot to go there. My friends took my money like Jesse James robbed a bank; they were skilful cardplayers, congenital handicappers. In any case, there were always lovely girls around.

But, for the life of me, I couldn't recall any Betty Hansen with whom I was supposed to have gone to bed—whom I had raped.

"What am I supposed to do?" I asked them.

"We'd like you to come down with us to Juvenile Hall and identify the girl."

"But I don't know any such girl."

"Well, look," they said, "we just want to clear this matter up. It might be nothing, it might be something, we don't know. She says that you were all playing tennis. She seemed to know everybody at the house there, all your friends. She gave a detailed description of the act."

"What did she say?"

"She said she could even describe you. You got undressed, but you kept your socks on."

"Good God! Tell me, what does she look like?"

"She described you as sitting on your chair, then you took her upstairs and——"

All of a sudden a picture flashed before me, and I saw again the scene that was behind this horrible accusation. I could remember somebody sitting on the edge of my chair. Many of the girls had sat on the edge of the chair or around it. I recalled this particular one being over-friendly and I recollected getting up out of the chair.

"You don't mean that frowsy little blonde?—Is she a frowsy little blonde?"

"Yes, that's the one!"

Those were the worst words I could ever have said, because eventually they were repeated to her, and, being feminine, she naturally resented this description. Also, as it turned out, she had been threatened by the authorities with four years of detention in Juvenile Hall, and, with these two things, she would swear to anything—and she did.

"Look," I said to the two dicks, "I must call my lawyer right away."

"You don't need a lawyer."

When you hear a cop tell you that, brother, always get the lawyer!

"This is my house," I said. "Sit down, have another coffee, or drink, whatever you want!"

My mind was in absolute turmoil.

I called up Robert Ford, a young Irish lawyer just beginning his practice. He was the son of a famous lawyer, a fine guy, a guardian of my interests.

"Bob, there are a couple of boys here, from . . ." I turned to them and asked them where they were from. From Downtown Los Angeles Police Department, they said. "That's where they are from, Bob, Downtown Police Department. What am I to do? They want me to go down to Juvenile Hall. They say I screwed somebody. I know I didn't. It's very late and I don't know if you're in bed, but if you are, Bob, I don't give a damn. Get out of it! Get on down there. They said they'll arrest me if I don't come under my own steam."

It was late at night, but down we went to Juvenile Hall. That was a long ride, done in silence now, no more fishing from them, no more biting by me. Why I should have been called upon at this hour I don't know; they could have waited till the daytime, but I discovered then that there is sometimes a narrow line between how crooks and police find it necessary to work. Get the guy when he's tired—his mind isn't with it.

As we entered Juvenile Hall, I asked, "You won't mind waiting till my attorney gets here?"

"Oh, he's here already, waiting outside."

Bob took over from there.

"What's the charge?" he asked, inside a gloomy-looking office.

They told him. He wanted to know what was the idea of their bringing me down here.

"Under the law," they explained, "the accuser and the accused must confront each other."

They brought in a girl, dressed in some kind of uniform which they put on kids unfortunate enough to get into this kind of place. At once I recognised her as the one who had indeed sat on the arm of my chair. To my utter astonishment. I said, "It can't be!"

I mean, she was gruesome-looking.

They said to her, "Will you repeat the charge?"

She hung her head and said, "Yes. He took me upstairs." She talked in a low, monotonous voice, as if by rote. "They had been playing tennis, then they played some cards. He took me upstairs, undressed me, and then he—he—he——" She ran out of words. "You know what I told you," she said to the police.

Bob Ford asked, "Did you put up a fight?"

"No, no. Why should I?"

They turned to me. "Well, what do you say about this, Mr Flynn?"

"Utterly untrue. Certainly I met her. True she was at the house. I don't know how she got there."

Actually I was thinking very fast. I did remember that there was a young fellow called Sevow, somebody who was more or less in charge of inviting girls to this house for the boys who were living in it. I am not suggesting that this was a den of animals. On the contrary, it was mainly devoted to sports, and gambling, but it was a bachelor's house and 'ladies' rarely object to visiting a bachelor's house in Hollywood.

The officer said, "That's all."

The girl was led out.

I drove home with Bob. "How did I get into all this?"

"Did you or didn't you?" he asked me.

I said no.

"I believe you."

The Los Angeles District Attorney's office apparently decided that they had a very weak case against me on Betty Hansen, but, having levelled this charge, they got a bit frantic. They dug up another girl whom I knew, a certain Peggy Satterlee, and my lawyer phoned me to get set for a second charge.

At two o'clock in the morning they went to the night club where this girl was dancing, brought her down to headquarters and, by whatever means and through whatever threats they used, they got her to tell of her meeting with me a year earlier. It had taken her a year to discover that she also had been raped by me. Now there was no question that I knew this second young lady very well, and I did not deny it. Peggy Satterlee had been out on my yacht, the *Sirocco*, for a weekend.

If you meet a young lady who, in fact, invites herself for a trip on your yacht—"I'd love to cru," she said, in the vernacular unknown to yachtsmen—knowing in advance full well what the risks are, who the hell asks her for her birth certificate, especially when she is built like Venus? And if afterwards she tells you she has had the most wonderful time in her life, who has been hurt? What is all the fuss about? Why international headlines? Who approaches a prospective sweetheart by asking her to whip out her birth certificate, or driver's license, or show a letter from her mother? Naturally I had no knowledge of how old she was, nor did I know the difference between rape and statutory rape.

Statutory rape as it is now defined is actually a nineteenth-century improvement on an older law designed to protect infant girls against degenerates. The law is quite clear. If you have had carnal knowledge of a person or persons under the age of eighteen, you can go to jail for five years or more, whether or not—and this is important—she consented. It doesn't matter if you had no way of knowing she was under eighteen, or even if she actually tells you she is over the so-called age of consent. Broadly interpreted, it could even mean that should a powerful girl under the age of eighteen knock down a man, sit on his chest, put a knife to his jugular vein, and say that if he didn't overpower her she would cut his throat, he could still get five years in jail for doing as ordered. That would be stretching the law, but that is actually what the law says.

While this hadn't happened to me, they could definitely prove that Betty Hansen was under age—she was seventeen. Yet to this day nobody knows for certain how old Peggy Satterlee was; although it appeared later, from a driver's license she owned, that she was twenty-one.

So here I was faced with four charges of statutory rape, two on each count, and scheduled to go before the Grand Jury two days later.

The District Attorney's office lost no time in giving the story to the newspapers. It caused, at once, national, even international, headlines.

ERROL FLYNN CHARGED WITH RAPE

I didn't sleep much in the period before the Grand Jury session. I tried to imagine what effect my troubles would have on my father, who was Dean of the Faculty of Science at Belfast. What would my mother, my sister, think of it?

Crowds swarmed around the courthouse. The people were strung out in front of the place, and I wanted to shrink into the ground with shame. The mere idea of force or rape was unthinkable. Who had to hit somebody over the head with a chair, or trip them up, or smuggle them across a border? On the contrary, where was my baseball bat to ward them off?

Women banged on the doors of Mulholland House like ice-drops in a hailstorm. I had to bolt the doors against them. I had proposals of marriage every day. I got letters from women setting up dates, hours and places where they would be waiting for me, ripe and ready, and they didn't wait for a written reply. They went ahead with their plans, and when I wouldn't show up I suppose they were disappointed. But this wasn't New Guinea, where I was alone with palm trees. I was a big Hollywood star, and female flak burst around me all the time. So what the hell was this charge of RAPE?

Somebody was out to put the screws into me. Who was it? What was it?

Still I held my head up, I must go into this with a fairly dignified demeanour. It came back to me how, as a younger man, I had set out to acquire a dignified look, the manner of a man of means, of stature and pride, how I had deliberately squared my shoulders, stood erect, held my head up imperially, and practised moving about with a certain hauteur—in the belief that you can make yourself what you feel, what you want to be, that if you act great you may become great. Now I needed this force again, needed to see over the heads of this crowd, of this situation, and face it with an air of courage, even if I didn't feel confident inside.

The girls told their story to the Grand Jury. I told mine. Freddie McEvoy gave evidence supporting what I said about my knowledge of the Hansen girl—and the Grand Jury was swift about it. They saw something stank. They promptly returned what is called a 'No True Bill'.

This meant they believed me; not the prosecution.

So—rather quickly—it was over with.

Freddie and I went back to Mulholland House. The load was off my mind. We celebrated my acquittal by opening a bottle of champagne. Freddie said, "Christ, you're lucky, pal!"

Still it had been turbulent, and I tramped around my place loosing profanity at the walls, at the mystic forces that seemed to have been out to get me. It was all goddamned torture, and I hollered, "The hell with Christ!"

Freddie, a devout Catholic when he felt like being so, shouted back, "That's blasphemy! Don't say that. You will be sorry."

"To hell with God too! This is a crooked thing!"

I couldn't sleep. I stayed awake, hanging around the fireplace, wondering why I had been singled out for this business.

Maybe I shouldn't have cursed God.

Freddie had gone to bed, so had Alexandre. I was alone, stewing over the incident, when the phone rang. My number was unlisted, so I presumed some friend was calling.

"Hello."

The voice at the other end said, "Hello, Flynn?"

"Yes, who is this?"

"That don't matter. Listen, Flynn, you got a lucky break—"

"Lucky about what?"

"You know about what—downtown. You got a lucky break."

"That's a matter of opinion. Anyway, what's on your mind? Who are you?"

"I am not identifying myself," this man said. "But I will tell you something. If you know what's good for you——" Then he asked, "Do you know Jack Warner?"

"Of course."

"Well, just ask Jack if he knows Joe. Just say 'Joe'."

"Joe. He must know a million Joes. Why should I?"

"Just tell him Joe called you. If Warner only knows what's good for him and if you know what's good for you, you will just drop a little thing called ten G's at the corner of Melrose and La Cienega."

"Repeat that, will you?"

"Okay. I'm telling you now, if you think you have been hit, don't wait. Get ten G's down there, or, brother, you will never know what really hit you. Today is Monday. I will give you two nights to get it there, otherwise, brother, on Wednesday you will have had it."

I figured I was talking to some crank, so, before hanging up, I said, "Oh, sure. Ten thousand dollars? How would you like it? In nickels or dimes?"

"Okay, wise guy, I guess you don't know what's good for you. You'll find out."

"Why don't you go to hell?"—And I hung up.

I paid no attention to this. I figured it was just some crank.

I supposed I was a free man. The charges took only a few minutes for the Grand Jury to throw out. In cases like that, where the Grand Jury has refused to indict, perhaps not in a hundred years has the District Attorney's office gone any further—although, under the law, the District Attorney could proceed.

That mysterious telephone call couldn't have hit the nail more on the head.

On Wednesday the District Attorney's office announced that they were going to over-ride the Grand Jury's decision and proceed against me on the same charges.

Everyone was flabbergasted—the studio, my lawyer, my friends. When I heard about this I was holding in my hands a cablegram from my father. He had indulged in a bit of whimsy. He had learned of my acquittal, and he cabled: 'HOW WAS IT, ANYWAY?'

When this new announcement was made, Bob Ford quickly realised that he shouldn't handle it himself. "This is very serious," he said. "There is only one man for it—Jerry Geisler. I'm going to retain him if I can."

"Bob, do what you think best."

Geisler had a wonderful reputation. But he did not come cheap. I was told that when Geisler took the case of Busby Berkeley, who was charged with manslaughter for being drunk and killing three people, it cost Berkeley a fortune to have Geisler defend him.

Geisler agreed to take the case.

I was taken down to the police station and finger-printed.

I found myself sitting on a long bench next to a fellow, and at once he gave me the low-down on jail conditions in the vicinity.

"What are you here for, Errol?"

"Rape."

"Ahh, that's nothing."

"What are you here for, brother?" I asked.

"Kidnapping. That's ten."

"Ten what?"

"Ten years," he said, "but of course I'm innocent."

I turned to a coloured fellow sitting on the other side of me. "What are you here for, pal?"

"Murder, but of course I'm innocent."

Then he asked me, "What are you here for?"

"I'm innocent too, chum."

Bob Ford was in another part of the courthouse trying to arrange bail. Jerry Geisler was in conference with the District Attorney's men, and my colleagues with charges against them continued chummy with me. One guy said, "Errol, don't get down to Lincoln. They don't give you a break down there. The County Jail is the best. You can't get it better, kid. For Christ's sake, a guy lives well here. The boys get a break. And they ain't a bad bunch of guys . . ."

"Who?"

"The wardens. Who else? They're all crooks, like us——"

Jesus! I thought, am I one of the 'boys' already?

The same information went on. "Of course the best thing can happen to you, you are sent to the Honor Farm. There it is fine. You are out in the sunshine. All you have to do is try to get a rake, and scratch up something."

I listened appreciatively, wondered whether I had influence enough left around town to get a rake. He went on, "You ought to be able to make a rake job, Errol. Don't get none of them shovels. Jesus, you've got to dig! I have blisters on my hands——"

Somebody else cut in. "Nah, nahnah. A soft spot's the dispensary. A big shot like him, he could get into the dispensary maybe. Another soft spot is the library. Jesus! That's a good idea. Try and make the library, Errol. Sit down on your arse and you read."

On all sides I could see and feel nothing but disaster. The idea of books cheered me up a little, but not much.

They took me up to the top floor to measure me. If I went to prison, I was going to have a nice striped suit, one that fitted me well, and if I tried to make a prison break, maybe a coffin.

What nobody knew but Freddie and myself was that I had made up my mind that I would never let them send me to jail on this deal.

I had made arrangement to have a two-motor Beachcraft sitting out at the Burbank airport, because I knew I could get out on bail—and if the thing looked bad, unbeatable, I was going to leave the United States for ever. I would head first for Mexico . . . and from there . . .

Jerry Geisler never asked me whether I was guilty or innocent. Not once in the next five months of trial operations. Maybe he was afraid I was guilty, and didn't want to know it. But at the outset, in my first talk with him, I told him of the mysterious telephone call I had, and I pointed out to him that things had happened just as the guy on the phone predicted they would.

All that he said was, "Very interesting." Nothing more.

Geisler, with his own special genius, discovered by talking with the District Attorney's office, knowing downtown politics, looking into the present and recent political picture in Los Angeles, that there appeared to be a whole political force at work to get me—men with their own axes, ambitions, motives.

He didn't tell me what he uncovered, but he did tell Bob Ford. He discovered the following:

The previous District Attorney, Buron Fitts, had been the protector of Hollywood's big names in squashing any kind of complaints. The big studios naturally supported him generously in his political campaigns: so much so that he had been in office three terms, and that was an almost unheard-of thing. Since he had made three terms, it looked likely that he might win a fourth, so the big studios supported him in a race against an opponent, John Dockwiler, called 'Honest John Dockwiler'. The studios, while they made large contributions to Fitts's election, had only made small token ones to 'Honest John's' campaign, which was worse than giving nothing.

But in a landslide victory Fitts was knocked out, and 'Honest John' moved in. He brought in with him, of course, a lot of subdistrict attorneys who had to make their reputations. They had won the hard way, and they had vengeance in their hearts. They said, 'Okay, instead of getting any preferential treatment the first guy of your lot who gets in trouble has had it. Watch.'

I was the first guy.

Soon after the 'Honest John' administration came into office these moves against me began.

Moreover, after this began, I had a very strong feeling—which by now was widely shared—that I was being railroaded for some unknown reason. I couldn't figure it out. At that time neither could anyone else.

But supposing there is a big political force, with its own objectives, out to get someone, out to make an example, out to get revenge for some party politics? You still have to do what Jerry Geisler had to do: you have to conduct your defence on the basis of the actual charges, the merit in the case, the specific counts. You couldn't try a political grouping. You might see and understand that this 'throwing of the book' at someone was a consequence of internecine local politics, but a defence had to be conducted on the basis of the actual complaints.

I had never been in trouble in Hollywood. But I was known as a roisterer. I was vulnerable, an ideal scapegoat.

For what went on trial, there in the Los Angeles Courthouse, was my personality, and above all my way of life. Certainly it was a much more complicated thing than has ever been presented by the press, the magazine writers, the clowns who joke about me on radio and television, and the fellows around saloons who tell salacious stories.

Bear in mind that at this time, although married, I was technically a bachelor, a man living alone. I had no evil practices. I did no one any injury. I wasn't even drinking much. I would have champagne around, and if people wanted it they could have it, and I'd take a bit with them, but that was it. I was thirty-four, in my prime; women liked me, I liked them; nobody got hurt. I thought, 'Let's have fun, let's live by the sunshine, let's swim and play; let's make love, let's cruise in the Pacific, let's have pleasant parties, gay chatter; let's work, let's make pictures, let's entertain the people, let's be artists, if we can.'

This was my balls, my way of living, breathing and exulting in this short swift act called Creation. Am I supposed to live as other people? Are they supposed to do what I do? Do I have to be made over into their image, and they into mine?

A man who is so overwhelmed by willing females has a special problem. But [Flynn's aviator friend Bud] Ernst ribbed me unmercifully, saying it was the girls who were taking me—over and over again—and that I was incapable of 'making' them. In fact, he provoked my manhood by this, for it was true. My problem was not to get girls into my life, but to get them out—once they had 'had' me. A strange story, of course, and one perhaps that men all over may envy, but it has been true, and it was why I got into this scrape of the five months that shook the world's glands. . . .

For months the case drifted, with postponement after postponement. Geisler wanted and needed time. He had to prepare his defence the way a general plots a campaign. He told me later, "The whole secret of my success is preparation. You cannot go too far with preparation." He dug up everything he could on the young ladies; he manœuvred, he studied the law.

These delays seemed not to disturb the prosecution. They liked the big newspaper play. The new prosecutors were getting known about California.

But the Press, remarkably fair to me, began to ask questions. What is going on downtown? Who is out to get Flynn? Why has this specific actor been chosen for a going-over?

Hollywood's morals had often been criticised: now it seemed the incident had appeared which was to set off the whole question of the cinema capital's morality. This was the exterior look of the case as it loomed; but behind it was simply this local political hassle, a pay-off deal to get even with the big studios for not coughing up properly—Dockwiler and a few prosecuting attorneys out to make their names over somebody's dead body. . . .

The word 'swordsman' had a double-edged meaning now.

All over the country people didn't know or care about the difference between statutory rape and rape. There prevailed in people's minds somehow the thought that I had forced these girls, made them surrender to my wicked way by getting them to do something they didn't want to do. Headlines never said or explained the statutory aspect of the charge; only they used that anciently harsh word which men and women all over the world depise: *rape*.

The war against Nazism went on to pages two and three, and my case covered five and six and seven columns of front-page space in papers all over the land. In New York—I have always been sensitive to the mood of the people there, the life of the press, and the cultural world located there—in that city the tabloid papers shot their circulation skyward. People came out, I was told, in queues each evening at eight o'clock to get the papers, to read the latest testimony. . . .

Jerry Geisler dressed immaculately, but in a plain way. Here was a man with force, but with no overbearing personality. His power lay in his latent strength. He kept his forces in reserve, for his work in court. To me he always seemed a bit distrait, which may have meant only that he was concentrating on the job: he wore a far-away look and usually he went about with a nice smile. He wore dignity as some wear fine clothes; and he had a high-pitched offbeat voice with charm and command to it. You couldn't easily define his mentality, except of course, as the legal community knows, he almost never loses—*almost*. He advised me beforehand, "Bear in mind that the District Attorney's office will say, 'This man is an actor', and they will expect the jury to discount your testimony because you are trained as a performer." To this Geisler had his own answer. If and when this arose he intended saying—and he did—"Hasn't this man the right to his day in court—as any of us?"

The trial opened. Inside the court all seats were taken, outside there was a jam of humanity. On one side of the room sat the Press, by and large friendly to me, so friendly that I couldn't fully understand it. Geisler had advised me to cooperate with the Press, and he talked to the newspapers freely. My legal help was limited to two men: Geisler and Ford. The prosecution had a battery of eight attorneys headed by a prosecutor named Cochrane.

Some not surprising instinct guided Geisler into selecting a nearly all-female jury: nine out of twelve of the 'good men and true'.

Prosecutor Cochrane put Peggy Larne Satterlee on the stand. She was a beautiful girl. Her upholstery was sensational. Her waist was a lovely moulding. She had long, dark, silky hair, and could have passed for anywhere between twenty and twenty-five.

Yet when she came in, I hardly recognised her. They had put her in bobby socks, flat-heeled shoes, and *pigtails*. She could have looked like my kid sister. My heart sank when I beheld her. Migod, I thought, she looks like a baby. Yet a week or two earlier she had been in a chorus dressed scantily, to say the least.

While Peggy gave her testimony I sat at my desk, listening hard and concentrating on a pad of paper on to which I wrote notes. Occasionally I looked at her or at Cochrane—a furtive glance—and I seemed to need the actual physical warmth of Geisler on my right and the young Irish lawyer on my left.

Cochrane asked her to tell how, nearly two years before, she had yielded to me on board the *Sirocco*. We were cruising to Catalina, a weekend jaunt, she said, and I had kissed her at the companionway of the yacht. Then, she said, she had gone into her stateroom, and I followed her.

Then came the juicy dialogue that the newspaper boys—and the public—were waiting for. The White House must have been a little grateful to have the war news taken off Page One and some of the fire deflected elsewhere.

Question: *Who kissed you?*
Answer: *Why, Mr Flynn.*
Q. *What did you do?*
A. *I went to the stateroom and went to bed.*
Q. *What happened then?*
A. *In about ten minutes there was a knock at the door. At the same time Flynn walked in, clad in pyjamas. He asked if he could talk to me. I said it was not very nice for a gentleman to be in a lady's bedroom, especially if she was in bed.*
Q. *What did he say?*
A. *'If you let me get in bed with you, I won't bother you. I just want to talk with you.'*

Then, she testified, I was intimate with her.

(At just about that time, when Peggy said it wasn't very gentlemanly of me to call at her bedroom, Warners released *Gentleman Jim*. A lot of merriment went around all through the country and elsewhere. Because I had a certain very apposite line of dialogue at the close of that picture. Alexis Smith, the girl, is almost in my arms and I say to her, *"How could I marry you? You are a lady."*

She says, *"I am no lady."*

Gentleman Jim slaps her, grabs her in his arms, kisses her and says, *"I am no gentleman."*

The wartime public was thrown into mild hysterics over this. In some parts of the country they even had to throw out the last line so as to prevent anything too raucous happening in the theatres.)

Peggy also testified that on returning to port we were standing at the rail and she remarked how beautiful the moon was. 'He said it would look much more beautiful through a porthole.'

Apparently, she testified, we actually looked at the moon through the porthole. We went below, she said, I took a yachting outfit off her, and we had another session.

Question: *How did you feel about this?*
Answer: *I was just plain mad this time, instead of scared as before.*

I don't have to defend myself as I recount the trial. My lawyers did that and the jury arrived at its decision. Nonetheless the trial was an American drama, and Jerry Geisler produced much of it as he handled the young ladies and the legal opposition.

When he cross-examined Peggy, employing a soft voice, and not at all the harsh accuser, he said, "Miss Satterlee, I am a little bit mystified. I have here a picture. Is this you?"

He showed her the picture.

"Yes."

He made a clucking sound with his tongue two or three times, as if expressing surprise. He didn't show the picture to anybody in the court except her. But he said, "What a difference! Tell me, do you always dress like this?"

"Like what?"

"In bobby socks and pigtails?"

"Sometimes, if I feel like it."

"That's all."

Yet the effect on the jury must have been fantastic. They could only have wondered, "What has he got there?"—a picture she admitted was herself.

Peggy was smart, very smart. She stuck to her story. She described in minute details how I lured her into the after-cabin and, as she said, pushed her on the bunk.

In other words, she did not admit consent.

She was implying a knock-her-down-drag-her-out rape.

I pushed her up on to the bunk, she said, where I forcefully took her. Meanwhile I said to her, 'Darling, look out the porthole. You see that glorious moon?'

That remark followed me around for years: 'Oh Errol, look at the porthole and the glorious moon.' I rather suppose that that expression had become the dividing line of my life—everything that went on before the porthole and the glorious moon, and everything that has gone on since.

Geisler began his attack. He brought out a picture of the *Sirocco's* interior, and he drew a counterpart of it on a blackboard. He asked Peggy how high the bunk was. She indicated a height not much above the knees. Geisler proved that the bunk was at least five feet off the floorboard. He wondered, before the jury, if I had enough strength to get her up there forcibly, or whether or not she had enough strength to resist being put up there or enough strength to get down.

This kind of testimony went on for days. Yet slowly, steadily, the talented Geisler convinced everybody that these two young ladies knew what they were doing, that they were amibitious to become show girls, they knew and understood the risks of visiting a famous bachelor's house, or yacht, in Hollywood.

Thereafter Geisler battered down Peggy's claim of intercourse without consent.

January 1943 ended. The trial moved into February. Day after day the law dragged us all into this court. These poor girls were pawns in the local political wrangle as much as I was. They were being drained and wrung out and so was I. There, behind all this, was an age-old political pitch: a threatening of the big studios, someone getting even with them, saying, 'You didn't shell out enough dough to us for the protection you want from an administration, we'll show you, we'll teach you not to buck us.' There was my head on the block because Warners and the other studios had not picked the right political horse to back, hadn't paid off right.

Letters poured in from all over the world. One would say: *That is an outrage. You are being swindled by two gold-digging girls. They ought to be strung up.* Another said: *You lecherous swine! You ought to be hung. I hope they send you away for twenty years!* But few people then, and not even now, know how plaintiff and defendant were both caught up in a political whirlpool: how corruption, money, power, graft, stood in the rear, symbolically and actually, and ran the show.

But they didn't run everything.

I still had some will left: quite a lot of it, in fact, and some of that I directed to a very lovely-looking redhead who occupied a cubicle in the lobby entrance of the City Hall. Day by day I passed by her and watched how she sold chewing-gum, cigarettes, cigars. It was easier to look at her loveliness than to stare into the wilderness of the mob that hung about the courthouse waiting to get a look at me. As I walked past there'd be shouts of 'Attaboy, Errol.' 'Let her go, kid!' 'You got 'em whipped, Errol.' I hoped some of that would rub off on the jury. I listened to these cries of encouragement but glanced over to the cigarette counter at this slender girl with the lovely complexion, the bluish-green eyes that slanted up at the corner.

I didn't get a look at her figure for quite some time. Finally I stopped and bought some cigarettes. I stared beneath the lovely complexion and spotted just enough freckles to make it interesting. I craned my neck a bit over the counter, and saw that all was well. She had about a nineteen- or twenty-inch waist, hips to go with it and slender ankles and wrists. All my life I have been partial to slender ankles.

The case was drawing near to its close. I would either be sentenced to jail or not. Under the law there was no such thing as a suspended sentence or a fine. None of these nice amenities. You either had it or you hadn't. I had no intention of going to jail. My two-engine plane was out at Burbank, waiting, so that if I got a bum rap I'd get out of there, hop in, and leave America and my screen career for ever. Meantime, the redhead behind the counter interested me to the point where something had to be done. . . .

I had a friend, Buster Wiles, a bald-headed fellow aged about twenty-nine, a stunt man and a daredevil—one of the best in movies. He had a Tennessee drawl, very thick, and he had a sense of humour and more charm than most cowboys or stunt men. I knew I had to meet this girl; it might be my last companionship of the sort prior to a flight over Mexico or, if I couldn't make it, a long spell in the clink. Apparently I hadn't lost my faith in the opposite sex. But I didn't have enough guts to make any advances myself, so it was Buster into the breach.

He charmed her into agreeing to come to Mulholland House for 'tea'—which would turn out to be a slug of champagne. She was invited to come up with a girl friend, just to put her mind at ease—and up she came.

I had to go about this very slowly. She had read the papers like everyone else, and I had to watch my technique—do no rushing whatever. I treated her with what I can only now think of as exaggerated courtesy. I even greeted her with a hand-kiss on arrival and the same hand-kiss upon her departure. Very bad manners, of course, since she would presumably be a virgin. In the Kissing-of-the-Hand Department, you only kiss the hand of married women. I skipped this point of protocol, knowing she would never know the difference. I was rewarded for my gallantry with a shy simper.

Having decided to take things slowly—bear in mind this was in the middle of the double statutory rape trial—it took me about a week to advance the hand-kissing stage up her arm. However, I was careful not to make the deadly proposition, or at least not to rush it.

There was a certain precaution that I took before all of this. I carefully checked her age. She was eighteen, safe ground. Her name, it turned out, was Nora Eddington.

What I didn't know was that her father was Captain Jack Eddington of the Los Angeles County Sheriff's office.

Betty Hansen had her day in court.

It was now February 15th. I understand that throughout the nation the newspapers were feeling the pinch of a newsprint shortage, partly because of the war effort and its needs, and partly because their pages were being filled with extra columns of testimony at my trial. I may or may not be joking about that.

Geisler had the seventeen-year-old Betty on the stand and was most kindly and sympathetic towards her as she began her testimony by identifying herself as a drugstore clerk. He was almost fatherly as he led her to admit that the prosecutor had stressed to her that she could be held in Juvenile Hall for four years if she didn't testify properly. All this he brought out by indirect cross-examination without even seeming to try, and it appeared to me that what he said was having its effect upon the jury.

He examined her about the alleged act, almost as if he were her lawyer, not mine.

Q. *What did he do when he came into the den, as you call it?*
A. *He told me he was going to take me upstairs and lie me down.*
Q. *Then what did you do?*
A. *We went upstairs.*
Q. *Then what did you do?*
A. *We went into a little bedroom off the big bedroom where there were two twin beds. He sat me down on the bed and told me he was going to put me to bed. I said I didn't want to go to bed and that I wanted to go downstairs around with the others. Then he said, 'You don't think I'm really going to let you go downstairs, do you?' And then he got up and went into the big room and I heard a click and I don't know if he locked the door or not.*
Q. *Then what did he do?*
A. *He came back and he started to undress me. I thought he was just going to put me to bed, like he said.*
Q. *What did you have on?*
A. *I had on slacks, a blouse, brassière and teddies. He took off everything but my shoes and stockings. Then he took off his clothes, all but his shoes.*
Q. *Did he have on socks?*
A. *No.*

(Right then they had released *They Died With Their Boots On.* The press had a circus with this testimony.)

Q. *Then what happened?*
A. *Then we had an act of intercourse.*

Geisler tore into her at this point. He was out to show consent. Hadn't she been going around saying that Flynn was good-looking? Hadn't she been playing up to Flynn?

A. *Yes.*
Q. *But you didn't mean to play up to him all the way?*

A. *No, I didn't.*

Q. *You thought you'd played up to him far enough when you let him remove your clothes?*

A. *Yes.*

Geisler said, "You say that Flynn removed your slacks. Didn't you want him to take them off?"

She hesitated a minute. Then she made the remark that may have endeared her to the grammarians but not the jury:

"I didn't have no objections."

Through all such testimony I sat with clammy hands. I felt I was growing greyer by the day. Downstairs, in the lobby, I had a new-found red-headed friend, but this wasn't enough. The unrevealing face of Judge Stone was always before me, and I prayed for the day when this horror would end.

There were technical delays; twice they tried to throw off the jury one man who spoke out of turn. The prosecutor wanted to get him bounced, but Geisler didn't want a re-trial, knowing the kind of cost and misery involved, so he blocked those motions. Naturally the politicos in and around the DA's office would have liked this case to drag on for years while they stayed in control.

Betty Hansen said I had locked the door before getting undressed. Geisler set out to prove that there was no lock on this door, or that it wouldn't work. The prosecution sent sleuths around and they found evidence of steel scrapings on the floor, proving somebody had tampered with the lock. Actually I am pretty sure somebody had. It was none of my doing. But it caused a great outcry when they brought in these steel scrapings and swore they found them under this supposed lock that wouldn't lock. That was a dark day. It looked as if my legal help had somebody go out there and frame this thing.

Another time there was an incident that sent everyone in America to their dictionaries. Somebody, in testimony, used the word 'crumpet', which I think is an English cookie. But this was construed as strumpet, which is a different kind of cookie. There was a debate in court over whether the girls were crumpets or strumpets, and there was a spill-over of this row to the press, which sent everybody skedaddling to Webster's to see what he had to say.

In the midst of all this I had a the-show-must-go-on stint to do. I remember working with David Butler, the director, on a film called *Thank Your Lucky Stars*. Warner Brothers convinced the stars that it was their patriotic duty to do this picture for nothing. Each of us had an act to provide. We were not to get paid and the proceeds were to go to the Hollywood Canteen. And while the motors spun out at Burbank, and the trial raged on, I had to fit in some time to go and do this number, sing and dance and try to look gay and carefree.

A song-and-dance routine, when, to pile on the contradictions, I had never been a song-and-dance man. David Butler was astounded. He said, "I don't see how you can do it." I still don't.

One day the judge ordered the jury to consider the evidence and come in with a decision.

The jury was out about four hours. I looked out into the streets. The way the crowd was massed outside reminded me of a mob scene that Cecil DeMille might have been filming. Would I be thrown to the lions or not? Would the old Spanish statute, of another day, hold for Hollywood in 1943?

As the jury filed back in I felt myself go numb. There were four counts and each had to be read out.

I felt Jerry's hand on my leg, gripping me like an eagle grasping a rabbit. He didn't know, or wasn't sure, what was going to happen, any more than I, but this was his way of showing his feeling for me, and his gesture took away some of the numbness.

I heard voices.

"On the first count—Not Guilty." Jerry's hand gripped tighter.

"On the second count—Not Guilty." Again his hand tightened.

"On the third count—Not Guilty." He gripped so hard that I felt the circulation had stopped in my leg.

"On the fourth count—Not Guilty!"

The courtroom broke into cheers. Judge Stone didn't even try to quiet them. He let the outbursts go on. When the noise inside court settled, I heard a din from the street.

I got a strange choked feeling, a stopped-up emotion that seemed to hold on. I couldn't talk: only sit there and gulp and choke and try to smile at Jerry.

I wasn't wearing a hat, but I touched my hair—to the ladies—as if I were wearing one.

When the air settled, Judge Stone congratulated the jury on what he considered a fair decision. I was grateful to hear that, and grateful for the applause in the court.

It left an enduring scar but also another kind of emotion: the thought that the common sense of people will always prevail. I might have been as guilty as hell— under the law, that is—but in the world of day-to-day common sense, where the ebb and flow of existence can't always be measured to the dotted i and the crossed t of living, everybody knew that the girls had asked for it, whether or not I had my wicked ways with them. . . .

I supposed that Jerry Geisler was going to charge me a hundred grand, as he did others.

On the contrary, his fee was only $30,000. It cost, of course, another $20,000 for expenses. . . .

Ostensibly I won the case. The people had vindicated me. There was applause for the verdict, and the crowds thronged into the theatres to see my pictures and get a double laugh: to laugh at the film fare and to enjoy seeing the man who gave them so much entertainment over and beyond the call of picture-making. A new legend was born, and new terms went into the national idiom. . . .

A GI or Marine or sailor went out at night sparking and the next day he reported to his cronies, who asked him how he made out, and the fellow said, with a sly grin, *"I'm in like Flynn."*

Edward Albert, Errol Flynn, Ava Gardner and Tyrone Power in The Sun Also Rises *(1957), 20th Century-Fox.*

JOAN FONTAINE

Joan Fontaine and Robert Ryan in Born To Be Bad *(1950), RKO.*

**Born Joan de Beauvoir de Havilland on October 22, 1917 in Tokyo, Japan
. . . Sister Olivia de Havilland . . . Married Brian Aherne 1939 . . . Divorced
1944 . . . Married Producer William Dozier 1946 . . . Divorced 1951 . . . Movie
Debut:** *No More Ladies* **(1935) . . . Oscar nomination for** *Rebecca* **(1940) and for**
The Constant Nymph **(1943) . . . Oscar for** *Suspicion* **(1941) beat out sister
Olivia . . . Pursued by Howard Hughes during filming of** *Born To Be Bad*
(1950) . . . Balloonist, pilot, deep sea fisherman, golfer, interior decorator, and
Cordon Bleu **chef.**

Money is Sexy

The first film I made after the birth of my daughter was *Born To Be Bad*. Joan Harrison, Hitchcock's writer, had shown me the novel *All Kneeling*, by Anne Parrish, and suggested it might make an interesting vehicle for me, one that would give me a chance to break away from the English lady heroines that I'd been playing. I bought the rights to the book and sold them to R.K.O. Despite a cast that included Robert Ryan, Zachary Scott, and Mel Ferrer, direction by Nicholas Ray, the only acceptable part of the film was my wardrobe designed by Tina Leser.

During the making of *Born To Be Bad*, Howard Hughes bought the R.K.O. Studios . . . lock, stock, and Fontaine's contract, too. My boss was now the same man who had been proposing to me for over ten years. I was summoned to his office.

There Howard informed me that we were to see the rushes together every evening and that he had heard the Doziers were breaking up. Was it true? Again he proposed.

"Why me, Howard? Why *me*?"

"Because you know the business, because you like to travel, you like to fly . . . why, I haven't even been to South America! We could read scripts together, play golf, see the world." Then he added a remark that was to explain his reclusiveness. "Since my accident in 1946, I can't bear to look at my face in the mirror when I shave. I'm getting ugly and don't want to be seen. And with my deafness, I haven't much more time to be among people."

At Fordyce [The Dozier-Fontaine house in Brentwood] that evening, I recounted to Bill the entire conversation I'd had with Howard. He looked thoughtful. "I'd like to run R.K.O. again," he confessed, "and our marriage isn't any good anyway. . . ."

I was never in love with Howard. As a matter of fact, I was a little afraid of him. Certainly one could not be relaxed and at ease with a man of so much wealth, power, and influence. He had no humor, no gaiety, no sense of joy, no vivacity that was apparent to me. Everything seemed to be a "deal," a business arrangement, regardless of the picture he had tried to paint of our future together—but money is sexy and he certainly had a blinding overabundance of cash appeal.

The next afternoon I went into Howard's office again to explain that Bill might be willing to give me a divorce under certain terms. But before I could even consider another marriage, I would have to get to know Howard much better, to see if the life he envisioned for us was possible. And there was Debbie [Fontaine's daughter]. What about her?

Howard pressed the intercom button on his desk, mumbled into it, and said, "Let's go." A shabby, inconspicuous car was waiting below. We got into it, Howard driving along Sunset Boulevard, eventually turning toward the hills. At a white stucco, red-tiled house, he got out and ushered me into an indifferently furnished living room. The front door had been unlocked.

"What's all this, Howard? Whom are we visiting?"

Cocking his head to one side as he so often did to hear better, in his quiet, level monotone, he answered, "It's yours. Until your divorce is final, we can meet here."

I turned quickly and raced out the front door. Back in his car, Howard soon learned that I had my own house, thank you, and was not about to lead a shady double life with anyone. Even though I was not a lawyer, it was obvious to me that if I did so, Debbie's father would have justifiable grounds to gain custody. Howard obviously couldn't have cared less.

Undeterred, Howard began telephoning me at the house, undoubtedly to bring matters between the Doziers to a head. Sometimes Bill would answer and hand me the phone. "God calling." Bill even seemed amused by the situation. I was not. California laws are very protective about children. If it could be proved that I was having an affair, even after divorce proceedings had begun, I most certainly would have lost custody of my child. Too, the newspapers could have had a field day, and I would end up in a monumental scandal: no child, no anything.

One evening Howard telephoned me to say he wanted to discuss our situation further and would meet me in his car in Brentwood. Bill agreed to have dinner with his friends while I was out. At eight o'clock, I parked my car behind Howard's and we set off in his along the coast highway. Howard had a solution. Because of his own legal situation, a year-long California divorce would be less chancy than a quick one obtained in Reno or Mexico. I was to live at a ranch he would rent for me in Nevada or Arizona while I got the divorce. He would fly in on weekends to visit me.

What! Coop me up for a year? No friends, no films? And what about Debbie? I thought of the Cole Porter song "Don't Fence Me In."

"Sorry, Howard, it won't do."

Howard kept looking in the rearview mirror as we approached Malibu. I, too, could see exceptionally bright lights that shone steadily in the mirror. Howard abruptly turned the car southward. We were being followed. I saw a black limousine with whitewall tires turn in the half circle we had made and resume its tail behind us.

Back in my own car again, I waved good-bye to Howard as the limousine stopped at the corner. Howard had a fair idea of who had had us followed. So did I. I recognized the driver. I was to see him again.

Ten minutes later, back at Fordyce, I telephoned Bill at the number he had given me and told him of the conversation with Howard and of the black limousine. He was not pleased. His bewildering comment was "You've botched it." Then silence. He hung up the receiver abruptly.

Bill did, eventually, get his old office back at R.K.O., but I was to wait for some time before getting a divorce. I was one of the few girls pursued by Howard Hughes who never had an affair with him.

Joan Fontaine in Rebecca *(1940), United Artists.*

LILLIAN GISH

Lillian Gish in The Birth of a Nation *(1915).*

Born Lillian de Guiche on October 14, 1896 in Springfield, Ohio . . . "The First Lady of the Silent Screen" . . . Introduced by Mary Pickford to D. W. Griffith in 1912 . . . Films include: *Birth of a Nation* **(1915) . . .** *Intolerance* **(1916) . . .** *The Scarlet Letter* **(1926) . . .** *The Night of the Hunter* **(1955) . . .** *A Wedding* **(1978) . . . Never married . . . Griffith: "She is not only the best actress in her profession, but she has the best mind of any woman I have ever met."**

The Birth of *The Birth of a Nation*

One afternoon during the spring of 1914, while we were still working in California, Mr. Griffith took me aside on the set and said in an undertone, "After the others leave tonight, would you please stay."

Later, as some of the company drifted out, I realized that a similiar message had been given to a few others. This procedure was typical of Mr. Griffith when he was planning a new film. He observed us with a smile, amused perhaps by our curiosity over the mystery that he had created.

I suspected what the meeting was about. A few days before, we had been having lunch at The White Kitchen, and I had noticed that his pockets were crammed with papers and pamphlets. My curiosity was aroused, but it would have been presumptuous of me to ask about them. With Mr. Griffith one did not ask; one only answered. Besides, I had learned that if I waited long enough he would tell me.

"I've bought a book by Thomas Dixon, called *The Clansman*. I'm going to use it to tell the truth about the War between the States. It hasn't been told accurately in history books. Only the winning side in a war ever gets to tell its story." He paused, watching the cluster of actors: Henry Walthall, Spottiswoode Aiken, Bobby Harron, Mae Marsh, Miriam Cooper, Elmer Clifton, George Siegmann, Walter Long, and me.

"The story concerns two families—the Stonemans from the North and the Camerons from the South." He added significantly, "I know I can trust you."

He swore us to secrecy, and to us his caution was understandable. Should his competitors learn of his new project, they would have films on the same subject completed before his work was released. He discussed his story plots freely only over lunch or dinner, often testing them out on me because I was close-mouthed and never repeated what anyone told me.

I heard later that "Daddy" Woods [Griffith's scenario department head] had called Mr. Griffith's attention to *The Clansman*. It had done well as a book and even better as a play, touring the country for five years. Mr. Griffith also drew on *The Leopard's Spots* for additional material for the new movie. Thomas Dixon, the author of both works, was a southerner who had been a college classmate of Woodrow Wilson. Mr. Griffith paid a $2,500 option for *The Clansman*, and it was agreed that Dixon was to receive $10,000 in all for the story, but when it came time to pay him no more money was available. In the end, he reluctantly agreed to accept instead of cash a 25 per cent interest in the picture, which resulted in the largest sum any author ever received for a motion-picture story. Dixon earned several million dollars as his share.

Mr. Griffith didn't need the Dixon book. His intention was to tell his version of the War between the States. But he evidently lacked the confidence to start production on a twelve-reel film without an established book as a basis for his story. After the film was completed and he had shown it to the so-called author, Dixon said: "This isn't my book at all." But Mr. Griffith was glad to use Dixon's name on the film as author, for, as he told me, "The public hates you if it thinks you wrote, directed, and produced the entire film yourself. It's the quickest way to make enemies."

After the first rehearsal, the pace increased. Mr. Griffith worked, as usual, without a script. But this time his pockets bulged with books, maps, and pamphlets, which he read during meals and the rare breaks in his hectic schedule. I rehearsed whatever part Mr. Griffith wanted to see at the moment. My sister and I had been the last to join the company, and we naturally supposed that the major assignments would go to the older members of the group. For a while, it looked as if I would be no more than an extra. But during one rehearsal Blanche Sweet, who we suspected would play the romantic part of Elsie Stoneman, was missing. Mr. Griffith pointed to me.

"Come on, Miss Damnyankee, let's see what you can do with Elsie."

My thin figure was quite a contrast to Blanche's ripe, full form. Mr. Griffith had us rehearse the near-rape scene between Elsie and Silas Lynch, the power-drunk mulatto in the film. George Siegmann was playing Lynch in blackface. In this scene Lynch proposes to Elsie and, when she rebuffs him, forces his attentions on her. During the hysterical chase around the room, the hairpins flew out of my hair, which tumbled below my waist as Lynch held my fainting body in his arms. I was very blonde and fragile-looking. The contrast with the dark man evidently pleased Mr. Griffith, for he said in front of everyone, "Maybe she would be more effective than the more mature figure I had in mind."

He didn't tell us then, but I think the role was mine from that moment. . . .

During his six years with Biograph, Mr. Griffith had taken strides toward his ultimate goal: filming his version of the Civil War. He had made a number of early pictures that touched on the War between the States. But it was soon obvious to everyone that this film was to be his most important statement yet. Billy Bitzer [Griffith's master cameraman] wrote of that time: "*The Birth of a Nation* changed D. W. Griffith's personality entirely. Where heretofore he was wont to refer in starting on a new picture to 'grinding out another sausage' and go at it lightly, his attitude in beginning on this one was all eagerness. He acted like here we have something worthwhile."

Although fact and legend were familiar to him, he did meticulous research for *The Birth*. The first half of *The Birth*, about the war itself, reflects his own point of view. I know that he also relied greatly on Harper's *Pictorial History of the Civil War*, Mathew Brady's *Civil War Photographs: Confederate and Union Veterans—Eyewit-*

nesses on Location; the Nicolay and Hay *Abraham Lincoln: A History;* and *The Soldier in Our Civil War: A Pictorial History of the Conflict 1861–1865.* For the second half, about Reconstruction, he consulted Thomas Dixon, and *A History of the American People* by Woodrow Wilson. President Wilson had taught history before going into politics, and Mr. Griffith had great respect for his erudition. For Klan material, he drew on a book called *Ku Klux Klan—Its Origin, Growth and Disbandment* by John C. Lester and D. L. Wilson. But he did not use the uniform that is worn by Klan members today. Instead he used the costumes that, according to Thomas Dixon, were worn by the earlier Klans—white and scarlet flowing robes with hood and mask to hide the features of rider and horse.

Brady's photographs were constantly consulted, and Mr. Griffith restaged many moments of history with complete fidelity to them. The photographs were used as guides for such scenes as Lee's surrender at Appomattox, the signing of the Emancipation Proclamation, and Sherman's march to the sea. He telegraphed a newspaper in Columbia, South Carolina, for photographs of the interior of the state capitol, which held a majority of Negro representatives after the war, and constructed the legislative chamber according to the photographs.

The largest interior was Ford's Theater, the setting of the assassination scene, which was done in one day on the lot. So great was Mr. Griffith's obsession with authenticity that he unearthed a copy of *Our American Cousin,* which had been performed at Ford's Theater on the night of the assassination, and restaged parts of it. In the actual filming, as Raoul Walsh, gun ready, steals into the Presidential box, the lines being spoken on the replica of the stage are precisely those spoken at the fateful moment on the night of April 14, 1865. This fidelity to facts was an innovation in films.

Mr. Griffith knew the terrain of the battle fields, and he hired several Civil War veterans to scout locations similar to the original ones. After exploring the southern California country, they chose what later became the Universal lot for the countryside around Petersburg, Virginia, site of the last prolonged siege and final battle of the war.

He had studied maps of the major battles of the Civil War and, with the help of the veterans, laid out the battle fields. Trenches, breastworks, roads, brooks, and buildings were constructed to duplicate those of the actual battle fields. Troop movements were planned with the advice of the veterans and two men from West Point Military Academy. Civil War artillery was obtained from West Point and the Smithsonian Institution, for use when the camera was close.

Mr. Griffith also sent to the Smithsonian for historical records and then went over the documents with his advisers. But in the end he came to his own conclusions about historical facts. He would never take the opinion of only one man as final.

The street in Piedmont on which the Cameron house was located was complete with brick walls and hitching and lamp posts. A small set, it achieved scope from violated perspective—an old stage technique in which each successive house and street lamp is a little shorter, so that the setting seems to "recede" without actually taking up much space or requiring the use of expensive lumber.

We had no stage designer, only the modest genius of a carpenter, Frank Wortman, known as "Huck." Huck, a short, rather heavyset man in his forties, with friendly blue eyes and a weakness for chewing tobacco, didn't talk much, but listened intently to Mr. Griffith. Even before rehearsals started Mr. Griffith explained to him what he wanted in the way of sets. He would show Huck a photograph that he wanted copied, or point out changes to be made in the reproduction. They would decide how the sun would hit a particular building three, four, even five weeks from then.

Men during the Civil War era were rather small in stature (it was before the age of proper nutrition), so genuine uniforms could not be used by the later generation. Uniforms for *The Birth* were therefore made by a small struggling company, which has since become the famous Western Costume Company.

The Brady photographs also served as models for the soldiers' hair styles.

To absorb the spirit of the film, we came down with a case of history nearly as intense as Mr. Griffith's. At first, between making other films during the day and rehearsing *The Birth* at night, we had scant time for reading. But Mr. Griffith's interest was contagious, and we began to read about the period. Soon it was the only subject we talked about. Mr. Griffith didn't ask us to do this; it stemmed out of our own interest. We pored over photographs of the Civil War and *Godey's Ladies' Book,* a periodical of the nineteenth century, for costumes, hair styles, and postures. We had to rehearse how to sit and how to move in the hoop skirts of the day.

My costumes were specially made. One of them had a tiny derby with a high plume. When I saw it, I rebelled.

But Mr. Griffith insisted that I wear it. He wanted the audience to be amused. "It's a darb!" he said, smiling.

In filming the battles, Mr. Griffith organized the action like a general. He stood at the top of a forty-foot tower, the commander-in-chief of both armies, his powerful voice, like Roarin' Jake's, thundering commands through a megaphone to his staff of assistants. Meetings were called before each major filmed sequence and a chain of command was developed from Mr. Griffith through his directors and their assistants. The last-in-command might have only four or five extras under him. These men, wearing uniforms and taking their places among the extras, also played parts in the film.

Griffith's camera was high on the platform looking down on the battle field, so that he could obtain a grand sweep of the action. This camera took the long shots. Hidden under bushes or in back of trees were cameras for closeups.

When the din of cannons, galloping horses, and charging men grew too great, no human voice, not even Mr. Griffith's, was powerful enough to be heard. Some of the extras were stationed as far as two miles from the camera. So a series of magnifying mirrors was used to flash signals to those actors working a great distance away. Each group of men had its number—one flash of the mirror for the first group, two for the second group, and so on. As group one started action, the mirror would flash a go-ahead to group two.

Care was taken to place the authentic old guns and the best horsemen in the first ranks. Other weapons, as well as poorer horsemen, were relegated to the background. Extras were painstakingly drilled in their parts until they knew when to charge, when to push cannons forward, when to fall.

Some of the artillery was loaded with real shells, and elaborate warnings were broadcast about their range of fire. Mr. Griffith's sense of order and control made it possible for the cast and extras to survive the broiling heat, pounding hoofs, naked bayonets, and exploding shells without a single injury. He was too thoughtful to the welfare of others to permit accidents.

In most war films it is difficult to distinguish between the enemies unless the film is in color and the two sides are wearing different-colored uniforms. But not in a Griffith movie. Mr. Griffith had the rare technical skill to keep each side distinct and clear cut. In *The Birth*, the Confederate army always entered from the left of the camera, the Union army from the right.

One day he said to Billy, "I want to show a whole army moving."

"What do you mean, a whole army?" Bitzer asked.

"Everyone we can muster."

"I'll have to move them back to get them all in view," Billy said. "They won't look much bigger than jackrabbits."

"That's all right. The audience will supply the details. Let's move up on this hill, Billy. Then we can shoot the whole valley and all the troops at once."

They never talked much, but they always seemed to understand each other. People around Mr. Griffith didn't bother him with idle talk.

When daylight disappeared, Mr. Griffith would order bonfires lit and film some amazing night scenes. Billy was pessimistic about the results; he kept insisting that they would be unsuccessful. But Mr. Griffith persisted. One big battle scene was filmed at night. The sub-title was to read, "It went on into the night." Nothing like it had ever been seen before. Those of us who had time were there—the women to watch, the men to help.

Although everything was carefully organized, whenever he saw a spontaneous gesture that looked good—like the soldier's leaning on his gun and looking at me during the hospital scene—he would call Billy over to film it.

In that scene, the wards were filled with wounded soldiers, and in the background nurses and orderlies attended their patients. In the doorway of the ward stood a Union sentry. As Elsie Stoneman, I was helping to entertain the wounded, singing and playing the banjo. The sentry watched me lovingly as I sang and then, after I had finished and was passing him, raised his hang-dog head and heaved a deep, love-sick sigh. The scene lasted only a minute, but it drew the biggest laugh of the film and became one of its best-remembered moments.

The scene came about in typical Griffith fashion. We players had no one to help us with our costumes. We had to carry our various changes to the set, as we could not afford the time to run back to our dressing rooms. Those period dresses, with their full skirts over hoops, were heavy. A kind young man who liked me helped me with my props and costumes. The young man, William Freeman, was playing the sentry, and he simply stood there, listening, as I sang. Seeing his expression, Mr. Griffith said to Bitzer, "Billy, get that picture on film right away." He knew that it would bring a laugh, which was needed to break the dramatic tension.

Since the release of *The Birth of a Nation*, I have often been asked by fans what happened to the sentry in the hospital. After *The Birth* was finished, I didn't see William Freeman again until the first World's Fair in New York. It was the day of the Fair's closing. I happened to be riding on a float for charity, and there, walking toward the float, was William Freeman. I recognized him immediately.

"My son is here," he said after we had greeted each other. "I would like you to meet him."

He disappeared into the crowd and returned shortly with a bright four-year-old, whom he proudly introduced to me. Then we said goodbye, and I haven't seen him since. . . .

In going through Mr. Griffith's papers recently, I came across some "facts" about *The Birth of a Nation* that read like most press releases of that day. Robert Edgar Long, in his soft-cover book *David Wark Griffith: A Brief Sketch of His Career*, published in 1920, suggests that professors of history from at least a half-dozen universities were called upon for facts and figures, so that no errors would mar the film's authenticity. He says that Mr. Griffith had plans to shoot some 5,000 scenes; to use 18,000 men as soldiers; to make 18,000 Union and Confederate uniforms for these men; to hire 3,000 horses; to build entire cities and destroy them by fire; to buy real shells that cost $10 apiece in order to re-enact the greatest battle of the Civil War; and to select fragments from about 500 separate musical compositions to synchronize perfectly with various scenes. Many scenes, he says, were photographed from fifteen to twenty times before Mr. Griffith was pleased with the results. He adds that the scene of Lincoln's assassination was rehearsed at least twenty times before it was actually filmed.

I know that in later years Mr. Griffith himself was prone to exaggerations that were a press agent's dream. Perhaps he too believed that these gross overstatements and inaccuracies would enhance the film's prestige.

It seems to me, however, that the truth is a much finer tribute to Mr. Griffith's skill. In the battle scenes there were never more than 300 to 500 extras. By starting with a closeup and then moving the camera back from the scene, which gave the illusion of depth and distance, and by having the same soldiers run around quickly to make a second entrance, Mr. Griffith created the impression of big armies. In the battles, clouds of smoke rising from the thickets gave the illusion of many soldiers camouflaged by the woods, although in actuality there were only a few.

The scene of Sherman's march to the sea opened with an iris shot—a small area in the upper left-hand corner of a black screen—of a mother holding her weeping children amid the ruins of a burned-out house. Slowly the iris opened wider to reveal a great panorama—troops, wagons, fires, and beyond, in the distance, Atlanta burning. Atlanta was actually a model, superimposed on the film.

The entire industry, always intensely curious about Mr. Griffith, was speculating about this new film. What was that crazy man Griffith up to? He was using the full repertoire of his earlier experiments and adding new ones. He tinted film to achieve dramatic results and to create mood. In the battle scene at Petersburg, the shots of Union and Confederate troops rushing in to replace the dead and wounded are tinted red, and the subtitle reads "In the red lane of death others take their places." And, at the climax of the film, there were the thrilling rides of the Klan. These riders were beautifully handled—first, the signal riders galloping to give warning; then, one by one and two by two, the galloping hordes merging into a white hooded mass, their peaked helmets and fiery crosses making them resemble knights of a crusade.

Before the filming of this scene Mr. Griffith decided to try a new kind of shot. He had a hole dug in the road directly in the path of the horsemen. There he placed Billy and the camera, and obtained shots of the horses approaching and galloping right over the camera, so that the audience could see the pounding hoofs. This shot has since become standard, but then it was the first time it had been done, and the effect was spectacular. Billy came through safely, and so did his precious camera, as Mr. Griffith must have known it would. He would never have taken a chance with a camera; it was far too costly.

Among the obstacles that cropped up during the filming was a lack of muslin needed for Klan uniforms. There was also a shortage of horses for battle scenes. Both were war scarcities. When the war in Europe broke out, the Allies were rounding up horses and shipping them to France. Mr. Griffith found himself in competition with French, English, Russian, and Italian agents, all in search of horses. Acting as his own agent, he was obliged to rent horses at higher prices from a dealer in the West.

We had outstanding riders like the Burns Brothers, who led the Klan riders and supervised any scene involving horses. Henry Walthall was a superb horseman, as were some of the other actors. The cowboy and circus riders beneath the Ku Klux sheets did a superb job. In the mob scenes they reared their horses until clouds mushroomed, but not one of them was hurt.

What I liked most about working on *The Birth* was the horses. I could always borrow a horse from the set, and during my lunch hour I would canter off alone to the hills.

I saw everything that Mr. Griffith put on film. My role in *The Birth* required about three weeks' work, but I was on call during the whole time that it was being filmed. I was in the studio every day—working on other films, being available for the next scene if needed, making myself useful in any way that was required.

My dressing room was just across the hall from the darkroom, where Jimmy Smith and Joe Aller worked. Whenever I had a few minutes I would join them, watching them develop the film and cut it. I would view the day's rushes and tell Jimmy my reactions to them. I saw the effects that Mr. Griffith obtained with his views of marching men, the ride of the Klan, the horrors of war. Watching these snatches of film was like trying to read a book whose pages had been shuffled. There was neither order nor continuity. Here was a touching bit from a scene with Mae; there was a long shot of a battle. It made me realize the job that Mr. Griffith had ahead of him after the filming was done.

The shooting was completed in nine weeks, but Mr. Griffith spent more than three months on cutting, editing and working on the musical score. I still remember how hard he worked on other films during the day and then at night on *The Birth*. Of all his pictures up to that time, none was more beset with difficulties. Without his spirit and faith, it might never have been completed.

John Cromwell and Lillian Gish in A Wedding *(1978), 20th Century-Fox.*

WILLIAM GOLDMAN

Dustin Hoffman and Robert Redford in All The President's Men *(1976), Warner Bros.*

Born August 12, 1931 in Chicago . . . pseudonym Harry Longbaugh . . . Oberlin College, B.A. (1952) . . . Fiction editor of literary magazine . . . Columbia University, M.A. (1956) . . . Prolific novelist and screenplay writer . . . *Harper* (1966) . . . Won Oscar for best original screenplay, *Butch Cassidy and the Sundance Kid* (1969) . . . 2nd Oscar, *All the President's Men* (1976) . . . *The Stepford Wives* (1975) . . . *Marathon Man* (1976) . . . *Magic* (1978) . . . "I'm not all that crazy about the act of writing . . . The sooner I'm done, the sooner I can go to the movies."

All the President's Men

"Have you heard about these two young guys on the *Washington Post?*"
The question was asked me over the phone early in the winter of 1974. By Robert Redford. And it began my association with *All the President's Men.*

I had not heard, at that point, of Carl Bernstein and Bob Woodward. Redford explained that they were young reporters (both in their late twenties when the break-in took place at the Watergate complex). And that they had been doing sensational work on the story and had written a book. He had taken an option and asked me to read it.

The version that I read was well prior to publication or even the proofing stages. It was Xerox copy, full of half pages and cross-outs, and it weighed a ton. I went through it quickly and I knew well before I finished that it was not a job I could conceivably turn down.

Nobody wants to be connected with a garbage film. I find it hard to believe that at the early meetings involving *The Green Slime* or *Jesse James Meets Frankenstein's Daughter* that the creative teams really thought they were in the *Citizen Kane* derby.

What you pray for is this: (1) a movie that people will remember and (2) a movie that people may actually go and see.

Movies with that double potential come along not too often, and when one does, and you're offered a shot, I think you have to take it.

I had no idea whether anyone would want to see a picture about Watergate, but Redford, then the number-one star in the world, was not just going to produce it, he was committed to playing the Woodward part, so obviously that didn't hurt. But the Watergate story had been so important to the country for so many months that I felt if it could be pulled off, people might remember.

Now, there were problems.

(1) Watergate had been so heavily dealt with in the media that a lot of people, rightly, were already sick of it.

(2) Certain kinds of subject matter were viewed with less than glee by studio executives: sports, for one; politics, for another. And *All the President's Men* certainly was a political story.

(3) The book had no structure that jumped out at me. And very little dialog.

(4) There were all those goddam names that no one could keep straight: Stans and Sturgis and Baker and Segretti and McCord and Kalmbach and Magruder and Kleindienst and Strachan and Abplanalp and Rebozo and backward reeled the mind.

(5) Great liberties could not be taken with the material. Not just for legal reasons, which were potentially enormous. But if there ever was a movie that had to be

authentic, it was this one. The importance of the subject matter obviously demanded that. More crucially was this: We were dealing here with probably the greatest triumph of the print media in many years, and every media person who would see the film, if there was a film—every columnist and commentator and reviewer—would have spent time at some point in their careers in a newspaper. And if we "Hollywood it up"—i.e., put in dancing girls—there was no way they would take it kindly. We had to be dead on, or we were dead.

(6) Redford himself. He was not to be a hired hand on the project. Being the producer meant that a lot of directors might shy from the job, since they don't like having their star be their boss.

Plus this: He wasn't just the star, he was the co-star. The Bernstein part would have to be equal. At least that. Because if you are a star, and your co-star is your producer, your part can disappear pretty quickly in the cutting room.

And we needed a *star.* If we had gone with a relative unknown—say, Robert De Niro at that time—not only would it have thrown the balance out of whack, Redford was very much aware that people would say he was afraid of an equal and wanted it all for himself. There were only two equals who had the proper ethnic qualities for Bernstein—Hoffman and Pacino. If we couldn't land either one of them, we were in trouble.

(7) And this turned out to be one of the great jokes—my wife remembers my telling her that my biggest problem would be somehow to make the ending work, since the public already knew the outcome.

Was ever a man so naive?

Before I went down to Washington to meet with the authors, I began my preliminary research, and one of the things I found that I hadn't known was the inept quality of so much of what went on.

The famous break-in of June 17, 1972, the event that triggered everything, was *not* their first attempt. The burglars had tried several times before, and they kept goofing it up. Once, they got trapped and had to hide for the night in an empty room in the complex. Better than that, another attempt failed because the keys they had made to get them into Democratic National Headquarters didn't fit. Now, they had had these keys made in Miami, and after their bungle some of them *went back* to Miami to have keys made all over again.

The reason I suppose I liked that stuff was my obsession with the likelihood that everyone assumed they knew everything about Watergate. So I felt whatever I could bring in that was surprising would help us.

Anyway, still winter, I shuttle to Washington to meet the *Post* editors and, most particularly, Woodward and Bernstein.

It was not a good meeting and I suspect it was my fault. Bernstein was late, but when he arrived the three of us began to talk and I remember talking about the incompetence of so much of what went on, and I said, "It's almost like a comic opera."

The look on Bernstein's face when "comic opera" came out was not one of joy. The story had taken him from being a young, not all that sucessful reporter and had already given him a certain amount of fame and was soon to make him rich. And here was this Hollywood asshole talking about it being something less than serious. (Not my intention, obviously, but it was not the best phrase for me to use on a first meeting.) At any rate, although I met with Berstein a couple of times in the months that followed, his contribution to the film was, for a while, nil.

And that doesn't make him wrong. When a movie company takes a property of yours, it's not yours anymore. I think it was Hemingway who advised "Take the money and run." Not without wisdom.

Woodward, on the other hand, was available to me constantly. I cannot overemphasize his importance to the screenplay. When he was in New York he would call and we'd often meet. When I was in Washington, he gave me everything I needed in the way of knowledge and support.

And I needed plenty. Because it was an incredibly complicated story and trying to find the handle was a bitch. He'd been working on it for close to two years and I was new. Forget, for now, trying to make a screenplay; I was struggling just trying to get the events straight.

If Gordon Willis, the cinematographer, was the hero of the film, Bob Woodward was the hero of the screenplay. I hacked away at the morass of material and finally reached one conclusion: Throw away the last half of the book.

Bernstein and Woodward had made one crucial mistake dealing with the knowledge of one of Nixon's top aides. It was a goof that, for a while, cost them momentum. I decided to end the story on their mistake, because the public already knew they had eventually been vindicated, and one mistake didn't stop them. The notion behind it was to go out with them down and let the audience supply their eventual triumph.

If I ended there, and I began around the break-in, I didn't have a whole structure but at least I had the start of one. I fiddled with the rest of the narrative, tucking things in as best I could, and then Woodward came to my office. I asked him to list the *crucial* events—not the most dramatic but the essentials—that enabled the story eventually to be told.

I think there were thirteen of them and he named them in order. I looked at what I'd written and saw that I'd included every one. So even if the screenplay stunk, at least the structure would be sound.

Then I went to work writing.

In August of '74 I delivered the screenplay to Redford in Utah, where he has a home and a ski resort. My family came along, we rented a house in the area. The month was to be spent working.

He read the first draft, liked it well enough, and copies were sent out. Obviously to Warner Bros., which was the studio that was to make the film—if they liked what they read. (If they didn't, they could have gotten rid of me and brought in another writer of their choice, but that would have been very damaging in terms of time. I'd been working for six months at least by August, and it wasn't the kind of material another screenwriter could have whipped off easily.)

And copies were sent to the editors of the *Washington Post*, who were portrayed in the movie. And, of course, to Woodward and Bernstein. I'm not sure as to whether we were legally bound to give them copies or whether it was done for goodwill and courtesy, but it was done.

Now Redford and I began to wait. We met each day usually near his house, and we talked about changes and who would be best for director, etc. But mainly he talked and I listened.

It was a very strange time. We had known each other now for half a dozen years, had worked on three pictures together—*Butch, Hot Rock, Waldo Pepper*.

Shortly after *Butch* opened he was on the cover of *Life*, which identified him as "Actor Robert Redford." I remember him saying to me that each time he looked at the cover he had to look twice because he was convinced it said "Asshole Robert Redford."

Well, he wasn't an asshole anymore. Now he was a phenomenon.

He'd also become secretive. Not only did I know him, our wives knew each other, so did our kids. And he had asked me to come to Utah for the month to work with him—

—and he wouldn't give me his phone number.

In order for me to contact him, I would have to call his secretary, and she would then call him and he would then call me.

None of this mattered, of course, once we heard from Warners that they liked the screenplay and we were a "go." The movie was to become a reality. *President's Men* had been the most difficult and complicated movie work I'd done till then and I felt a greater sense of accomplishment at that moment than ever before.

If only I could have ridden off into the sunset then and there.

One of the things I have tried to avoid in this book is to rewrite history. Some of what you're reading comes from talking to people, but the greater amount comes from memory. And I've blocked a lot of what happened between August of '74 when the news came from Warners and the following June when photography actually began.

The rest of this chapter is material I've been unable to block, no matter how hard I've tried.

It's still August, Redford begins the search for a director.

But we still haven't heard from the *Washington Post*.

And we still haven't heard from Woodward and Bernstein.

The first director we sent the script to—who must remain nameless for legal reasons—said yes.

Incredible.

Then things started getting funny. Phone calls weren't returned, meetings were delayed. Many weeks later I was finally told—who knows if it was true?—that the director was involved in litigation against Warner Bros. and had only said yes in order to do any little thing he could to take out his vengeance on the studio. He never had any intention of directing the film, he just wanted to cost Warners time.

By the time this news surfaced, we still hadn't heard from Woodward and Bernstein.

But we had heard from the editors of the *Washington Post*—

—and they *hated* all the jokes I'd put in their budget meetings.

A word now about just what a budget meeting is. The *Post* had two of them a day. And the main purpose was to budget space for articles—especially front-page articles. If you are a reporter or an editor, you want your stuff to appear on "page one above the fold."

When I was spending time at the *Post*, they were decent enough to allow me to attend their budget meetings. (They were all decent, by the way. Courteous and helpful as much as their very busy schedules allowed.)

Okay, I go to my first two budget meetings and they were, of course, fascinating. But afterward, the top editors came up and told me that they weren't as funny as they usually were. Because one of the editors—Harry Rosenfeld, the part played by Jack Warden in the movie—was out that day. They assured me that when Rosenfeld was back, and he would be tomorrow, I'd get a different picture.

The next day Rosenfeld was back and was, as advertised, hysterical. In these meetings, the various editors—metropolitan, national, foreign—all argue with each other about the importance of their stories and the prominence their stories should receive.

And every time one of these guys would tout a story, Rosenfeld would zap him. Funny, funny jokes. And sitting in a corner of the room, I copied down Rosenfeld's lines in my notebook.

And in the screenplay, when I wrote the budget meeting scenes, I used Rosenfeld's lines.

Which infuriated them, because now they felt they looked like a bunch of clowns.

So that was the *Washington Post*'s reaction.

Still nothing from Woodward and Bernstein.

It's now fall, I'm back in New York, in my office, and the phone rings. It's Redford. He says that Bob and Carl are with him and why don't I come over.

I go over to his apartment, elevator up, ring the bell, go inside. My mood was pretty good as I remember. And I had absolutely no warning bells going off in my head that I was about to begin experiencing the worst moments of my movie-writing life.

Redford's in the living room. Woodward's in the living room. Bernstein's in the living room.

And there is a script on the living-room table.

I say hello to Redford, shake hands with Woodward, shake hands with Bernstein.

And now there is this silence.

And that script is still on the living-room table.

Then Redford said really the most extraordinary thing: "Listen—Carl and Nora have written their version of the screenplay." (Nora being Nora Ephron, a writer, then Bernstein's girl friend, whom he was later to marry and divorce.)

I just stood there.

Probably I blinked.

But I sure couldn't think of anything to say.

As a screenwriter, I test very high on paranoia. I'm always convinced of any number of things: that my work is incompetent, that I'm about to get fired, that I've already *been* fired but don't know yet that half a dozen closet writers were typing away in their offices, that I *should* be fired because I've failed, on and on.

But all those nightmares—and on occasion they've all happened—are within the studio system. The producer goes to the executive and says, "Goldman can't cut it, let's get Bob Towne." And then the executive calls Towne's agent and a deal is struck and money changes hands and the first I hear about it is when my phone doesn't ring when it's supposed to.

But for two *outsiders*, a hotshot reporter and his girl friend, to take it upon themselves to change what I've done without telling anybody and then turn it in to the producer—a "go" project remember—

—not in this world possible.

But there was their script on the living-room table.

I stood silently, staring at the thing, and I wanted Redford to scream at Bernstein, "You asshole, get out of here, don't you know what you've done?"

Redford said, "I've gone over it a little and I think you ought to read it."

I wanted my producer to defend me—I'm eight months on the project now, and I've done a decent job—Warners said yes. I wanted to hear "You're a dumb arrogant fuck, Carl, and I'd like you to shove that script where the sun don't shine."

Redford said, "I think there might be some stuff in it we can use."

I'm up to here with Watergate, I'm going crazy with when did Haldeman talk to Mitchell and how can we fit Judge Sirica into the story and how can Erlichman be the perfect neighbor everyone described him as being and still do the things he did; I had fretted and drunk too much and stayed up nights because I couldn't make it work until finally I did make it work and I wanted acknowledgement that a terrible breach had been committed.

Redford said, "We all want the best screenplay possible, so why don't you look it over, we're all on the same side, we all want to make as good a movie as we can."

I said I couldn't look at a word of it until I had been told I could by lawyers. And I left as soon as I could.

I can make a case for my producer's behavior. After all, this was now a famous book, Woodward and Bernstein were the media darlings of the moment, and we needed all the help we could get from the *Washington Post*. A pitched battle with Bernstein wouldn't have been an aid to moving the project forward. I could go on longer and make a better case. Redford was in a bind, no question.

But I still think it was a gutless betrayal, and you know what else? I think I'm right.

Lawyers were called in, and eventually it was decided I could read the Bernstein/Ephron version. One scene from it is in the movie, a really nifty move by Bernstein where he outfakes a secretary to get in to see someone.

And it didn't happen—they made it up. It was a phony Hollywood moment. I have no aversion to such things, God knows I've written enough of them—but I never would have dreamed of using it in a movie about the fall of the President of the United States.

One other thing to note about their screenplay: I don't know about real life, but in what they wrote, Bernstein was sure catnip to the ladies.

One important positive moment came out of that, a moment so meaningful to me I've separated it here. When I next met Woodward to talk about the movie, he said the following, word for word: "I don't know what the six worst things I've ever done in my life are, but letting that happen, letting them write that, is one of them."

I was and am grateful.

The Bernstein/Ephron episode did not stay secret long. God knows I didn't talk about it, but Washington, like Hollywood, thrives on the gossip of its main industry.

It was eventually common knowledge that I had written a dud. Later, after Hoffman had been signed, *Time* wrote an article about the progress of the movie and mentioned the lack of quality in what I'd done, even though, as they pointed out, it had snared Dustin Hoffman. I wished then for the first and only moment of my life that I subscribed to *Time* so I could cancel.

I was at CBS once in the news department and Walter Cronkite was walking along a corridor. The guy I was with knew Cronkite and introduced us, which pleased me because during this Watergate time, when everyone was lying, he was among the few Americans you could trust. Following is the entire conversation:

> MY FRIEND
> Walter, this is Bill Goldman who's
> writing *All the President's Men.*

> ME
> How do you do, sir.

> CRONKITE
> I hear you've got script trouble.
> (and he continued on his
> way)

Spring of '75 was the most stomach-churning time I've ever had writing anything. I had been on the movie now for over a year, not as daisy-fresh as I might have been. And by now I was dealing not just with the producer, a director had been signed: Alan Pakula.

Alan is a gentleman. We had mutual acquaintances in the business and they said nothing but good things about him as a human being. Neither can I. He is well educated (Yale) and serious about work. He had been a top producer for years before he became a director—*To Kill a Mockingbird*, which he produced, was nominated for the Best Picture award for 1962. His biggest success as a director had been *Klute*, which got Jane Fonda her first Oscar. He's wonderful with actors.

But I, alas, was no thespian.

I've only met Warren Beatty once, and that was at a large gathering where everyone was shaking hands with everyone else and there wasn't much time for conversation. Beatty had just finished working with Pakula on *The Parallax View*. As Beatty and I shook hands I managed to get out that I was soon to meet and work with Pakula.

Novelists are always using the phrase "enigmatic smile." It's a staple. In all my life, I have only seen one such enigmatic smile. It came on Beatty's face and he said this: "Just make sure you've got it before you go on the floor."

I didn't know what he meant then, and although I wanted to pursue it, it wasn't possible in the crowd.

Had I know then, as they say, what I know now.

Pakula and I began with a series of meetings. Now, when a writer meets with the director of a movie that is gearing up, there is really only one subject: improving the script. Cut it, change it, fix it, add, the whole point is to make it better.

As I've said, I like to think of myself as being very supportive at this time. I don't want to be on the floor, so if you're going to get the best I can give, this is when.

We would meet and discuss a scene, any scene, it doesn't matter, and I would ask if it was okay, and if it wasn't, how did he want it changed, what direction? For example, I might ask, did he want this shorter or longer?

He would answer, "Do it both ways, I want to see it all."

Both ways?

Both ways.

I might ask, did he want me to rewrite a sequence and make it more or less hard-edged.

He would answer, "Do it both ways, I want to see it all."

Both ways?

Both ways, absolutely.

But why?

And now would come the answer that I always associate with Alan: "Don't deprive me of any riches."

God knows how often I heard that. "Don't deprive me of any riches."

What I didn't know then, of course, was simply this: Alan is notorious for being unable to make up his mind. So here I was, thirteen, fourteen, fifteen months on the Watergate story, and when things should be closing down in terms of script, irising in, if you will, it was going all over the goddam map.

I didn't know what the hell he wanted. So I was writing blind.

Alan is also genuinely creative. One day he spitballed a wonderful little scene for Bernstein and his ex-wife. He just ad-libbed it and I wrote it down and typed it up and felt very good about the whole thing; at least I'd pleased my director.

Mistake.

In doing so, I had also displeased my producer.

Redford was very much aware that his two greatest successes had been in "buddy" movies: *Butch* and *The Sting*. And here he was, locked in with another male co-star.

He had always wanted a love interest in the movie. I think he always knew a romance didn't belong in the picture and this picture always had a length problem. It wanted to center on the two reporters and there was more than too much for them to do.

But now Hoffman had a scene with a girl and Redford became obsessed. I can't remember at the time whether Woodward was married or not, but he was involved with a lovely girl named Francie.

And now "Francie scenes" entered my life. Redford didn't want *one*, he wanted *three*, to show the growth and eventual deterioration of a relationship under the pressure of the story. It wasn't an incorrect idea, it was just incorrect for this movie.

At least I thought it was.

But he was my producer and he would appear again and again with new and different notions for three Francie scenes. I don't know how many I eventually wrote—a dozen, probably closer to two.

And it was miserable, because I didn't believe a goddam word I was writing. And I suspect my belief showed in the quality of the work.

So every day for months I would go to my office to write one of two things: either scenes for the director, who wouldn't tell me what to write, or scenes for the producer, which I didn't have a lot of faith in.

Plus I was dealing with their problems with each other. Redford was disgruntled with Pakula's lack of decision. Pakula could have cared less about the Francie scenes.

I think it was the existentialist philosopher Søren Kierkegaard who wrote about man's condition on earth being one of being caught between "insoluble tensions."

Søren didn't know it, but he was talking about me.

I've never written as many versions for any movie as for *President's Men*. There was, in addition to all the standard names, the "revised second" version and the "prehearsal" version. God knows how many. And by now the media are really gearing up to cover the film. And I'm fifteen months hacking away and tired of it all but I'm still writing these insane scenes for the star that everyone knew would never see the day and probably wishy-washy stuff for the director, who won't tell me what he wants. I didn't want to deprive anybody of any riches, I just felt impoverished and wondered if it all would ever end.

It ended when the phone stopped ringing.

When they started shooting, maybe a week after I'd delivered my who-knows-what version, I found out Pakula had brought in someone else to be in Washington with him.

There is a very funny line, attributed to the late Peter Sellers, who was asked to answer the question "What would you change if you had your life to live over?" And Sellers replied, "I would do everything exactly the same except I wouldn't see *The Magus.*"

The Woodward-Bernstein book became a famous and successful film. I saw it at my local neighborhood theatre and it seemed very much to resemble what I'd done; of course there were changes but there are always changes. There was a lot of ad-libbing, scenes were placed in different locations, that kind of thing. But the structure of the piece remained unchanged. And it also seemed, with what objectivity I would bring to it, to be well directed and acted, especially by the stars. It won a bunch of Oscars and numberless other awards besides.

And if you were to ask me "What would you change if you had your movie life to live over?" I'd tell you that I'd have written exactly the screenplays I've written.

Only I wouldn't have come near *All the President's Men.* . . .

Cast, producer and director of All The President's Men *in front of* The Washington Post *offices: Robert Redford, Jason Robards, Jack Warden, Dustin Hoffman, Alan J. Pakula and Martin Balsam.*

CHARLTON HESTON

Charlton Heston in Ben Hur *(1959), MGM.*

Born Charles Carter on October 4, 1923 in Evanston, Illinois . . . Educated at Northwestern . . . Established reputation as stage actor in both modern and Shakespearean roles . . . Six times President of Screen Actor's Guild . . . First professional film: *Dark City* (1950) . . . Followed by: *Ten Commandments* (1956) . . . *Touch of Evil* (1958) . . . Oscar for *Ben Hur* (1959) . . . *The Agony and the Ecstasy* (1965) . . . *Planet of the Apes* (1967) . . . Married to Lydia Clarke for over 40 years . . . Began keeping a journal of his life as an actor in 1956.

An Actor's Life

I was born of poor but honest parents who lived in a hut in the very center of the deep, black forest. Well, you see, there you are. They weren't poor, though they were honest. They weren't *rich*, you understand. This was the depression; nobody was rich. And there wasn't any deep, black forest left in Michigan by then. The Paul Bunyan days were over, but where we lived was where it had all happened, and it was a fine place to be a boy in.

There were woods, all right. Thick, second growth pine-birch forest, grown back after the lumbering finished. Our house was in the middle of it, set back off a trail road, drifted thick with snow in the winter, and I had a big, cross-breed shepherd that pulled me on a sled and was later shot by an angry neighbor.

The town was called St. Helen. I went to an old-fashioned one-room school. Thirteen pupils in eight grades, and three of them were my cousins. I was the only kid in my grade. It's no wonder I got a part in the Christmas play. I was Santa Claus, which turned out to be a one-line bit. I spent the evening crouching in a cardboard fireplace, so I could come out at the end and say "Merry Christmas!"

No, I don't think that was the spark that kindled the creative flame. I spent most of my time by myself in the woods, running a trapline with no success, and fishing and hunting, with some. Or pretending to, sometimes. At ten years old, when you've been following rabbit tracks through the snow for two hours without seeing one rabbit, and your nose is running and your feet are numb in your boots (mail order every fall from Sears, Roebuck, laced to the knees, with a pocket on the side for a jackknife) and your right hand is even colder, because you have to keep your mitten off in case you *do* see a rabbit, it's just as much fun to switch from being a kid hunting rabbits with a twenty-two to Kit Carson with a Kentucky long rifle hunting for elk to feed the starving settlers stranded in a blizzard in Donner Pass, and is that a Blackfoot behind that tree? Half the time, it was more fun, for me.

All kids play pretend games, but I did it more than most. Even when we moved to Chicago, I was more or less a loner. We lived in a North Shore suburb, where I was a skinny hick from the woods, and all the other kids seemed to be rich and know about girls. I'd never seen a football up in Michigan, but I went out for the team. All I got out of it was a broken nose, which has been a great asset to me ever since. I did make the rifle team, but that makes for a fairly limited social life. Discontented with who I was, I spent a lot of time pretending to be other people. In Chicago, there were movies to go to, so I could be Gary Cooper and Errol Flynn, which was fine with me.

There were plays, too. I saw a few, downtown, and then I found they did them at the high school I went to, New Trier High School, which was supposed to be the best public high school in the country at the time. Maybe it was. It certainly was for me. I suddenly realized make-believe wasn't just something you did by yourself if you had no friends. You could do it *with* people, on a stage, and even take classes in it. That was it; that's when it hooked me.

So I did. Took classes and did plays, in school and in the suburban little theaters. From one of them, the Winnetka Drama Club, I won a scholarship to Northwestern which was another lucky break for me, because I couldn't afford to go away to college, and I could *walk* to Northwestern. It also had one of the best theater schools in the country, in which I buried myself. My freshman year, I did seven plays. I also met a girl.

Lydia Clarke wasn't going to be an actress, she was going to be lawyer. She wasn't going to get married, either, but I wore her down on both counts. Before I finally talked her around, I was in the army and practically on my way overseas. We got married, Lydia was thrown out of her dormitory, and I went to the Aleutians. I'm told the first year of marriage is supposed to be the hardest. If so, this was the answer. I never laid eyes on her again for a year and a half, during which time she succeeded in getting her degree and I succeeded in not getting shot. When the atom bomb suddenly ended the war in the summer of 1945, it meant that instead of spending 1946 assaulting the main islands of Japan, I was able to assault New York, in civilian clothes.

I guess Dickens had it right. "It was the best of times, it was the worst of times." The war was over and we were finally where we wanted to be. We weren't acting, though. The thing you have to remember about acting is that you can't *practice* it. Van Gogh never sold a painting in his lifetime, but he painted masterpieces while being supported by his brother. You can write a great novel nights while you're pumping gas daytimes. Even the starving pianist can feed his soul playing sonatas in his garret. But the actor can only act if someone hands him a part and says, "There's the stage. Go fill it." This not only creates a basic problem for the out-of-work actor in learning to be better, but it can become an ultimate, consuming frustration.

Nevertheless, to be in New York at twenty-two, even with no parts and no money, but actually, honest-to-God making rounds in the actual honest-to-God professional *theater* was a shining time. (Don't trust this . . . remember . . . the altering power of memory.) I remember it that way, though. We weren't crazy about the cockroaches, and our cold-water walk-up had its shortcomings, but our friends had no money and no parts and roaches too. And you knew you were going to *get* the parts. I don't know . . . maybe at forty-two, you'd begin to wonder, but at twenty-two, you *knew*.

We were lucky, of course. Any actor who works is lucky. Lydia got a part first (never underestimate the value of a working wife), while I was serving the Muse by posing for life classes at the Art Students League. I worked in a neat little gray velour jockstrap Lydia made. I got a dollar and a half an hour, with free tea every two hours. And cookies. (Never underestimate the value of free cookies.)

Then I got a part with Katharine Cornell. A very small part, in very remote support of Miss Cornell, in *Antony and Cleopatra*. It was exactly the right first part. For one thing, it was a hit: It ran on Broadway longer than that play's ever run anywhere. For another, it's a great play. It can be very boring to play in a long run, but not if it's Shakespeare. Finally, working in Miss Cornell's company was an ideal apprenticeship. She was a consummate professional, so was her husband, Guthrie McClintic, who directed her. And you had to be a professional to work for them, or you didn't work long.

I think I got the part because of my size. Miss Cornell was very tall and she liked big men in her companies. It wasn't the last part I got for that reason, but it made a problem for me, too. One night, well into the New York run, I got to the theater a half hour before curtain. The stage manager told me, "Miss Cornell wants to see you in her dressing room, Heston."

"I'm fired," I thought, walking sweating down the hall to her suite instead of climbing the four flights to my cubicle. "No, it can't be that. McClintic'd have Gert Macy do that." Then vanity took over. "What if she wants to go to bed with me?" By this time I was at her dressing room door. "If she's wearing her robe," I thought, "and she sees me in the inside room, that's it."

"Go on inside," her dresser said. "Miss Cornell's anxious to see you."

There she was, in a red silk robe, looking fabulous. "Oh, Chuck," she said, sounding fabulous. "I want to show you something." She *parted the robe*. My mouth went dry. There, on her thigh (also pretty fabulous) was a bruise the size of my hand. "When you capture me in the monument scene, you bend me back over your hip, and your sword hits me every night. Do you suppose you could leave it off for that scene?" she said. Well, at least I didn't get fired.

So *Antony* closed, and Lydia and I both got other parts. The next season I ended up playing the lead in a play for which I'd been hired as the understudy. It only ran three performances on Broadway, but I learned from it. Mainly that when the playwright comes up to you in Boston and says, "Could you go on in this part tomorrow night?" the only possible answer is "You bet."

Then there was television. No, no, not like now. LIVE television, now eulogized as the Golden Age, though I recall at the time Newton Minow described it as a vast wasteland. It may have been, but it was also a superb opportunity for a whole generation of actors, writers, and directors. Half of them are household names now, but what they were then was out of work. And itching. Movie people weren't allowed to do television, and theater people of any reputation wouldn't do it because it didn't pay anything. The rest of us were untrammeled by these petty considerations, and for quite a while, we had the whole, brand-new medium to ourselves. Jack Lemmon and Anne Bancroft. Walter Matthau and Joanne Woodward. Directors like Frank Schaffner and Arthur Penn, George Roy Hill and John Frankenheimer. Mel Brooks, Rod Serling, Paddy Chayefsky, Neil Simon.

The thing was, no one had figured TV *out* then. The networks and the sponsors hadn't realized yet that the whole point was really the commercials. They didn't have the comic strip series, and the cost-per-thousand, and the reruns, and the laugh tracks then. All they had was this new audience, and some shows to do for them, and they let us do them. There hasn't been a chance like that since sound first came to movies.

I got my chance when they decided to do *Julius Caesar*, and use only actors who'd played Shakespeare on Broadway (in retrospect, this seems an arbitrary criterion, but there it was, and there I was, fresh out of *Antony*). I only got a small part, but there I was again, when the actor playing Brutus was sent home from rehearsal one day to rest his bad throat. "Can one of you guys read Brutus so we can work on the funeral oration scene for the rest of the day?" Well, I *mean*. So I read the part, which any actor is going to sound good reading, in those circumstances. I didn't play it, of course, but over the next sixteen months I played a few others, just as good. *Jane Eyre*, *Macbeth*, *Of Human Bondage*, *Taming of the Shrew*, *Wuthering Heights*. Some Henry James, some Turgenev. The actor doesn't draw breath who wouldn't look bloody good in at least one of those parts.

I did some plays, too, but not as good, and it's probably just as well Hal Wallis didn't see them. He did see me on television, though . . . I forget in what. *Jane Eyre*, I think, and a 16mm film of *Julius Caesar*. (I played Antony in that.) I wasn't really all that keen to do movies. I was getting good parts on Broadway and marvelous parts on live TV, and we all more or less assumed film acting was kind of low-class, anyway. I mean, *serious* actors worked in New York, not in the *movies*. Besides, the only film offers I'd had so far were standard studio contracts, and I didn't want any of that. The studio contract system was really ending by then, but the studios didn't know it. Hal Wallis did, though. Already established as an independent producer, he saw that the future of film lay with the independent film makers. He offered me a contract with the independence I needed to do plays, and films for other producers. I grabbed it. Lydia was running in a leading role on Broadway, so I came out alone for the first film. I lived in a furnished apartment up behind Grauman's Chinese. Merv Griffin lived just down the hall, but a high proportion of the other tenants seemed to be hookers.

I don't remember finding it very hard to adjust to films, but I suppose it must've been. It *should've* been. When you're a kid, things seem easy because you don't know they're hard. I finished the film, and spent a good part of the summer doing a publicity tour as the latest of God's gifts to the American cinema (nineteen cities in twenty-six days, as I recall), and went back to New York, where Lydia was still ticking along, in her play, to resume my life as God's gift to the American stage.

The first film didn't set the town on fire, but the second one, *The Greatest Show on Earth*, won the Academy Award for Best Picture, which comes to the same thing. Of course the fact that it was made by Cecil B. De Mille and starred Jimmy Stewart, Betty Hutton, Cornel Wilde and the complete Ringling Brothers, Barnum and Bailey Circus had a good deal to do with this, but my role as the circus manager set me off and running. I also got the best compliment I've ever received on my work from a lady who wrote a letter to Mr. De Mille. She thought the picture had captured the feeling of the circus wonderfully, and that Hutton and Wilde, and particularly Jimmy Stewart, had been fine in their roles. "I also was amazed at how well the circus manager fitted in with the real actors," she said.

Lydia came out for that film, and we commuted between both coasts for quite a while, doing plays in New York and films out here. I was lucky with some of the early films, and had more and more chances at character parts, and period parts, and learned a little. Then, just about the same time, Lydia got pregnant and I got cast as Moses. Both were events of some significance in my life. If you can't make a career out of two De Mille pictures, you'd better turn in your suit. And the experience of fatherhood changes your life. Acting is a very uncertain trade, but it was beginning to look like permanent employment for me. Our son, Fraser, was born while we were shooting *Ten Commandments*. (He played the infant Moses at the age of three months and immediately retired, displaying an acute judgment of the acting profession.)

It *is* a hard trade, you know. Most actors don't get to act at all, most of the time, and they have to act in whatever they can get all of the time, and act it to fill out someone else's vision, not their own. By 1956, I was able to choose, a little. In my work, and in my life. I think that really may be why I started these journals: to teach myself to choose better. Anyway, that's more or less what they're about. Making choices.

VERONICA LAKE

Alan Ladd and Veronica Lake in The Blue Dahlia *(1946), Paramount.*

Born Constance Francis Ockleman on November 14, 1909 in Brooklyn . . . Under stage name Constance Keane, broke into films as an extra in *Sorority House* (1938) . . . First box office success: *I Wanted Wings* (1941) . . . As she put it: "created, designed, and manufactured by Hollywood" . . . Voted by *Harvard Lampoon* worst actress of 1941 . . . *This Gun For Hire* with Alan Ladd (1942) . . . Made "peek-a-boo" hair style the rage . . . Favorite role: in director Preston Sturges' *Sullivan's Travels* (1941) . . . Groucho Marx: "I opened up my mop closet the other day and I thought Veronica Lake fell out."

You've Got to Have a Gimmick

Arthur Hornblow, Jr., one of the most respected and active producers of the period, was about to produce one of the big films of the year, *I Wanted Wings*. It was to be a salute to our nation's aviators, and Hornblow had already signed Ray Milland, Brian Donlevy, William Holden, Wayne Morris and Constance Moore to star in the film. It was adapted for the screen by Richard Maibaum from the book by Lieutenant Beirne Lay, Jr.

With all that powerful male box-office lure, Hornblow felt he could take a chance with a newcomer in the role of Sally Vaughn, an out-and-out and unsympathetic siren nightclub singer.

My agent at William Morris took my Metro screen test to Hornblow and asked him to screen it and consider me for the part. Hornblow declined, certainly with justification when you consider the fact that my agent told him the test was lousy but he should look anyway. If my own agent didn't think I was good, why should Hornblow waste his time looking at me?

But Arthur Hornblow, Jr., had a secretary Isabel, who pulled a lot of weight with the big man. She persuaded him to look at the test. He did, hated it as much as I did, but decided for reasons of his own to give me another test at Paramount.

I was more frightened at the Paramount test than I'd ever been for the Metro test. And again, that damned hair drove me crazy.

We did a scene in which I was supposed to be tipsy at a table in a small nightclub. Things were going fairly nicely until I leaned my elbows on the edge of the table. I was beginning to gesture in an unsure, drunken manner when my right elbow slipped off the table edge sending my long, thin blonde hair falling over my left eye. I spent the next few minutes trying to continue with the scene as I kept shaking my head to get the hair out of my eyes. I could feel myself getting madder and madder and when the test was completed, I stormed off the set, my lips a thin line against the tears.

God, how I cried in my dressing-room.

'This goddamned shitty hair,' I yelled at my image in the mirror, shaking my head back and forth violently in physical defiance of it.

I didn't even go to the screening room a few days later when the test was run. I couldn't face it.

But then came the phone call from Arthur Hornblow's secretary.

'Mr. Hornblow would like to see you, Miss Keane.'

Why? Why would he ever want to see me again?

I went of course.

'Constance,' he said, after we'd exchanged the usual opening amenities, 'I'm going to cast you as Sally Vaughn in *I Wanted Wings*.'

I didn't cry. I laughed nervously, thanked him too many times and raced home to spread the good news.

I received professional acknowledgment of pleasure from my mother and that's when it set in hard. I could not come up with even the slightest and most remote reason why anyone would cast me after that terrible, botched-up screen test. And what about my hair? Surely that must have frightened even the most hardened Hollywood producer. The thought crossed my mind that maybe they were going to rewrite the part of Sally Vaughn into a low comedy role for an ugly starlet with unmanageable hair. But even that was all right, I decided, because who was I to question any reason for putting me into an important film with so many popular leading men of the day. I'd take the role under any circumstances and with any strings attached they would see fit to attach. Constance Keane was going to be a movie star, just as her mother wanted her to be.

I learned later from the film's assistant director that the screening room reaction to my screen test was less than unanimous in approval and enthusiasm. Everyone at that screening did feel, however, that I projected some sort of magnetism, the kind that stars emit on the screen. My hair had been a smash; it gave me something that would be remembered, imitated and talked about. It gave the studio's publicity people something to peg their stories on. And let's face it—all those things are great big plus factors for anyone looking for stardom in Hollywood.

You've got to have a gimmick, even in the nicest sense of the word. When you think about it, every big name from Hollywood has possessed something, even a little something besides his or her talent. Gable's ears, Widmark's wild and wicked laugh, Cagney's slipping pants that his elbows always managed to hitch up, Davis' swishy hand and hip roll, etc. Just watch any impressionist on television and you'll see capital being made of a mannerism or physical feature. The same with cartoons and caricatures of celebrities. Durante's marvellous nose gave artists something to work with. Hope's nose and its famed 'swoop' configuration and Mitchum's bedroom eyes—and on and on with virtually everyone of star ranking.

And my gimmick, my featured feature was my hair, fine blonde hair hanging loose over one eye. Something I always considered a detriment to my appearance became my greatest asset. That's Hollywood, folks. And that's the nature of the film fan. Who am I to fight it?

You can't imagine the silly thoughts that go through your head when you realize you're about to appear in a major Hollywood feature film as a lead player, one that will play in theatres all over the world—and Brooklyn, your home town.

It occurred to me one day that with my hair over one eye and the few years I'd gained since leaving Brooklyn, it would probably be impossible for anyone back home to know it was me, Connie Ockleman. After all, I was now called Constance Keane.

But what I didn't realize at the time was that even my Miami friends who knew Constance Keane were to be thrown a curve.

Arthur Hornblow, Jr., didn't like the name Constance Keane. The first time I was made aware of his feelings on the subject was in his office. He'd summoned me early that morning and I raced to his office assuming he had decided to change his mind. I'd had a long and bitter fight with my mother the night before and had cried a lot. I smeared my puffy eyelids with make-up and tried to look as cheerful as possible when I entered his office.

Mr. Hornblow looked as though he'd been up all night. He had.

'Connie,' he began as I sat nervously on the couch, 'it's pretty well agreed around here that we want a different name for you. *I Wanted Wings* is going to be one of the year's big ones, and it could launch you into a very large and important career. And the name you begin that career with is very crucial.'

'Whatever you think, Mr. Hornblow.'

'Now don't misunderstand me, Connie. Connie Keane is a fine name. It's fine as just a name and as a professional name.'

I smiled.

'It always seemed all right to me, Mr. Hornblow.'

He smiled.

'Of course it's all right. But you do realize how many factors are involved in the making of a star, don't you?'

'I guess I really don't.'

'Well, you'll learn, Connie. But believe me, the right name, a name that the public can latch on to and remember can make all the difference. It isn't just a matter, though, of creating a name that can be remembered. If that were all it took, we'd just name you Maude Mudpie or Tilly Tits or something and they'd remember the name.'

I nodded that I understood.

'No, Connie, picking a name involves coming up with something that associates in the fan's mind the person attached to that name. The name has to . . . well, it has to be the person, or at least what the fan thinks that person is. You know what I mean?'

'Yes.' I didn't, but that was irrelevant.

'It has to do with images.'

I nodded.

He sat back in his chair and rubbed his eyes.

'I've been up here all night, Connie, trying to come up with the right name for you. All night. And about five this morning, I knew I had it.'

I sat up straight and came to the edge of the couch. A new name was an exciting thing. It's not an exciting event when your name changes because you lose a father and your mother supplies a new one. But when it's created for you to project a desired image, it's damned exciting.

'Connie, here's how I came to choose your new name. I believe that when people look into those navy blue eyes of yours, they'll see a calm coolness—the calm coolness of a lake.'

The first thing that crossed my mind was that I was going to be named Lake something or other. That doesn't sound very outlandish these days with Tab and Rock, but in those days names stuck closer to the norm.

Arthur Hornblow, Jr., continued.

'And your features, Connie, are classic features. And when I think of classic features, I think of Veronica.'

Lake Veronica?

Oh!

Veronica Lake.

Of course.

And then it hit me. My mother was sometimes called Veronica. Of all the goddamn names in the world to choose. I could feel the tears welling up and the lump forming in my throat. I tried so hard to hold everything back but I didn't make it. I broke down and bawled like a baby into the couch cushions.

There had been no way for Arthur Hornblow to know about my mother. Nor could he have known we spent so many summers at Saranac Lake while my stepfather recovered from TB at nearby Saranac.

I never told him why I was crying. My feelings were deep but quickly soothed. I really didn't care about having my mother's name. It was just such a shock for the moment.

I told my mother when I got home and I'm certain she considered it the rightful will of Hollywood's gods.

But there are bad gods, too.

Veronica Lake and Joel McCrea in Sullivan's Travels *(1941), Paramount.*

JANET LEIGH

Alfred Hitchcock, Janet Leigh and wardrobe mistress on the set of Psycho *(1960), Universal.*

Born Jeanette Helen Morison on July 26, 1927 in Merced, California . . . Father a laborer . . . Marriage at 14 annulled . . . Big break when Norma Shearer accidentally spotted the 19-year-old's photo . . . First film, *The Romance of Rosy Ridge* (1946), co-star Van Johnson gave her her screen name . . . *Little Women* (1949) . . . *That Forsyte Woman* (1949) . . . *Houdini* (1953) . . . *Pete Kelly's Blues* (1955) . . . *My Sister Eileen* (1955) . . . *Touch of Evil* (1958) . . . *Psycho* (1960) . . . *The Manchurian Candidate* (1962) . . . *Bye Bye Birdie* (1962) . . . *Harper* (1966) . . . Married Tony Curtis 1951 . . . Hollywood's "perfect couple" . . . Jamie Lee Curtis born 1958 . . . Divorced Curtis 1961 . . . Married businessman Bob Brandt in 1962 . . . In Howard Hughes' *Jet Pilot* (1951), she played a Soviet spy converted to democracy by—who else?—John Wayne.

Psycho: What to Wear in the Shower?

Alfred Hitchcock! Descriptions and depictions skirmished for admittance to my head. Genius. Suspense. Girth. Clever. Witty. Master. Naughty. Cameo. Mystery. Pretty ladies. Debonair men. Evil. Controversial.

Alfred Hitchock sent me a book to peruse, a novel entitled *Psycho* by Robert Bloch, that was to be his next film. I was to consider the role of Marion. I would have said yes without reading the manuscript or without his assurance that Marion would be improved and upgraded. The size of the part had no bearing. Alfred Hitchcock was enough incentive for me.

The first in-person encounter was tea in Hitchcock's home on Bellagio Road, in November 1959. His deportment was cordial, matter-of-fact and academic. He outlined his modus operandi. The angles and shots of each scene were predetermined, carefully charted before the picture began. There could be no deviations. His camera was absolute. Within the boundary of the lens circumference, the player was given freedom, as long as the performance didn't interfere with the already designed move. "I hired you because you are an actress! I will only direct you if A, you attempt to take more than your share of the pie, or B, if you don't take enough, or C, if you are having trouble motivating the necessary timed motion."

I could see how this method might incur the indignation of some actors, be considered too set, hindering, confining. But I thought of it in a different light. This was the way the man worked. And since I had profound respect for his results, I would earnestly comply. As I reflected, I realized he was in actuality complimenting our profession, giving credit to our ability to inspire our own reasons behind a given movement. He was proposing a challenge, throwing down the gauntlet to our ingenuity. And I intended to be a contestant. Marion was on the screen only a short time, but she was a focal point and offered unlimited potentials in characterization.

Much has been written about Hitchcock, pro and con. I am in accord with some documents and take exception to others. The basis for my opinions rests solely on my individual exposure and observation. I've had no inside tunnel to the mine of facts and figures of others. I hope biographers of Hitchcock and *any* late personages who chose a negative approach *did* have access to pertinent information, or they would be guilty of grave injustice to the memory of the dignitary in question, and to the legion of admirers whose hero they have tarnished.

Days on the set with Hitch were surprisingly calm, pleasant, swift. Because the work was already delineated, he was relatively relaxed. The crew functioned quickly because he was prepared. Once he knew my sense of humor, he enjoyed being the raconteur. Sometimes I would still be laughing from a story (usually risqué), and the A.D. would inform him the camera was ready, he would give the signal to roll, and I would have to call a halt, to get my head straight for Marion.

He relished scaring me. He experimented with the mother's corpse, using me as his gauge. I would return from lunch, open the door to the dressing room, and propped in my chair would be this hideous monstrosity. The horror in my scream, registered on his Richter scale, decided his choice of the Madame.

He was very thoughtful in regard to comfort and safety. His first impulse was to have me wear contact lenses for the close shot of the dead eye. When we went to the optometrist to select the lens and be fitted, the doctor explained he would need a few weeks with me to demonstrate the insertion procedure and accustom my organs to the foreign objects, or else my eye surface could be damaged. We didn't have the time, and Hitch wouldn't permit the risk, so he scrapped that idea. "You'll just have to go it alone, ole girl." And he was adamant about the temperature of the shower water, tested it himself to insure its warmth. Which caused me a slight embarrassment.

What I was to wear in the shower gave the wardrobe supervisor migraines. I had to appear nude, without being nude. She and I pored over striptease magazines, hoping one of their costumes would be the answer. Every male on the set tried to donate his services in the search. We had popular literature. There was an impressive display of pinwheels, feathers, sequins, toy propellers, balloons, etc., but nothing suitable for our needs. Finally the supervisor came up with a simple solution: flesh-colored moleskin. Perfect! So each morning for seven shooting days and seventy-one setups, we covered my private parts, and we were in business.

The lengthy shot, starting with the eye in full frame and gradually easing back to disclose the draped body still clutching the torn curtain, the running water, the entire bathroom, was a thorny intricacy, from the technical side and from my side. I had to fix and maintain that empty glazed stare. Hitch found the spot where the camera wouldn't pick up a blink and snapped his fingers to let me know. (Mrs. Hitchcock always claimed, "I saw Janet blink in the film." I didn't see anything, but I couldn't be positive it wasn't there.) For sundry reasons we had to do it over and over. At long last a take was near completion without a mishap. Abruptly I felt something strange happening around my breasts. The steam from the hot water had melted the adhesive on the moleskin, and I sensed the napped cotton fabric peeling away from my skin. What to do? Decisions, decisions! To spoil the so far successful shot and be modest? Or get it over with and be immodest? I opted for immodesty. No one there would see anything they hadn't seen before—it was below the edge of the tub and out of the camera's view—and I had had enough of that gauche position. I made the correct judgment. That was the printed take, and no one noticed my bareness before I could cover up. I think!

Brilliant artist Saul Bass designed the titles, and also did a thorough storyboard for the shower-scene montage. Hitchcock diligently adhered to Bass's blueprint. Some of the prescribed angles required the construction of elaborate scaffolding, just for a few seconds' flash on the screen. But there was no compromising. Certainly that is one reason why the sequence had such impact. The combined endowments of these two gave us a course in fantasy. Did we see the knife penetrate? Or didn't we? Did we see complete nudity? Or didn't we? Our mind's fantasy will swear we saw both. That demonstrated their skill and our entrapment. I believe that class of film making was more effective than the current standard. The censorship obliged creators to find a way to show, without showing, thus giving the viewers liberal range for their imaginations. This was much more demanding for the architects. It's fairly uncomplicated to take a picture of the lethal weapon apparently slashing an obviously naked body with blood gushing in full view, which is tolerated today, but far more complex to present the *illusion* of that happening.

Even with the existent strict code, Hitchcock was cunning in getting certain heretofore taboo images on the screen. He traded. He deliberately inserted more questionable shots in the script, knowning quite well they would be unacceptable, but with each disallowed one, he gained leverage in his bargaining for the ones he had really wanted all along. He argued that the unprecedented shot and sound of a toilet flushing was a vital component of the plot. Lila Crane (Vera Miles) found the scrap of paper that had refused to go down and substantiated that her sister, Marion, had been in the motel. Marion's half-clad appearance in the opening shot with her lover Sam (John Gavin) was necessary to prove the furtiveness and futility of the affair, which prompted her theft. The mixed blood and water gurgling down the drain was the necessary chilling substitute for any blood spurting or bloodstains.

There have been conjectures for two decades about the use or nonuse of a nude model in the shower sequence. This is what I know:

When Norman Bates (Anthony Perkins) cleaned the bathroom after the murder and put the body in a sheet and dragged it to the car, that was a model. Hitch told me there was no reason to subject me to the discomfort since it was a distant high angle anyway. He also told me his original intent, as discussed with the writer Joseph Stefano and whomever, had been to employ a professional model for some of the shower shots. But he said he abandoned that thought because we had already accomplished what was essential. I have observed the film many times, and I can't find any glimpse of an unfamiliar shot in that montage.

Hitchcock made films for us to enjoy on varying levels of insight. You might see one the first time and appreciate just the entertainment, enough in itself of course. Then you might see the same picture a second time and discover a sublayer of meaning. The third time could uncover even deeper values. . . .

There are endless examples of what can be discerned in Hitchcock's movies, and they are all there, waiting to surprise us.

Psycho was an enormously commercial success, but oddly not critically acclaimed in the beginning. It is interesting, and gratifying, that over twenty years later, the imprint of that film is still vividly etched in most minds. And, for the record, *no, I do not take showers.*

Janet Leigh and Van Johnson in The Romance of Rosy Ridge *(1946), MGM.*

JERRY LEWIS

Dean Martin and Jerry Lewis in My Friend Irma *(1949), Paramount.*

Born Joseph Levitch March 16, 1926, Newark, New Jersey . . . From age 5 performed with parents in the Catskills "Borscht Belt" . . . Quit high school after one year . . . Worked as soda jerk, movie theater usher, shipping clerk . . . Married singer Patty Palmer in 1944 . . . Small-time comic until he teamed up with small-time singer Dean Martin ("Dino") in 1946 . . . Most popular comedy team in the world made 16 wacky blockbusters with Paramount (1949-1956) . . . Chairman of Muscular Dystrophy Drive since 1950 . . . His own films include *The Sad Sack* (1957), *The Bell Boy* (1960), *The Nutty Professor* (1963), *The Patsy* (1964), *The Big Mouth* (1967) . . . Highly lauded in France where he is known as "*Le Roi du Crazy.*"

A Handsome Man
and a Monkey

S onny King was a singer and a pal of mine. I'd known him since the Sunday night talent shows at Leon and Eddie's, where we'd stick around at the bar all night waiting for a chance to get up and do a big ten minutes before the joint closed at dawn. Then we'd take ourselves over to the B & G coffee shop to sit there with eyes half-shut and the happy, incessant chatter still going on as if we had blown into town after a sensational national tour.

Early one March morning, Sonny and I were walking into a cold wind toward Broadway. My date at the Glass Hat would soon end. There were no jobs ahead, so Sonny, knowing I couldn't afford the Belmont Plaza rates, had invited me to stay at his place, a cubicle of a room at the Bryant Hotel. We were on our way there when I saw Dean crossing Forty-ninth Street with an older man. He waved at Sonny. "Come on over!" And we did.

Inescapable fate.

We were introduced. "Jerry Lewis, meet Dean Martin; Dean—Jerry." The first time in my life I was to hear what would be spoken around the world: Dean and Jerry.

The other man was Lou Perry, his agent. Short and slightly built, with a thin mouth and deep-set eyes, he gave me a quick glance, then listened quietly while Dean and Sonny talked about everything from broads to singing and work, and back to broads again.

When we shook hands in farewell, I thought it would be the last I'd ever see of Dean. Such an Adonis. And look at me, weighing 115 pounds—still fighting acne. Standing there in my bumpkin mackinaw jacket, T-shirt underneath and suspenders that held the pants two inches above my Flagg Brothers shoes. The heels made me five foot ten. When I took them off I lost the two inches, but I had a pompadour that brought me back up again. There was enough pomade on my hair to grease all the flapjacks in Hanson's drugstore.

So, tall and handsome, with my hair shining like Broadway itself, I find myself in Sonny's room a few nights later, the two of us tranquilly catching the flow while Dean spins a yarn, retracing his past, seeing himself in boyhood in Steubenville, Ohio. . . . Steel-mill town of immigrants and cheap labor and rowdy pleasures: a little house standing close to the Weirton and Wheeling mills; and a barbershop in the neighborhood where his father gives twenty-five-cent haircuts ten hours a day, and Saturdays, too. And his mother cooks big pots of spaghetti and meatballs, all kinds of Italian food, every evening a fantastic, mouth-watering meal. The smell of it—"Beautiful . . . the best . . . nothing like it in the entire world!"—Mom and Pop, and his older brother Bill, eating and gabbing at the kitchen table. Then the after-supper stories on the front steps of their little house. Pretty soon going to bed, listening to cats meowing on back fences and more cats joining in, the garbage cans rattling in the alley; the neighbors wrangling, their moans lowering into the dark Steubenville night.

He was born Paul Dino Crocetti on June 17, 1917. He quit school in the tenth grade—"It wasn't fun. I hated it, hated the system. All I wanted was to get out and go to work."

Sonny says, "Righto, Dean. You must've been profound in your early youth."

"Yeah, a real sonofagun." And he slides into it: delivering milk for his Uncle Joe, pumping gas at a filling station, working at the Weirton mill . . . sledging coils of hot steel, flipping them into boxcars and nearly getting killed when a four-ton coil dropped from a crane . . . Remembers one haunted afternoon in a broken-down, overheated poolroom, as gray as slate from the tobacco smoke. "I was chalking my cue, ready to take anybody on for a game, when along comes this kid, Ruzzi. He sticks his face in my ear and says, 'Do you wanta make some real dough?' Well, the next night me and Ruzzi and another buddy of mine called Slick drive into Cannonsburg, Pennsylvania, with ten cases of bootleg whiskey. Terrible hooch, man! The fumes could have run our car straight through to Los Angeles."

I laugh and applaud. Dean winks, makes a circle with his forefinger and thumb. I begin to suspect he likes me.

Now his eyes dim. A different note creeps into his voice. He says, "They're in jail . . . I could've been there myself."

Sonny coughs. "That's a drag, man. C'mon, tell Jerry about your ring career. You know, when you were just a regular kid like the rest of us Eyetalians."

Dean fakes a grimace and asks me, "You wanna hear that shit?"

"Yeah, I'll listen; sure, that's cool."

"OK, pallie. Ask me a question and I'll tell you no lies."

"Well, ah . . . how many fights did you have?"

"Oh, about thirty. Mostly amateur stuff in West Virginia and Ohio. It wasn't that rewarding. They paid me off in Mickey Mouse watches. In the semipros I made ten-fifteen dollars a fight—bought Mom some extra pots for the spaghetti. Anyway, I quit the racket after taking a hard shot to the old beagle."

He gingerly touches his new-look nose. "Before the operation, it was five times bigger."

Sonny giggles and throws a pillow at him. "Schmuck, you could've been Jimmy Durante!"

Wham-bam, a barrage of pillows goes sailing across the room, and I'm bent over hugging myself smack in the middle of the whole rumpus. And life just then is a magnificent goof, moving in one rhythm, made of a single energy; we're clowning around like lunatics, but everything we do and say is positively the best.

And there are dreamy lapses in conversation while we listen to a tinny phonograph that spins 78s of Benny Goodman, Coleman Hawkins, Louis Armstrong, Tommy Dorsey, Billie Holiday. . . . We sit relaxed, reflecting off each other, our eyes hitting on internal images, our thoughts spilling over in pure honest enjoyment. And by now I've learned how Dean grew up and made his way through hard times.

He had a job at one of the toughest gambling establishments in Steubenville. The Rex Cigar Store. A front for the Ohio wise guys, a place where Dean clerked and sold punchboard chances over the counter, while in the back room a team of muscular hoodlums in gray fedoras watched suspiciously with their shoulders pressed against the wall as the gamblers shot craps, played blackjack and roulette. Lots of fast action, plenty of people who had come from poverty and threw big tips around to show everyone they had made it. Dean saw the potential. He studied the games. He became so good at them, the bosses hired him as a croupier.

"I pulled down between twenty and thirty bucks a day," he was saying to Sonny and me in the early A.M. "And at night I'd go to swinging parties with my pals. . . ." Well, Sonny is buzzing off in his chair, having heard all this many times before, no doubt, but I'm sitting like a kindergarten schoolboy, eyes and ears wide open while Dean goes on talking of one of his Steubenville adventures: partying one night at a roadside club called Walker's and being pushed up to sing a couple of songs, gin-drinking crowd giving him heavy applause and the band leader, Ernie McKay, offering him a job right then and there. That's how Dean got his start. . . . In Cleveland a few months later, singing with the Sammy Watkins band at the Hollendon Hotel, he meets a Pennsylvania girl named Betty McDonald— "Great figure," he reminisces. "I took her home to Steubenville and showed her off to all the guys who worked with me at the Rex. Yeah, she carried herself proud, man. Everybody said she looked like a movie star."

He went into his wallet, held up a picture of Betty; dark-eyed, long black hair, engaging smile, an Irish beauty in a white-lace wedding gown.

"We were married at St. Ann's Church in Cleveland and the next morning lit out on a bus to Louisville with Sammy and the whole band—"

"When was that, Dean?"

He smiles. "October 1940. Since then we've had three kids, two girls and a boy."

I say, "We have a little boy."

"Hey-hey crazy! No, wait a minute—you married?"

I lock my arms, grin at him, sort of embarrassed.

He looks puzzled. "How old are you?"

"I was twenty this month."

"You look younger—like twelve."

And now Sonny stands up on shaky legs. He does a Leon Errol bit around the room in one turn. "What the hell time is it?" he yawns.

I glance at my watch. "It's a quarter to four."

* * *

First morning light filling the room, and I'm thinking that Dean has come along at the right time. I'm thinking he's going to be someone special: the big brother I never had.

[2]

On July 24, 1946, I pulled into Atlantic City to play the 500 Club, a flashy boardwalk spot that showcased unknown comics and singers. The place was owned by Paul "Skinny" D'Amato, so-called because of his pencil-thin silhouette. From head to toe he personified the jaunty, debonair nightclub operator. He wore London-crafted shoes, Parisian silk ties, and each of his made-to-order suits cost more than he was paying me as an opening act. But why complain? At a hundred and fifty bucks a week I could afford to bring Patti and Gary along. We stayed at the Princess Hotel, one block off the beach.

The first afternoon is retained in kaleidoscope memories of wild laughter trailing down from the roller-coaster ride; and the smell of sarsaparilla, hot dogs and buttered corn; the long, pleasurable walk we took on the boardwalk while lifting our faces to the sun; getting high watching Gary dig for shells, watching him splash in the surf and tumble in the sand—on that afternoon it seemed that nothing could go wrong. Sure as life itself, I felt that my luck would change for the better in this town.

Maybe the salty air had something to do with it, but as we prepared to leave the beach, I said to Patti, "Let's see what it's like in Acapulco."

She grabbed my ankle. I sprawled onto the blanket in mock horror, and she hitched up beside me, snuggled against my chest. "Oh, Joey, if *anywhere* is half as good as this, it will be wonderful."

At the 500 Club that night, I did my record act in front of two hundred tables and thirty customers. I bowed off to desultory applause, and there was Skinny waiting in the wings with a hypersuspicious smile. So I wasn't about to ask him if he loved the act. I recalled some pretty sage advice, my father saying: "The minute you start looking hard to please 'em, that's when you can't see your own faults."

"You're running a little short," said Skinny. "Give them more jokes, maybe a couple more impressions; just stretch it to twenty minutes. Other than that, kid, you did good."

"Gee, thanks, Mr. D'Amato. I'll get my records and pick something. I do a Deanna Durbin. That oughta—"

"Relax. Wait awhile—let's see what's happening out front. I want to catch the singer."

We sat at a corner table. Skinny's thumbs were revolving in a definite sign of agitation as this gut-stabbing sound ripped across the room.

By the second number I knew the singer was in serious trouble when Skinny almost soared out of his chair.

"I can't believe it—the guy sings as if his nuts are caught in a zipper!"

All the illogical pitfalls of running a respectable nightclub suddenly crashed in on him. "The guy's bad . . . oh, my . . . he's so bad I'm gonna kill his agent."

"Maybe he'll get better."

"Yeah, kid, right after they operate on his neck. I can't wait around. I gotta get somebody else in here, and quick."

I thought of Dean. Instantly, without effort. We had been corresponding. His last postcard had been sent from Chicago: *Working with Buddy Lester at the Rio Cabana. Buddy is great, but the spaghetti is lousy. Closing on the twenty-second. Open for a job on the twenty-third. Your pal.*

I took a shot. "Why don't you book my friend, Dean Martin? He's not working."

Skinny put a hand on my shoulder. "Tell me, just for my own edification, what's a Dean Martin?"

"He's a terrific singer. He's played some good places, like the Havana Madrid, the Rio Cabana, and, uhh . . . listen, you can call his agent, Lou Perry. He'll tell you."

Skinny pushed forward in his seat, anchored his elbows on the table, cradled his jaws and began meditating, wincing now and then as the noise from the stage kept battering his eardrums. At last—"Dean Martin, huh?"

I had him. "You'll see, Mr. D'Amato. Dean is not only terrific, but we've worked together."

"You have?"

"Sure. We do a lot of funny stuff." It seemed like years ago at the Bryant. Ah, such nonsense, such a nutty time. Only, it was all play, and all for free.

Skinny placed a call to Lou Perry. On the twenty-fifth, Dean arrived in Atlantic City.

That night he does his first show. He sings five songs, then gets off. I go on with my record act, and when I leave the stage Skinny is waiting for me, looking somewhat perturbed. He's muttering something about "cement waistcoats." The next thing I know, he's pointing in the general direction of his office.

And for five minutes tops, Dean and I are in there with him.

"Where's the funny shit?"

"Hmm . . ."

"I said, where's the stuff you guys were going to do together? If you're not doing it by the next show, you're both out on your asses."

So Dean and I retired to our dressing room. Our dressing room is a nail hammered in the wall. Two guys and a nail. And Dean speaks to the nail. "So what are we supposed to be doing together, pal?"

"I'm thinking, I'm thinking . . ."

In the alleyway leading to the stage, I say, "Here's the plan. You sing, and I'll put on a busboy's jacket. Then we'll grab some things out of the kitchen and make a lot of noise."

He says, "Where is that gonna get us?"

"I don't know. But if we don't do something funny, I'm gonna blow a hundred and fifty bucks."

The next show starts. The audience sits up, anticipating. All four of them. Literally, an audience of four, not including the maître d', nine waiters, five busboys, one cigarette girl and Skinny. If one of the customers snaps his fingers to order a drink, sixteen people are there in a flash, clomping all over him.

We do a three-hour show.

We juggle and drop dishes and try a few handstands. I conduct the three-piece band with one of my shoes, burn their music, jump offstage, run around the tables, sit with the customers and spill things while Dean keeps singing. That takes eight minutes. Then it takes another eight minutes to stagger up to the piano, and I don't know how much more time to remove the fat man from his stool so I can sit down. Finally, after I sit down, Dean gives me a withering stare. "Hey, kid, can you play that thing?" And when I say, "No," he says, "Then get the hell away from there!"

Screams from the two tables of two each, and on and on it goes. I'm looking gleefully at Dean, feeling the lightning, the whole world thundering down before us right there in that room.

And at four o'clock in the morning we leave the club, head down the shadowy boardwalk kicking up our heels and cackling nonsensically because everything is so wonderful we can hardly believe it. Then, all of a sudden, about a mile past the Steel Pier, we find ourselves standing quietly by a rail, cigarettes lit and eyes peering into the inky black sea.

Dean tosses his butt away. "It's really phenomenal."

"You mean out there—the ocean?"

"Yeah."

"Y'know, during the war I used to think of all those torpedoes zinging through the water in the darkness. Man, no wonder sailors get drunk."

"You ever been on ship?"

"Oh, sure. The Staten Island Ferry. Five cents from the Battery to Hoboken."

"Wise guy. Anyway, when they book us to play the Palladium in England, we'll go by plane."

"Hey! It's a deal! And you wanta know what else?"

"What?"

"No bull, Dean. I have this feeling that pretty soon we'll be playing Hollywood, and the best clubs in New York and Chicago and everywhere. The main rooms! I tell ya, it's in the bag!"

He grins. "I don't know about that, pardner, but we're sure gonna have a lot of fun wherever it is."

"You bet. Wherever it is . . ." I echo softly. And after a while we start back to the hotel, whistling like a couple of goofs.

*   *   *

In the afternoon of the same day, I rented a typewriter and went to work shaping the act. After writing down the title, which I called "Sex and Slapstick," I laboriously typed out these words: *Since the time immemorium, there has never been a two-act in show business that weren't two milkmen, two food operators, two electricians, two plumbers, and for the first time here we have a handsome man and a monkey.* . . .

That was the premise.

And that is precisely how we played it. Not only onstage, but whenever the mood struck. Everybody was fair game, especially the unsuspecting targets we sighted at boardwalk novelty shops, shooting parlors, all sorts of ethnic restaurants and the swarming beach itself.

For instance, at a booth in a Chinese restaurant I ordered chicken chow mein, then stuck the noodles up my nose while Dean nonchalantly sipped his Chinese tea. The Chinese waitress watched with her tongue lolling out. Behind her, three other Chinese waitresses and the Greek proprietor stood riveted to the floor until a guy in the opposite booth hollered, "Waddya know, it's those two *meshugeners* from the 500 Club!"

One afternoon it was the beach, a plan to do something really crazy. In the midst of hundreds of sunworshippers, I took off across the sand, kept going and finally dove into a roaring wave. Seconds later, I called for help. Of course, Dean was only a few yards away, churning toward me with forceful butterfly strokes. A moment later he had an arm around my shoulder. "Play dead. Don't move." He dragged me to the shore.

It grew to more dramatic proportions when a lifeguard pushed his way through the crowd. "Step aside—give him some air, folks."

I jumped up. "If you don't mind, sir, I'd rather have a malted."

His mouth fell open. "How's that again?"

Now it was Dean's turn. He looked at me curiously. "What'll it be, kid? Vanilla or chocolate?"

"Chocolate, you dummy."

"I'm no dummy—you dummy. The name is Martin. Dean Martin."

"Hi. I'm Jerry Lewis. Are you working in town, sir?"

"Sure. With you—you idiot!"

We skipped past the lifeguard, saying for all to hear, "Get dressed and see us at the 500 Club!"

Three nights into our engagement, the lines began to form. By the weekend the lines stretched down the boardwalk. So Skinny D'Amato raised our salaries to $750 and held us over for four weeks. Meanwhile, people from every part of the country were calling in reservations, some willing to pay any price for a ringside table. The press helped by whetting their appetites. Ed Sullivan raved about the act, as did Walter Winchell, Leonard Lyons and Bob Sylvester. They all touted us as the comedy finds of the year.

An added boost came from Sophie Tucker, the Last of the Red-Hot Mammas. She talked us up after one of our shows, telling a group of reporters, "These two crazy kids are a combination of the Keystone Kops, the Marx Brothers and Abbott and Costello." Heady stuff.

Sometimes, alone in my hotel room, trying to assess what had happened, thinking of what Dean and I had accomplished, of what we were capable of becoming, the adrenaline would pump so hard I'd jump around shouting, "There's no way to fail— no way!"

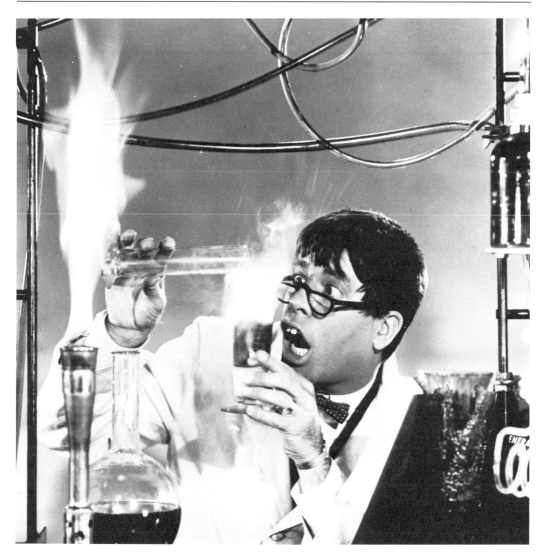

Jerry Lewis in The Nutty Professor *(1963), Paramount.*

HAROLD LLOYD

Harold Lloyd in Safety Last *(1923), Pathé.*

Born April 20, 1893 in Burchard, Nebraska . . . Died in 1971, leaving a huge fortune . . . Grew up in San Diego, where his father ran a pool hall . . . Film debut 1912 as a nearly naked Indian . . . Met Hal Roach when they both worked as extras for Keystone comedies in 1913 . . . Invented the average clean-cut young man with horn-rimmed glasses in 1917 . . . By the '20s was one of highest paid movie stars . . . Outdrew Chaplin at the box office . . . Performed his own stunts . . . Master of the "comedy of terrors" . . . *Safety Last* (1923) . . . Happily married to leading lady Mildred Davis from 1923 until her death in 1969 . . . Last film *Mad Wednesday* (1947) for Howard Hughes.

A Laugh, a Scream, and a Laugh

*S*afety Last, which followed *Doctor Jack,* was seven reels long. It has its partisans who hold that we never have made a better, and they are not far wrong in my judgment. It was a thrill picture, if you remember my climbing the face of the twelve-story building, and thrill pictures have an unfair advantage over straight comedies.

The old formula for comedy drama of the David Warfield school was "a laugh, a tear and a laugh." The recipe for thrill pictures is a laugh, a scream and a laugh. Combine screams of apprehension with stomach laughs of comedy and it is hard to fail.

Safety Last came of an old family. Its original progenitor was a one-reel glass character picture called *Look Out Below.* For it we built a frame of wooden girders, painted to likeness of steel, two and a half stories high, over the southern portal of the Hill Street tunnel, which the city conveniently had bored through the bluff on which the Bradbury mansion stands. It was our first thrill picture depending upon height for its effects, and was original with us as far as I know. Neither it nor any of its three descendants contained any doubling, double exposure or trick photography in the usual sense. The illusion lay in deceptive camera angles of drop and height.

The second member of the family was a two-reeler called *High and Dizzy,* taken on the same scene, but presumably on the ledge of a completed ten-story hotel instead of bare girders, and having nothing in common with *Look Out Below* except the height theme.

The third generation of the family was *Never Weaken,* a three-reel *de luxe* edition of *Look Out Below.* The thrills came of my efforts to commit suicide in the belief that Mildred had thrown me down. This time we built our framework of girders on the roof of the Ville de Paris department store, the owner of which, Bernal Dyas, is a close friend of Roach. We used the interior of the same store for the department-store scenes in *Safety Last,* the next thrill picture, working from closing time until two and three o'clock the next morning.

The success of the thrill idea in one, two and three lengths suggested trying it at full-program distance. One afternoon in downtown Los Angeles I stopped to watch Bill Strothers, who called himself the Human Spider, scale the sheer walls of a high office building. The higher he climbed the more nervous I grew, until, when he came to a difficult ledge twelve stories up, I had to cut around a corner out of sight of him and peek back to see if he was over the ledge.

If it makes me this jumpy, what would it do to a picture audience, I asked myself. The more I thought of it the better I liked it. Once I feel like this about a story, all the staff like to work on it, for they can count upon my enthusiasm; whereas, if the story is another's and doubts linger in my mind, it takes some of the zest out of my work.

When we have a story to build, the three gag men, the director and I get in the gag room and work it out. All we had to begin with here was the human-fly idea. Obviously I must not be a professional human fly in the picture; if I am an expert there is no comedy in the situation. We would hire Bill Strothers himself for that rôle and I must be a fool boy roped, in some comedy fashion, into climbing the building in Bill's stead, which is a comedy situation. The plot gradually worked out this way: I was to be a country boy new to the city. I get a job clerking in a department store. The pompous floor walker is my enemy. I room with Strothers. He innocently makes an enemy of a policeman. After much comedy business in the store, gags suggested by the locale, I sell the manager on the idea of having a human fly climb the building as an advertising stunt. When the time comes for Strothers to climb, his enemy, the cop, is found to be patrolling the beat in front of the store. He gives chase to Strothers. The store manager impatiently demands to know where my human fly is. The crowd is waiting, and in order to save the situation I reluctantly start the climb for Strothers, who tells me that he will take my place at the second story. But the cop pursues him to the second floor, then to the third and on. Meanwhile I have to continue, finally making the entire ascent myself, the cop having run Strothers to the roof and over an adjacent roof.

Not that we waited to start shooting until we had such a finished plot. All we ask to know when we begin is our general direction. The chinks can be filled in as we go along.

The dizzy drops in the picture were partly illusion. Although you saw the city's traffic crawling many stories below, at no time could I have fallen more than three stories, but who wants to fall three stories for that matter? I have no desire to break my neck and it would be very foolish of me from a business standpoint. All the staff, the company officers, the distributors and others have a like business interest in keeping me alive and whole. So the amount of risk I take in a thrill picture becomes a compromise between the necessity of taking some and the foolishness of taking too much.

As it was, I threw my shoulder out of joint in the scene—probably the loudest scream of the picture—where I grab frantically at the minute hand of the building clock, many stories up, and the face of the clock is pulled out and down by my weight. At Ocean Park, one night just after we had finished this sequence of *Safety Last*, a party of us stopped at a fortune teller's booth. The reader of the stars felt the calluses of my hand and told me that I earned my living at manual labor. She was not far wrong.

Harold Lloyd in Mad Wednesday *(1947), RKO, released through United Artists as* The Sin of Harold Diddlebock.

ANITA LOOS

John Emerson and Anita Loos, ca. 1920s.

Born April 26, 1893 in Sisson, California . . . Child actress with D.W. Griffith before becoming writer . . . 1925 novel *Gentlemen Prefer Blondes* was kept by Winston Churchill at his bedside . . . Movie versions 1928 and 1953, the latter starring Marilyn Monroe . . . Close friend of Aldous Huxley and William Randolph Hearst . . . H.L. Mencken: "Young lady, you're the first American writer ever to make fun of sex."

What Killed Jean Harlow

One afternoon while Hoppy [screenwriter Bob Hopkins] and I were having coffee in the Trap, he thought of a colorful character on which to base a movie for Jean Harlow. She would play the daughter of a horsetrader, born and raised in an environment of race tracks. The locale would be Saratoga, which would also be the title of the film.

We told our idea to our producer, Bernie Hyman, who said, "That sounds like a possibility. Go ahead!"

When our story was ready to be put into script form, Bernie hired a jockey from the Santa Anita track to supply a proper vernacular for the dialogue. (Our pal Bernie was a stickler for authenticity. When he produced *The Great Waltz* he rented a Stradivari violin at $1000 a day for an actor who couldn't have played a bazooka.)

Our jockey was a wizened little man of about forty who bore out my contention that jockeys are among the most civilized men in the world. Sitting over coffee in the Trap, he gave me a lesson I couldn't have gotten in a Yale drama course.

"Look, honey," he said, "if you use jockey terms in your dialogue, you'll be writing a movie for jockeys and just between the two of us, folks who spend their time with horses don't care very much about films. Write your dialogue in your own words and it'll sound okay even to a jockey."

The filming of *Saratoga* had been completed except for its final scene, when Jean was suddenly taken with what seemed to be a mild sort of ailment that kept her home. Jack Conway [the director] started "shooting around her," as they say in films.

One afternoon, a group of us were sitting in Bernie's outer office: there were Clark Gable; Bernie's secretary, Goldie; and the switchboard operator, who happened to be a boy. We began to talk of Jean and to wonder what her ailment was. No use asking her Ma because Ma didn't believe in the existence of disease. "Probably drunk again," said Clark, making a pretty stupid joke because Jean was not given to drinking when on the job.

"Let's call up and ask her when she's coming back," I suggested. The boy at the switchboard got through to Jean's house, talked briefly to a servant, and then hung up.

"They've taken Jean to Cedars of Lebanon!" he said with apprehension. We all began to be disturbed; because for Ma to allow her precious baby to be hospitalized was a pretty radical move. Clark suggested we call the hospital. The call went through. Presently, the boy's face turned deathly white and the receiver clattered onto the desk. We knew what had happened before he told us. "Jean's dead!"

Then was the studio thrown into dismay; Jean had earned millions for MGM and stood to make many more. L. B. [Mayer] took the tragedy as a personal affront, but just the same he issued a humanitarian edict. "The next time one of our valuable properties gets sick, the studio's got to find out what's the matter."

Jean's funeral at Forest Lawn was an orgy of grief, with mobs of weeping fans, monitored by the police. L. B. sent a heart of red roses five feet tall pierced by a golden arrow. But those of us who were close to the bier were more impressed when one of Jean's former costars, Bill Powell, strode up to place a single white rose on her breast.

After it was too late, the studio tried to find some reason for Jean's death. She'd always enjoyed the best of health. When stricken, her symptoms seemed to be merely those of fatigue. One theory was that overexposure to sun might have poisoned her. The strangely iridescent skin, which was the reason Jean's platinum hair looked so natural, was as sensitive as an albino's. But then, she never went into the sunlight unless protected by long sleeves, a high neckline, a big floppy hat, and a parasol. Ma *could* be relied on for that!

Another notion was that excessive use of bleach might have brought on a fatal uremia. But the doctors and nurses who had hovered over Jean at the hospital agreed on one thing; she had refused to put up a fight. And this fact bolstered a theory of my own on what caused Jean to die.

Unlike Marilyn Monroe, Jean was not a narcissist. To her, sex had come to be an incessant matter-of-talk that would have bored Messalina. She recognized her looks as an accident of birth. The platinum hair that brought her to fame was a nuisance because she had to spend an hour in the make-up department every second day for its roots to be touched up. Jean's attitude toward clothes was that of a small boy who balks at being dressed up. I never knew her to go shopping. Jean's mother bought everything for her. Jean would slip into a new dress without bothering to glance in the mirror. Why bother? She always looked the same . . . terrific.

So all right! She *was* terrific. But to whom? To her distant public, to a trio of husbands that included a Kansas City playboy, a German psycho, and a mild little MGM cameraman, all of them the dull type of gentlemen who prefer blondes.

Between those three disastrous episodes which Jean philosophically called "marriages of *inconvenience*," she lived with her mother, who was her replica in looks, platinum hair and all, except in a more opulent form. Ma was married to a florid gentleman of Italian descent named Marino Bello, who was equipped with all the gigolo tricks to make a female happy. But Marino was given to writing Jean unwelcome love notes that had to be kept secret from her mother.

Jean was always lonely; she longed to find companionship in a lover, one with wit enough to respond to her compulsive wisecracks. But very early in life she realized she was doomed to failure. Irving [Thalberg], for instance, found her nothing more than a booby trap for male stupidity.

Because Jean granted so little importance to sex, she could be thoughtlessly cruel at times. Soon after she married Paul Bern he took Jean and me to a football match.

That day Paul made a great issue of his bride's comfort; supplying her with a cushion, a lap robe, a hot dog, a bottle of soda. Finally, he asked if he could get her anything more. Jean indicated a husky fullback down on the field and said. "Yes, Daddy. Get me that one!" Jean and I laughed, having no inkling how the joke must have tortured her impotent bridegroom.

But the same impotence that could so easily be a joke ultimately caught Jean up in the most horrifying experience a girl in Hollywood ever had to go through.

Bern adored Jean as abjectly as only a German psycho might. But expecting no return of his ardor, he had had to woo her with arguments unrelated to sex. He maintained that, as a producer, he'd devote all his talents to her career.

He was good and kind and gentle and Jean had had too many experiences with men who were weak, selfish, or evil. At that very moment, she was living under the same roof with one of the worst, her own mother's husband. "It'll be a relief to get away from the rat before Mom finds him out," Jean told me.

In short, for Jean to marry someone as respectful as Paul Bern seemed a very bright thing to do. "Paul's so sweet," Jean said to me, "he'd cut out his own heart before he'd ever do me in."

And then, even *Bern* did Jean in.

He may have counted on his marriage producing a miracle and that, with an inspiration like Jean, he could conquer his impotence. Well—he couldn't.

As time went on, the poor man tried to assuage his guilt by practices which Jean was too normal to accept. But she understood; didn't blame her husband; assured him how little sex meant to her. Jean's tolerance went even further; "Just do any thing you like, sweetheart," she said, "but count me out of those sessions. Find yourself someone else. I won't object; I'll understand."

Still putting up a bluff at manhood, Bern agreed. And then one evening, to bolster his pretenses, he told Jean of a rendezvous he'd made. When he was leaving for his date she kissed him tolerantly and wished him a good night.

Next morning Jean found a note under her bedroom door. It said, in essence, "I hope you'll understand that last night was a farce. Now I'm yours forever. Paul."

Puzzled, Jean went to ask for an explanation. Bern lay sprawled on his bedroom floor in a pool of blood. There was a bullet hole in his head and his squat, fat body, so ill-equipped for marriage, was shamefully naked. Paul Bern's suicide was the very apotheosis of masochism, for he had killed himself while looking in a full-length mirror.

Jean's role in that tragedy of Beauty-and-the-Beast must have destroyed the last small vestige of faith she may have had in men. But then, prior to filming *Saratoga*, she had costarred in a picture with William Powell. Bill had all the qualities which Jean despaired of ever finding in a sweetheart. He was a gentleman—urbane, witty, and charming. It began to flash on her consciousness that sex need not be snide and degrading. She turned her full battery of feminine charms on Bill.

But Bill happened to have been the victim of another dynamic blonde. He had been married to Carole Lombard whose incredible glamour made him feel inferior, reduced his ego practically to the situation of a Paul Bern. Bill needed some Little-Miss-Nobody in order to regain his polarity. So he walked out on Jean and, about three years after her death, he finally discovered just what he'd been looking for: a blonde as cute and pretty as Jean but with the one virtue Jean lacked, anonymity. Bill married his charmer without more ado and they began to live happily ever after.

After Bill's rejection, Jean seemed to lose interest in everything; and, when stricken, she refused to put up a fight. It was as if Jean took advantage of a minor ailment to escape from life. Her mother's reason was saved by her faith; she never admitted that Jean was gone.

The filming of *Saratoga* was completed with an actress in a platinum wig substituting for Jean. The camera angles featured Clark fullface, with the substitute's back to the camera.

Saratoga confounded all the experts who claimed that Jean's tragedy would keep people out of the theaters. The movie stacked up a fortune which, to L. B. at least, made for a happy ending.

To become a star an actress must be sensitive. A letter Jean wrote me after the Bern tragedy could only have been written by a woman of warmth and sensitivity.

Anita Dear,

Could I but make you know the depths of gratitude I have for your most wonderful letter with its expressions of loyalty, friendship, and understanding. Without friends, I could not have gone on. Please know I shall always treasure your wonderful faith in me and will never disappoint you.

Devotedly and gratefully,
Jean.

Jean had all the sensitivity required of a star. But to remain one, an actress also has to be an egomaniac. Jean didn't have enough ego to survive, and so the movies' greatest *femme fatale* simply died of sex starvation.

Clark Gable and Jean Harlow in Saratoga *(1937), MGM.*

SHIRLEY MACLAINE

Frank Sinatra and Shirley MacLaine in Some Came Running *(1958), MGM.*

Born Shirley Maclean Beatty on April 24, 1934 in Richmond, Virginia . . . Sister of Warren Beatty . . . Began dancing at age 2 . . . Broke into Broadway as chorus girl in '50s . . . Signed to movie contract by Hal Wallis when he spotted her stand-in performance in *Pajama Game* in 1954 . . . First film: *The Trouble With Harry* (1955) . . . *Around the World in Eighty Days* (1956) . . . *Some Came Running* (1958) . . . *The Apartment* (1960) . . . *Irma La Douce* (1963) . . . *The Turning Point* (1977) . . . *Being There* (1979) . . . California delegate to Democratic convention in 1968 . . . Oscar for *Terms of Endearment* (1984).

Jackpot

T he biggest surprise brought by success was that suddenly people were interested in what I thought, not because I was older—I was still in my twenties—or because I knew what I was doing, but because I made $800,000 a picture. It was suddenly O.K. for me to call Samuel Goldwyn "Sam," and William Wyler "Willy." They had been people with a Mr. before their names when I was young-and-nobody, but now that stardom was mine I had become *somebody* and we could communicate as equals.

Success in Hollywood forced me to come face to face with certain things: young or not, ready or not, success forced me to evaluate myself.

Take money for instance. Before Hollywood, I had never had more than fifty dollars I could call "spendable." True, I had never lacked the money for necessities—food and a place to sleep—but luxury money was unknown to me. Now suddenly I had all the luxury money I wanted, but I still acted as though I had only the fifty dollars. I shopped in bargain basements and more often than not bought nothing. Several times I found myself haggling over something that had a fixed price, finally paying the money and leaving the purchase behind on the counter. I felt guilty because I could have what I wanted. I was reluctant to indulge myself, even though I had worked hard for it and economic security had become a reality.

I also found I wanted success and recognition without losing my anonymity. I was haunted by my psychological conditioning as a child to be inconspicuous. It was impossible. I had to adjust to shocking, baseless adulation and an enraging loss of privacy.

Unreasonably, I resented the attention I attracted even though I had fought for it. The most pleasant strangers provoked my fury because they simply looked at me, or watched how I picked up a fork, or stared while I spoke quietly with my daughter, or told me that they had seen the same facial expression on the screen. I felt that it was not their right to stare or to be interested in me. I was wrong, but regardless of how full of admiration their interest might be, I still resented it. I resented my enforced and constant awareness of self; I didn't want to live in a world of only "me."

At first, I reacted with stony hostility, hardly smiling when someone approached me with a compliment. For a while I denied that I was Shirley MacLaine—and I always felt ashamed afterward. After all, how could I call it an invasion of privacy when I had chosen to splash myself across the screen, seeking the applause and approval and attention of strangers?

But I did. I wanted to stand in a supermarket line again with people who were unaware of being observed. I wanted to hear the snatches of personal conversation, notice the way people dressed, the attitudes of their children, and observe the interplay between those who seemed happily married and between those who were miserable. It was all part of what had kept me alive, and it was gone.

I wanted to splash in the waves at Malibu again with Steve and Sachie [her children] without being stared at by passersby. Suddenly I felt exposed in a bathing suit, acutely conscious of my white skin that wouldn't tan, embarrassed by my masses of freckles, afraid that my figure might not be what people expected. "Is your mother Shirley MacLaine?" people would ask Sachie. And Sachie would say, "Yes, but she says she's really Shirley Parker." And then she would ask me, "Why are you so special, Mom?" And I would try to explain that I wasn't really special—it was my work that was special. And she would say, "I wish they would leave us alone so we could play again."

But the stardom I had fought for meant that "they" would not leave me alone again. And of course I didn't really want them to. I wanted to be wanted. I needed to be appreciated. I did what I did to win their approval. Behind all my resentment, I was terrified that I would disappoint them.

Instinctively I knew that, if I wanted to maintain an honest level in my work, I would have to remain vulnerable inside myself. If I built a shell and crawled into it, I would fail. People want to see reflections of true human feelings—their own. An actor can only hope to be a mirror of humanity, a mirror to be looked into by audiences. My problem was how to keep myself vulnerable and sensitive while remaining resilient. How to be tough and tender.

As my new values emerged I began to realize that I had *power*. Money was one thing, fame and recognition another; both had to be dealt with. But to feel power was devastating.

I found myself with the power to hire and fire people, to impose my opinions on others—to be listened to. What did I think of so-and-so? Did I like his story and the way it was written? Would I accept so-and-so as my director? So-and-so needs a job; would I accept him as co-star or collaborator?

I found myself making decisions because they were part of my new responsibility. Sometimes my decision would wreck the life of someone I'd never met. Although I didn't want to express my opinion—I had never really learned to respect my own opinion because I always believed someone else knew better—I was forced to because I was a *star*. And stars, for some reason, are supposed to know. If they don't, they're supposed to act as though they do.

The power of my position changed the people I had known before. Some who had been direct and honest became wary—wary of offending in my presence, and anxious to be assured of my respect and high evaluation. Others, reacting, became my harshest critics, afraid I might think they were kowtowing to me. I tried to put my old acquaintances at ease, to let them know that nothing basic in me had changed. And I was distressed to discover that often it was they whom I had changed. My success was too much for them. They couldn't handle it. I wondered what they would be like if success had happened to them instead of to me.

In the years before success and for some time after, I didn't hear much from or about my brother Warren. He was busy finishing high school, playing football, and serving as president of his senior class. When he went to Northwestern University on a football scholarship, I assumed that, like most college students, he would decide what he wanted to do with his life after he graduated. But he left Northwestern before he graduated and went to live in New York. He worked as a sandhog in a tunnel-digging project and later played the piano in a night club.

When Warren decided to become an actor, it did not surprise me. Nor did the fact that when he came to Hollywood, chosen by Elia Kazan to play the lead in *Splendor in the Grass*, he decided he wasn't going to be thought of as Shirley MacLaine's brother. From the outset he announced that as far as he was concerned "she is Warren Beatty's sister." I was amused, and thought he was right to do so. The newspapers thought they smelled conflict. They tried to create a sibling rivalry, à la Fontaine-De Havilland or something like that. They would call Warren and tell him something I supposedly had said about him. If he said nothing they would call it a "pregnant pause fraught with meaning." If he said anything at all, usually out of embarrassment at the personal invasion, wham, the comment would appear in a newspaper story. So for a while there was a so-called feud going on that neither of us knew anything about.

It was true that we didn't see a great deal of each other. I was usually traveling or in Japan, and Hollywood was not one of my favorite places to spend free time, whether Warren was there or not. When I was working on a film I rarely saw anybody. So the rumors persisted.

Of course, the times we did spend together went unnoticed because we wanted it that way. We valued our privacy more than anything else. We would reminisce about Washington-Lee High School, the neighborhood pranks, and of course about what had happened to some of our old boy friends and girl friends.

One evening, Warren and Julie Christie had come to dinner at my home in California. We talked far into the evening about each other's childhood—ours in Virginia and hers in India. I heard a car pull up in front of the house. It was about one o'clock in the morning and I wasn't expecting anyone. Suddenly, without knocking or ringing the doorbell, a man opened the front door and walked straight across the living room to me. He put out his hand and said, "Hi, Shirley. Remember me? I'm Jim Hall from the Washington-Lee High School basketball team, and my friends bet me I wouldn't have the guts to drive clear across the country and do this."

I jumped out of the chair, glad my dogs were asleep—they would have chewed him up—and ran to hide behind Warren because I didn't recognize the intruder. When Jim saw Warren he screamed, "My God, I've really hit the jackpot—Shirley MacLaine and Warren Beatty on the same bet!"

It was almost as though Warren and I were two celebrity freaks instead of a brother and sister who wished to be alone, hoping that whoever wanted to call on us would at least ring the bell.

But after we had both made it in the movies everyone reacted that way. They all seemed fascinated that two people they considered to be of opposing natures could come from the same family. Dad told everybody that was easy to answer. He'd say, "I've always done my best work in bed." Mother would smile, either confirming his statement or wishing that it were true.

Then the curious would say, "But did they both plan to be what they are?" or "Did you know they were that talented then?" or "Did show business run in your family?" Dad always said he had acted as inspiration. He had, in a reverse sort of way. Warren and I usually said it was "just life."

Jack Nicholson and Shirley MacLaine in Terms of Endearment *(1983), Paramount.*

GROUCHO MARX

Groucho Marx (right) in Horse Feathers *(1932), Paramount.*

Born Julius Henry Marx on October 2, 1890 in New York City . . . Father a tailor . . . Dropped out of P.S. 84 . . . Began professional career as a singer at age 11 . . . Mother Minnie put brothers Chico, Harpo, Groucho, and Zeppo together as an act . . . Brother Gummo went his own way . . . First film *Cocoanuts* (1929) . . . *Animal Crackers* (1930) . . . *Monkey Business* (1931) . . . *Horse Feathers* (1932) . . . *Duck Soup* (1933) . . . *A Night at the Opera* (1935) . . . *A Day at the Races* (1937) . . . *Room Service* (1938) . . . Hosted radio and TV quiz show *You Bet Your Life* in the '40s and '50s . . . Wrote three autobiographies . . . Died 1977 . . . Fellow man-of-letters Thomas Stearns Eliot died in 1965.

Duck Soup Meets *The Waste Land*

26th April, 1961

Dear Groucho Marx,

This is to let you know that your portrait has arrived and has given me great joy and will soon appear in its frame on my wall with other famous friends such as W. B. Yeats and Paul Valéry. Whether you really want a photograph of me or whether you merely asked for it out of politeness, you are going to get one anyway. I am ordering a copy of one of my better ones and I shall certainly inscribe it with my gratitude and assurance of admiration. You will have learned that you are my most coveted pin-up. I shall be happy to occupy a much humbler place in your collection.

And incidentally, if and when you and Mrs. Marx are in London, my wife and I hope that you will dine with us.

Yours very sincerely,

T. S. Eliot

P.S. I like cigars too but there isn't any cigar in my portrait either.

June 19, 1961

Dear T. S.:

Your photograph arrived in good shape and I hope this note of thanks finds you in the same condition.

I had no idea you were so handsome. Why you haven't been offered the lead in some sexy movies I can only attribute to the stupidity of the casting directors.

Should I come to London I will certainly take advantage of your kind invitation and if you come to California I hope you will allow me to do the same.

Cordially,

Groucho Marx

January 25, 1963

Dear Mr. Eliot:

I read in the current Time Magazine that you are ill. I just want you to know that I am rooting for your quick recovery. First because of your contributions to literature and, then, the fact that under the most trying conditions you never stopped smoking cigars.

Hurry up and get well.

Regards,
Groucho Marx

23rd February, 1963

Dear Groucho Marx,

It seems more of an impertinence to address Groucho Marx as "Dear Mr. Marx" than it would be to address any other celebrity by his first name. It is out of respect, my dear Groucho, that I address you as I do. I should only be too happy to have a letter from Groucho Marx beginning "Dear T.S.E." However, this is to thank you for your letter and to say that I am convalescing as fast as the awful winter weather permits, that my wife and I hope to get to Bermuda later next month for warmth and fresh air and to be back in London in time to greet you in the spring. So come, let us say, about the beginning of May.

Will Mrs. Groucho be with you? (We think we saw you both in Jamaica early in 1961, about to embark in that glass-bottomed boat from which we had just escaped.) You ought to bring a secretary, a public relations official and a couple of private detectives, to protect you from the London press; but however numerous your engagements, we hope you will give us the honour of taking a meal with us.

Yours very sincerely,
T.S. Eliot

P.S. Your portrait is framed on my office mantelpiece, but I have to point you out to my visitors as nobody recognises you without the cigar and rolling eyes. I shall try to provide a cigar worthy of you.

16th May, 1963

Dear Groucho,

I ought to have written at once on my return from Bermuda to thank you for the second beautiful photograph of Groucho, but after being in hospital for five weeks at the end of the year, and then at home for as many under my wife's care, I was shipped off to Bermuda in the hope of getting warmer weather and have only just returned. Still not quite normal activity, but hope to be about when you and Mrs. Groucho turn up. Is there any date known? We shall be away in Yorkshire at the end of June and the early part of July, but are here all the rest of the summer.

Meanwhile, your splendid new portrait is at the framers. I like them both very much and I cannot make up my mind which one to take home and which one to put on my office wall. The new one would impress visitors more, especially those I want to impress, as it is unmistakably Groucho. The only solution may be to carry them both with me every day.

Whether I can produce as good a cigar for you as the one in the portrait appears to be, I do not know, but I will do my best.

Gratefully,
Your admirer,

T.S.

June 11, 1963

Dear Mr. Eliot:

I am a pretty shabby correspondent. I have your letter of May 16th in front of me and I am just getting around to it.

The fact is, the best laid plans of mice and men, etc. Soon after your letter arrived I was struck down by a mild infection. I'm still not over it, but all plans on getting away this summer have gone by the board.

My plan now is to visit Israel the first part of October when all the tourists are back from their various journeys. Then, on my way back from Israel, I will stop off in London to see you.

I hope you have fully recovered from your illness, and don't let anything else happen to you. In October, remember you and I will get drunk together.

Cordially,
Groucho

24th June 1963

Dear Groucho,

This is not altogether bad news because I shall be in better condition for drinking in October than I am now. I envy you going to Israel and I wish I could go there too if the winter climate is good as I have a keen admiration for that country. I hope to hear about your visit when I see you and I hope, that, meanwhile, we shall both be in the best of health.

One of your portraits is on the wall of my office room and the other one on my desk at home.

Salutations,

T.S.

October 1, 1963

Dear Tom:

If this isn't your first name, I'm in a hell of a fix! But I think I read somewhere that your first name is the same as Tom Gibbons', a prizefighter who once lived in St. Paul.

I had no idea you were seventy-five. There's a magnificent tribute to you in the New York Times Book Review Section of the September 29th issue. If you don't get the New York Times let me know and I'll send you my copy. There is an excellent photograph of you by a Mr. Gerald Kelly. I would say, judging from this picture, that you are about sixty and two weeks.

There was also a paragraph mentioning the many portraits that are housed in your study. One name was conspicuous by its absence. I trust this was an oversight on the part of Stephen Spender.

My illness which, three months ago, my three doctors described as trivial, is having quite a run in my system. The three medics, I regret to say, are living on the fat of the land. So far, they've hooked me for eight thousand bucks. I only mention this to explain why I can't get over there in October. However, by next May or thereabouts, I hope to be well enough to eat that free meal you've been promising me for the past two years.

My best to you and your lovely wife, whoever she may be.

I hope you are well again.

Kindest regards,
Groucho

16th October, 1963

Dear Groucho,

Yours of October 1st to hand. I cannot recall the name of Tom Gibbons at present, but if he helps you to remember my name that is all right with me.

I think that Stephen Spender was only attempting to enumerate oil and water colour pictures and not photographs—I trust so. But, there are a good many photographs of relatives and friends in my study, although I do not recall Stephen going in there. He sent me what he wrote for the New York Times and I helped him a bit and reminded him that I had a good many books, as he might have seen if he had looked about him.

There is also a conspicuous and important portrait in my office room which has been identified by many of my visitors together with other friends of both sexes.

I am sorry that you are not coming over here this year, and still sorrier for the reason for it. I hope, however, that you will turn up in the spring if your doctors leave you a few nickels to pay your way. If you do not turn up, I am afraid all the people to whom I have boasted of knowing you (and on being on first name terms at that) will take me for a four flusher. There will be a free meal and free drinks for you by next May. Meanwhile, we shall be in New York for the month of December and if you should happen to be passing through there at that time of year, I hope you will take a free meal there on me. I would be delighted to see you wherever we are and proud to be seen in your company. My lovely wife joins me in sending you our best, but she didn't add 'whoever he may be'—she knows. It was I who introduced her in the first place to the Marx Brothers films and she is now as keen a fan as I am. Not long ago we went to see a revival of "The Marx Brothers Go West," which I had never seen before. It was certainly worth it.

Ever yours,
Tom

P.S. The photograph is of an oil portrait, done 2 years ago, not a photograph direct from life. It is very good-looking and my wife thinks it is a very accurate representation of me.

November 1, 1963

Dear Tom,

Since you are actually an early American, (I don't mean that you are an old piece of furniture, but you are a fugitive from St. Louis), you should have heard of Tom Gibbons. For your edification, Tom Gibbons was a native of St. Paul, Minnesota, which is only a stone's throw from Missouri. That is, if the stone is encased in a missile. Tom was, at one time, the light-heavyweight champion of the world, and, although outweighed by twenty pounds by Jack Dempsey, he fought him to a standstill in Shelby, Montana.

The name Tom fits many things. There was once a famous Jewish actor named Thomashevsky. All male cats are named Tom—unless they have been fixed. In that case they are just neutral and, as the upheaval in Saigon has just proved, there is no place any more for neutrals.

There is an old nursery rhyme that begins "Tom, Tom, the piper's son," etc. The third President of the United States first name was Tom . . . in case you've forgotten Jefferson.

So, when I call you Tom, this means you are a mixture of a heavyweight prizefighter, a male alley cat and the third President of the United States.

I have just finished my latest opus, "Memoirs of a Mangy Lover." Most of it is autobiographical and very little of it is fiction. I doubt whether it will live through the ages, but if you are in a sexy mood the night you read it, it may stimulate you beyond recognition and rekindle memories that you haven't recalled in years.

Sex, as an industry, is big business in this country, as it is in England. It's something everyone is deeply interested in even if only theoretically. I suppose it's always been this way, but I believe that in the old days it was discussed and practiced in a more surreptitious manner. However, the new school of writers have finally brought the bedroom and the lavatory out into the open for everyone to see. You can blame the whole thing on Havelock Ellis, Krafft-Ebing and Brill, Jung and Freud. (Now there's a trio for you!) Plus, of course, the late Mr. Kinsey who, not satisfied with hearsay, trundled from house to house, sticking his nose in where angels have always feared to tread.

However I would be interested in reading your views on sex, so don't hesitate. Confide in me. Though admittedly unreliable, I can be trusted with matters as important as that.

If there is a possibility of my being in New York in December, I will certainly try to make it and will let you know in time.

My best to you and Mrs. Tom.

Yours,
Groucho

3rd June, 1964

Dear Groucho,

This is to let you know that we have arranged for a car from International Car Hire (a firm of whom we make a good deal of use) to collect you and Mrs. Groucho at 6:40 P.M. on Saturday from the Savoy, and to bring you to us for dinner and take you home at the end of the evening. You are, of course, our guests entirely, and we look forward to seeing you both with great pleasure.

The picture of you in the newspapers saying that, amongst other reasons, you have come to London to see me has greatly enhanced my credit in the neighbourhood, and particularly with the greengrocer across the street. Obviously I am now someone of importance.

Ever Yours,

Tom

*   *   *

June, 1964

Dear Gummo:

Last night Eden and I had dinner with my celebrated pen pal, T.S. Eliot. It was a memorable evening.

The poet met us at the door with Mrs. Eliot, a good-looking, middle-aged blonde whose eyes seemed to fill up with adoration everytime she looked at her husband. He, by the way, is tall, lean and rather stooped over; but whether this is from age, illness or both, I don't know.

At any rate, your correspondent arrived at the Eliots' fully prepared for a literary evening. During the week I had read "Murder in the Cathedral" twice; "The Waste Land" three times, and just in case of a conversational bottleneck, I brushed up on "King Lear."

Well, sir, as cocktails were served, there was a momentary lull—the kind that is more or less inevitable when strangers meet for the first time. So, apropos of practically nothing (and "not with a bang but a whimper") I tossed in a quotation from "The Waste Land." That, I thought, will show him I've read a thing or two besides my press notices from vaudeville.

Eliot smiled faintly—as though to say he was thoroughly familiar with his poems and didn't need me to recite them. So I took a whack at "King Lear." I said the king was an incredibly foolish old man, which God knows he *was;* and that if he'd been *my* father I would have run away from home at the age of eight—instead of waiting until I was ten.

That, too, failed to bowl over the poet. He seemed more interested in discussing "Animal Crackers" and "A Night at the Opera." He quoted a joke— one of mine—that I had long since forgotten. Now it was my turn to smile faintly. I was not going to let anyone—not even the British poet from St. Louis—spoil my Literary Evening. I pointed out that King Lear's opening speech was the height of idiocy. Imagine (I said) a father asking his three children: Which of you kids loves me the most? And then disowning the youngest—the sweet, honest Cordelia—because, unlike her wicked sister, she couldn't bring herself to gush out insincere flattery. And Cordelia, mind you, had been her father's favorite!

The Eliots listened politely. Mrs. Eliot then defended Shakespeare; and Eden, too, I regret to say, was on King Lear's side, even though I am the one who supports her. (In all fairness to my wife, I must say that, having played the Princess in a high school production of "The Swan," she has retained a rather warm feeling for all royalty.)

As for Eliot, he asked if I remembered the courtroom scene in "Duck Soup." Fortunately I'd forgotten every word. It was obviously the end of the Literary Evening, but very pleasant none the less. I discovered that Eliot and I had three things in common: (1) an affection for good cigars and (2) cats; and (3) a weakness for making puns—a weakness that for many years I have tried to overcome. T.S., on the other hand, is an unashamed—even proud—punster. For example, there's his Gus, the Theater Cat, whose "real name was Asparagus."

Speaking of asparagus, the dinner included good, solid English beef, very well prepared. And, although they had a semi-butler serving, Eliot insisted on pouring the wine himself. It was an excellent wine and no maitre d' could have served it more graciously. He is a dear man and a charming host.

When I told him that my daughter Melinda was studying his poetry at Beverly High, he said he regretted that, because he had no wish to become compulsory reading.

We didn't stay late, for we both felt that he wasn't up to a long evening of conversation—especially mine.

Did I tell you we called him Tom?—possibly because that's his name. I, of course, asked him to call me Tom too, but only because I loathe the name Julius.

Yours,
Tom Marx

MARILYN MONROE

Marilyn Monroe in Niagara *(1952), 20th Century-Fox.*

Born Norma Jean Baker (Mortenson on birth certificate—an illegitimate child) on June 1, 1926 in Los Angeles . . . Raped at age 8 . . . Married at 14 . . . Signed with Fox for $125 per week in 1946 . . . First film: bit part in *Scudda-Hoo! Scudda-Hay!* (1948) . . . Other films include: *Asphalt Jungle* (1950) . . . *Niagara* (1952) . . . *Gentleman Prefer Blondes* (1953) . . . *The Seven Year Itch* (1955) . . . *Bus Stop* (1956) . . . *Some Like it Hot* (1959) . . . *The Misfits* (1961) . . . First *Playboy* centerfold, 1952 . . . Married Joe DiMaggio 1954 . . . Divorced after 9 months . . . Married Arthur Miller 1956 . . . Divorced 1961 . . . Suicide 1962 . . . Constance Bennett: "There's a broad with a future behind her."

A Gentleman From Center Field

I
t was a balmy night, and I was late as usual.

When the dinner host said, "Miss Monroe, this is Joe DiMaggio," I was quite surprised. Mr. Joe DiMaggio was unexpected.

I had thought I was going to meet a loud, sporty fellow. Instead I found myself smiling at a reserved gentleman in a gray suit, with a gray tie and a sprinkle of gray in his hair. There were a few blue polka dots in his tie. If I hadn't been told he was some sort of a ball player, I would have guessed he was either a steel magnate or a congressman.

He said, "I'm glad to meet you," and then fell silent for the whole rest of the evening. We sat next to each other at the table. I addressed only one remark to him.

"There's a blue polka dot exactly in the middle of your tie knot," I said. "Did it take you long to fix it like that?"

Mr. DiMaggio shook his head. I could see right away he was not a man to waste words. Acting mysterious and far away while in company was my own sort of specialty. I didn't see how it was going to work on somebody who was busy being mysterious and far away himself.

I learned during the next year that I was mistaken about this baseball idol. Joe wasn't putting on an act when he was silent, and he was the least far away man I had ever known. It was just his way of being on the ball.

But to return to my first meal with Mr. DiMaggio—he didn't try to impress me or anybody else. The other men talked and threw their personalities around. Mr. DiMaggio just sat there. Yet somehow he was the most exciting man at the table. The excitement was in his eyes. They were sharp and alert.

Then I became aware of something odd. The men at the table weren't showing off for me or telling their stories for my attention. It was Mr. DiMaggio they were wooing. This was a novelty. No *woman* had ever put me so much in the shade before.

But as far as I was concerned, Mr. DiMaggio was all novelty. In Hollywood, the more important a man is the more he talks. The better he is at his job the more he brags. By these Hollywood standards of male greatness my dinner companion was a nobody. Yet I had never met any man in Hollywood who got so much respect and attention at a dinner table. Sitting next to Mr. DiMaggio was like sitting next to a peacock with its tail spread—that's how noticeable you were.

I had been dead tired when I arrived. Now suddenly I wasn't tired anymore. There was no denying I felt attracted. But I couldn't figure out by what. I was always able to tell what it was about a man that attracted me. Except this time with Mr. DiMaggio.

My feelings for this silent smiling man began to disturb me. What was the use of buzzing all over for a man who was like somebody sitting alone in the Observation Car?

Then I began to understand something. His silence wasn't an act. It was his way of being himself. And I thought, "You learn to be silent and smiling like that from having millions of people look at you with love and excitement while you stand alone getting ready to do something."

Only I wished I knew what it was Mr. DiMaggio did. I tried to remember what the football players did the time Jim Dougherty [her first husband] took me to a football game. I couldn't recall anything interesting.

I had never seen a baseball game; so there was no use trying to figure out what a baseball player did that was important. But I was sure now it was something. After one hour all the men at the table were still talking for Mr. DiMaggio's benefit.

Men are a lot different than women in this respect. They are always full of hero worship for a champion of their sex. It's hard to imagine a table full of women sitting for a whole hour flattering and wooing another woman if she were three champions.

Since my remark about the blue polka dot there had been no further conversation between my dinner partner and me. Even though I was attracted I couldn't help thinking. "I wonder if he knows I'm an actress? Probably not. And I'll probably never find out. He's the kind of egomaniac who would rather cut off an arm than express some curiosity about somebody else. The whole thing is a waste of time. The thing to do is to go home—and forget him—and without delay."

I told the host I was tired and had a hard day ahead at the studio. It was the truth. I was playing in a movie called *Don't Bother to Knock*.

Mr. DiMaggio stood up when I did.

"May I see you to the door?" he asked.

I didn't discourage him.

At the door he broke his silence again.

"I'll walk you to your car," he said.

When we got to my car he made an even longer speech.

"I don't live very far from here, and I haven't any transportation," he said. "Would you mind dropping me at my hotel?"

I said I would be happy to.

I drove for five minutes and began to feel depressed. I didn't want Mr. DiMaggio to step out of the car and out of my life in another two minutes, which was going to happen as soon as we reached his hotel. I slowed down to a crawl as we approached the place.

In the nick of time Mr. DiMaggio spoke up again.

"I don't feel like turning in," he said. "Would you mind driving around a little while?"

Would I mind! My heart jumped, and I felt full of happiness. But all I did was nod mysteriously and answer, "It's a lovely night for a drive."

We rode around for three hours. After the first hour I began to find out things about Joe DiMaggio. He was a baseball player and had belonged to the Yankee Ball Club of the American League in New York. And he always worried when he went out with a girl. He didn't mind going out once with her. It was the second time he didn't like. As for the third time, that very seldom happened. He had a loyal friend named George Solotaire who ran interference for him and pried the girl loose.

"Is Mr. Solotaire in Hollywood with you?" I asked.

He said he was.

"I'll try not to make him too much trouble when he starts prying me loose," I said.

"I don't think I will have use for Mr. Solotaire's services this trip," he replied.

After that we didn't talk for another half hour, but I didn't mind. I had an instinct that compliments from Mr. DiMaggio were going to be few and far between, so I was content to sit in silence and enjoy the one he had just paid me.

Then he spoke up again.

"I saw your picture the other day," he said.

"Which movie was it?" I asked.

"It wasn't a movie," he answered. "It was a photograph of you on the sports page."

I remembered the one. The Studio had sent me out on a publicity stunt to Pasadena where some team from Chicago called The Sox was clowning around getting ready for the eastern baseball season. I wore rather abbreviated shorts and a bra, and the ball players took turns lifting me up on their shoulders and playing piggyback with me while the publicity men took photographs.

"I imagine you must have had your picture taken doing publicity stunts like that a thousand times," I said.

"Not quite," Mr. DiMaggio answered. "The best I ever got was Ethel Barrymore or General MacArthur. You're prettier."

The admission had an odd effect on me. I had read reams on reams of writing about my good looks, and scores of men had told me I was beautiful. But this was the first time my heart had jumped to hear it. I knew what that meant, and I began to mope. Something was starting between Mr. DiMaggio and me. It was always nice when it started, always exciting. But it always ended up in dullness.

I began to feel silly driving around Beverly Hills like a prowl car.

But it wasn't silly.

LAURENCE OLIVIER

Laurence Olivier and Marilyn Monroe in The Prince and the Showgirl *(1956), Warner Bros.*

Born on May 22, 1907 in Surrey, England . . . Son of a clergyman . . . Royal
Navy flier . . . Married Jill Esmond in 1930 . . . Married Vivian Leigh in
1940 . . . Divorced 1960 . . . First film: *Too Many Crooks* (1930) . . . Other
credits include: *Wuthering Heights* (1939) . . . *Rebecca* (1940) . . . *Pride
and Prejudice* (1940) . . . Won special Academy Award for his role as an actor,
producer and director for *Henry V* . . . Oscar for *Hamlet* (1948) . . . *Richard III*
(1956) . . . *The Prince and the Showgirl* (1956) . . . *The Entertainer*
(1960) . . . *Othello* (1965) . . . *Sleuth* (1972) . . . *Marathon Man*
(1976) . . . 11 Oscar nominations in all . . . Knighted in 1947 . . . Took seat in
House of Lords in 1971 . . . First actor ever to achieve that honor . . . When
asked how he liked to be addressed, he said: "How about Lord Larry."

The Prince and the Showgirl

The first word came to [my manager] Cecil Tennant from Warners, I think, that Marilyn Monroe's company, run by Milton Greene, her stills photographer, would be very interested in filming *The Sleeping Prince*, and that she would like me to produce and direct her in it. So [playwright] Terry Rattigan, Cecil and I buzzed over to New York for the great meeting. We called on her in her apartment on Sutton Place for some jubilant conviviality.

There were two entirely unrelated sides to Marilyn. You would not be far out if you described her as a schizoid; the two people that she was could hardly have been more different. Her three visitors on this first meeting were a little the worse for wear by the time she vouchsafed her presence, as she had kept us waiting an hour, ably and liberally refreshing ourselves at the assiduous hands of Milton Greene. Eventually I went boldly to her door and said, "Marilyn, for the love of God, come in to us. We're dying of anxiety!" She came in. She had us all on the floor at her feet in a second. I have no memory of a single word that was uttered, except that all was as convivial and jubilant as could be.

The evening wore on to its self-congratulatory close; we were all making our departure when Marilyn, in the small voice she sometimes used to good effect, gently piped: "Just a minute. Shouldn't somebody say something about an agreement?" By George, the girl was right; we arranged for a purely business meeting in the morning, and I was then to take her to lunch at the "21" Club.

By the end of the day one thing was clear to me: I was going to fall most shatteringly in love with Marilyn, and *what* was going to happen? There was no question about it, it was inescapable, or so I thought; she was so adorable, so witty, such incredible fun and more physically attractive than anyone I could have imagined, apart from herself on the screen. I went home like a lamb reprieved from the slaughter just for now, but next time . . . Wow! For the first time now it threatened to be "poor Vivien"! (Almost twenty years earlier it had been "poor Jill.")

Vivien was really very sweet about being passed over for the role she had created, considering that in telling her I had chosen to be clumsily truculent. After all, it *was* her part, even if she did know that she had not been wildly successful in it at the Phoenix, and that the dazzling heights of fame that Marilyn had achieved were unchallengeable. But that is something that is never easy to accept, and she behaved with attractive understanding and shrugged it all off beautifully. I was grateful and relieved to find no cause for anxiety in that area.

The day of the great arrival dawned, and Marilyn was wafted onto this blessed plot in the illustrious charge of her new husband, Arthur Miller, a playwright both respected and popular; and so we were under starter's orders. I had arranged that we should have two weeks or so of rehearsals before starting the cameras rolling, so that strangenesses could wear off and we should all feel at home with each other. So many years at the job made it hard to believe that this might be impossible, but, by God, it was.

We started off with two days of press conferences. I had said last thing the night before, being already disturbed, that her famous reputation for unpunctuality somewhat belied the strict professionalism that I seemed to discern in the technique supporting her dazzling spontaneity. It sent up a host of question marks about the as yet undiscovered complexities of her psychological makeup. She had been pretty good at the huge press conference in New York, during which, making a gesture, her shoulder strap had broken, and one and all took it to be a gag. Now I said, "Marilyn, dear. Please, pretty please, we cannot be late tomorrow, we *cannot*. The press will take it very unkindly and half of them will be expecting it, so do me a favor and disappoint them, *please*."

She promised, and was one whole hour late. I don't think I've ever been so embarrassed. I filled in as best I could, answering personal questions about myself. My attitude to the giving of interviews was well known, so they had me where they wanted me for once; but interest was petering out a bit by the time she showed up. For the first twenty minutes all the questions started: "Why are you late?" The way she handled this difficult situation was an object lesson in charm, and in no time at all she had got this vast ballroomful of people nestling cozily in the hollow of her hand. To give her a chance, I spontaneously declared that since many of the questions could not be heard by more than a very few, I would take the liberty of repeating each question, thus making her answers more intelligible (and incidentally gaining for Marilyn a few more seconds to think out the answer).

She would always do exactly what was asked of her by any stills photographer. I marveled at first at this show of discipline and thought it augured well; my reaction only a few weeks later would have been: "Well, of course—she's a model." I think that wherever she gleaned that particular training, it taught her more about acting than did Lee Strasberg; my opinion of his school is that it did more harm than good to his students and that his influence on the American theatre was misapplied. Deliberately antitechnical, his Method offered instead an all-consuming passion for reality, and if you did not feel attuned to exactly the right images that would make you believe that you were actually *it* and *it* was actually going on, you might as well forget about the scene altogether. Our young American actors felt an aching void where there should have been some training or grounding from which they could leap or fly. In the ten years since the war there had been very little repertory training; Stanislavsky, upon whose philosophy Strasberg's Actors Studio was founded, was much in the mode in England at the time when we were in Rep in the 1920s. It was a gift we could take advantage of but should not be obsessed by.

I went along to Strasberg's Studio on two occasions early in 1958, when *The*

Entertainer was on in New York. On each occasion his judgments lengthened into a homily which, absolutely off the cuff as it was, mounted into an outpouring of spontaneous wise saws, all unthought out and probably unexpressed before, and therefore dangerously unreliable as information. But he was off, mounting into the skies of his own sudden visions. He was the revivalist minister of pure naturalism. The phrase "natural behaviorism" would have a different meaning dialectically and, to some of us, would lend that redeeming mite more technicality.

He was giving an unduly severe stream of criticism to one young man who seemed to me to have some sort of natural gift, and at the end of the session I ventured to say as much. Obviously only used to obsequious adulation, Strasberg waved me aside as an ignoramus, saying, "Aw, naw-naw-naw, he has many problems." More gently, I put it to him that removing any shred of confidence the boy might have wasn't likely to help many of them. "Aw, naw-naw-naw."

Only a very little time before the picture started was I told that Lee Strasberg's wife, Paula, "always came along with Marilyn." This alarmed me considerably as I had rarely found that coaches were helpful. Philosophically I clung to the thought, "Oh, well, perhaps she may bring out the better of those two halves." Marilyn was not used to rehearsing and obviously had no taste for it. She proclaimed this by her appearance—hair pulled back under a scarf, bad skin with no makeup, very dark glasses and an overly subdued manner, which I failed dismally to find the means to enliven. I just prayed that that miracle between the lens and the celluloid would happen for me, as I knew very well it must have done for half a dozen of my colleagues on the West Coast. I managed to contact two of them, Billy Wilder and Josh Logan; they commiserated with me cheerfully (their labors over) and said yes, it was hell, but that I would be getting a pleasant surprise when it was all over. When Paula arrived, I called off rehearsals for two days in order to go over and over the part, teaching *her* the way of it so that she could then teach Marilyn. Pride was a luxury I couldn't afford. Paula seemed willing to cooperate with every scrap of timing and whatever inflections or stress she thought Marilyn could cope with, "and make her feel it was her idea—you know what I mean?"

The truth came to light with uncanny speed: Paula knew nothing; she was no actress, no director, no teacher, no adviser—except in Marilyn's eyes, for she had one talent: she could butter Marilyn up. On one car journey I heard Paula play an innings in this, her special ploy, which pinned my ears back as I sat in the front with the two of them in the back. "My dear, you really must recognize your own potential; you haven't even yet any idea of the importance of your position in the world. You are the greatest sex symbol in human memory. Everybody knows and recognizes that, and you should too. It's a duty which you owe to yourself and to the world; it's ungrateful not to accept it. You are the greatest woman of your time, the greatest human being of your time; of any time, you name it. You can't think of anybody, I mean—no, not even Jesus—except you're more popular." Incredible as that must seem, it is no exaggeration; and it went on in unremitting supply for a good hour, with Marilyn swallowing every word.

This was Paula's unique gift to the art of acting, or rather the artful success of Marilyn's career, out of which the Strasbergs stood to make much capital. This was what, I realized in growing alarm, I was stuck with.

Nevertheless, I refused to treat Marilyn as a special case—I had too much pride in my trade—and would at all times treat her as a grown-up artist of merit, which in a sense she was. Her manner to me got steadily ruder and more insolent; whenever I patiently labored to make her understand an indication for some reading, business or timing she would listen with ill-disguised impatience, and when I had finished would turn to Paula and petulantly demand, "Wasseee mean?" A very short way into the filming, my humiliation had reached depths I would not have believed possible.

There was one relief from it: during the coronation sequence there was no dialogue except what was laid onto the effects sound track later; and so there was no need to go into long explanations before each take, and I could risk side-of-camera directions. To my intense relief she accepted these like a lamb. "Do a little curtsey as the King passes. Watch for when Dickie Wattis bows by your side, and I'll say when to rise. Now try to look up to your right where the altar is; now look back questioningly at Dickie. He'll hand you an open prayerbook for you to follow. Now look up and try to find the Regent towards the altar, find him, but of course he won't look at you, so, a wee bit disappointed, follow in the prayerbook a little while, feel moved by the music." I had a massive selection of records, but she would have nothing but the "Londonderry Air," which had perforce to go on for the whole day. The poor unit nearly went round the bend with it. "Now, catch sight of that stained glass window—it's the most beautiful picture you can imagine. Let some tears well into your eyes, Marilyn. . . ."

As if by magic, submissive and scrupulously obedient, she followed every instruction exactly and at once and, what is most important, quite perfectly. I had cause to reflect once more, this time with gratitude, "Of course, she's a model."

I had run a closed set, admitting no one who was not actually involved in the work, nobody that was even related to anyone of the press, sad to say thereby making enemies of many whom I had thought of as my friends in that profession. But the press of the entire world was screaming and tearing to get in; the set would have been a shambles. Besides these practical reasons, I had some more theoretical convictions of my own.

I had taken note of the fact that a few weeks after her wedding to Prince Rainier, Princess Grace (Kelly) was presented in a film production of Molnar's *The Swan*. There seemed to be no reason in the world why this should not have been a prodigious box-office success—unless one takes into consideration the fact that for months before her wedding the wealth of romance that surrounded this event ensured that her picture, together with some story or anecdote, would appear in almost every newspaper that could be bought. I believe the public was surfeited with the sight of her name in print, even with her beautiful features and, I am afraid, with her story—in fact anything that could be associated with her for some little time to come.

This taught me to be wary about Marilyn's promotion. If success has a limit, then so has the publicity which, it is claimed, brings it about. This thought prompted me to soft-pedal. But in spite of the most elaborate precautions there were leaks galore, all to do with the unhappy atmosphere on the set, with wildly exaggerated tales of screaming rows, *faute de mieux*. Our journalists did not lack for invention.

In the last shooting days, I was allowed one petty triumph in the Prince's first saunter down the chorus line backstage. It was fixed that Marilyn's shoulder strap should break as she made her first curtsey, to echo our first big press call in New York. It was fine, but Marilyn took it into her head that her breast had showed itself. "Nooooh, Marilyn. Nooooh," I said, and called in the boys on the rails as witnesses. The message came back: "They say they weren't looking at Miss Monroe; they were watching Sir Laurence." Knowing as I did the intensity of their appraising curiosity for the first few days of the work, this complete lack of interest was an object lesson in something or other.

The last word on Marilyn belongs to Irina Baronova, Cecil's wife, who had been watching quietly with her Russian intuitiveness from the darkness off the set: "She has a quite unconscious but basic resistance to acting. She loves to show herself, loves to be a star, loves all the success side of it. But to be an actress is something she does not want at all. They were wrong to try to make one of her. Her wit, her adorable charm, her sex appeal, her bewitching personality—are all part of *her*, not necessarily to be associated with any art or talent."

After the script had all been shot, I had feelings of vague disquiet. As a producer I was entirely satisfied with the picture, which was to be called *The Prince and the Showgirl*; as an actor, shamelessly unashamed of myself; but as a director, I wished I had got better stuff out of Marilyn. Other directors had, and it lay uneasily on my conscience that I had not. I began to admit to myself that I had not achieved greater perfection because I had shirked the probability of more rows. I asked Marilyn to see the picture run and to bring her husband, Arthur Miller, with her, after which would they please come and talk with me? They agreed and I talked with them sincerely and frankly. If she and Arthur found that they were entirely satisfied, then, God knows, I would be only too happy to leave it at that. They both agreed there was room for improvement, but what could be done now it was over? I told them that if Marilyn would undertake to contribute to a better atmosphere between us, discipline herself to absolute punctuality, accept my word when I passed something as OK and not insist on take after take more than was necessary, I would be willing to reshoot certain scenes. I would guarantee to get the work done in two days, but in no circumstances would I undertake more to help Marilyn. For once I had the other side by the short and curlies, and they knew they had to agree.

The first morning made my heart sink, a sensation I was getting profoundly sick of;

we had spent the whole time trying to inject a scintillating spirit into the scene of our first meeting. I had never dreamed up such a variety of expressions, examples, illustrations, images to help inspire the essential wit and sparkle needed to make a lively start to a picture from which a great deal would be expected. Marilyn made her inevitable way towards Paula, who said, "Honey, just think of Coca-Cola and Frankie Sinatra!" I suppose that might have been the Actors Studio approach. God! Don't tell me they would have been right and I wrong throughout this whole thing? Needless to say, it worked; enough to make a man cut his throat, enough for this man, anyway.

The day of the great farewell dawned. It had been agreed that whatever our personal feelings might be, a great act must be put on at the airport; our own crews were careful to take the right pictures of the right-looking embraces which assumed the right intensity of passion for any two great lovers of history: Marilyn and me kissing, Vivien and Arthur kissing, Vivien and Marilyn kissing, me and Arthur kissing—it deceived no one. An absurd show, the press called it; who did we think we were kidding? *L'envoi.*

Going home, I thought of all the excitement when the first news of the approaching partnership broke; how Josh Logan had declared it "the most exciting combination since black and white." I thought incredulously of our first meeting and how I had feared falling in love with her. Some weeks later I had to go across the waters to show the film to Jack Warner. Milton Greene grabbed hold of me and said, "Howbout a stills session tomorrow, huh?"

"By myself?"

"Oh, no, with Marilyn of course."

"*Oh, no*, Milton, *no, no, no*; you'll not get me with that dame again!"

"Oh, hell, she won't be that way t'morrow, you'll see. You won't recognize her. She'll be marvelous like she used to be. Besides, we want the picture t'make money, don' we? We've had no promotion at all."

It was as he said; he provided delicious caviar sandwiches, drinks of all kinds, the lushest music. He knew how to lay it on; after all, he'd managed to persuade Marilyn to sign up with him and form their own company—strictly business: his own wife was extremely attractive and intelligent.

Two years or so ago a couple of my Hollywood friends, as a sort of joke after a dinner party, ran this now-twenty-five-year-old picture for me on their library projection machine. I was a bit embarrassed as I didn't know how long it might be before the joke would begin to get a bit tired. However, the picture ran through, much to my surprise. At the finish everyone was clamorous in their praises; how such enchantment could have been poorly received defied imagination. I was as good as could be, and Marilyn! Marilyn was quite wonderful, the best of all. So.

What do you know?

Laurence Olivier in Marathon Man *(1976), Paramount.*

BASIL RATHBONE

Basil Rathbone and Nigel Bruce in The Hound of the Baskervilles *(1939), 20th Century-Fox.*

Born Philip St. John Basil Rathbone on June 13, 1892 in Johannesburg, South Africa, of British parents . . . On stage since 1911 . . . First film *Innocent* (1921) . . . Started out as romantic lead in 1920s . . . *Romeo and Juliet* (1936) . . . *If I Were King* (1938) . . . Played Sherlock Holmes in 16 films during the 1940s . . . Ended career as villain in *The Ghost of the Invisible Bikini* (1966) . . . *Prehistoric Planet Women* (1966) . . . *Hillbillies in the Haunted House* (1967) . . . Died 1967.

"Hi There, Sherlock"

T his greeting might quite easily prove to be my epitaph, if not in substance at least in effect. It is a greeting that in most cases I have not welcomed, for in general it has carried with it the connotation "We too are amused and entertained by your little game of sleuthing, how goes it, pal?" I do not remember a single instance from 1939 to 1962 where an interviewer from some newspaper or magazine, or a member of an audience, or a friend has not smiled somewhat indulgently when the subject of my association with Mr. Sherlock Holmes has arisen. In the upper echelon of my very considerable following as Mr. Holmes, there has always been a somewhat patronizing, if polite, recognition of my modest achievement. In the lower echelon I have experienced nothing but embarrassment in the familiar street-corner greeting of recognition, which is inevitably followed by horrendous imitations of my speech, loud laughter, and ridiculing quotes of famous lines such as "Quick, Watson, the needle" or "Elementary, my dear Watson," followed by more laughter at my obvious discomfiture. Quite frankly and realistically, over the years I have been forced to accept the fact that my impersonation of one of the most famous fictional characters in all literature has not received that respectful recognition to which I feel Sir Arthur Conan Doyle's masterpieces entitle him. Has it been my fault? I do not think so. And certainly it is not the fault of those who were responsible for producing sixteen pictures and some two hundred weekly radio broadcasts between 1939 and 1946. Professionally it has always been conceded that both pictures and broadcasts were of an exceptionally high quality. Could it be that our efforts somewhat resembled museum pieces? Here possibly may be a clue to the problem, i.e., the word "museum." With the development in talking pictures of a mass production of murder-mystery-sleuth-horror movies our audiences have been delighted and amused by the extravagant shock technique employed. Mr. Alfred Hitchcock is perhaps the prime "spoofer" of this type of storytelling, and he has contributed more than anyone else I know of to the acceptance of the murder-mystery-sleuth-horror as one of the most acceptable "jokes" of our time. Audiences are not really frightened by such pictures. They willfully indulge in a purely synthetic hysteria, which in some perverse way seems to entertain them momentarily. They are far too intelligent to accept anything but cacophony as the chocolate sauce that disguises their poisoned ice cream! . . . .

Had I made but the one Holmes picture, my first, *The Hound of the Baskervilles*, I should probably not be as well known as I am today. But within myself, as an artist, I should have been well content. Of all the "adventures" *The Hound* is my favorite story, and it was in this picture that I had the stimulating experience of creating, within my own limited framework, a character that has intrigued me as much as any I have ever played. But the continuous repetition of story after story after story left me virtually repeating myself each time in a character I had already conceived and developed. The stories varied but I was always the same character merely repeating myself in different situations. My first picture was, as it were, a negative from which I merely continued to produce endless positives of the same photograph.

In due course, and not unreasonably I think, these endless repetitions forced me into a critical analysis of Holmes that was often disturbing and sometimes destructive. For instance, toward the end of my life with him I came to the conclusion (as one may in living too closely and too long in seclusion with any one rather unique and difficult personality) that there was nothing lovable about Holmes. He himself seemed capable of transcending the weakness of mere mortals such as myself . . . understanding us perhaps, accepting us and even pitying us, but only and purely objectively. It would be impossible for such a man to know loneliness or love or sorrow because he was completely sufficient unto himself. His perpetual seeming assumption of infallibility; his interminable success; (could he not fail just once and prove himself a human being like the rest of us!) his ego that seemed at times to verge on the superman complex, while his "Elementary, my dear Watson," with its seeming condescension for the pupil by the master must have been a very trying experience at times for even so devoted a friend as was Dr. Watson. . . .

In John Dickson Carr's excellent biography of Sir Arthur Conan Doyle, he relates that Sir Arthur felt at one time that he had created a sort of Frankenstein that he could not escape from. And so he decided to kill Mr. Sherlock Holmes at the Reichenbach Falls and be done with him. Public outrage at this callous murder of Mr. Holmes by Sir Arthur was so great that Sir Arthur was literally forced to bring him back from the dead and continue the adventures.

I frankly admit that in 1946 I was placed in a somewhat similar predicament—but *I* could not kill Mr. Holmes. So I decided to run away from him. However, to all intents and purposes I might just as well have killed him. My friends excoriated me for my dastardly behavior, and for a while my long-time friendship with Nigel Bruce suffered severe and recurring shocks. The Music Corporation of America, who represented me at that time, treated me as if I were "sick-sick-sick."

My "sickness" was treated by Mr. Jules Stein, head of MCA, and by my friends as a temporary affliction—I was to be "babied" along until I had recovered my senses. It was in August, 1946, that Jules phoned me in Philadelphia, where I was appearing in a play and headed for a New York opening. A new seven-year Sherlock Holmes radio contract had been negotiated by MCA—was I about ready to return to the Coast? It was then that the seriousness of my "condition" became evident. The climax was reached in a long-distance telephone call from Jules in Los Angeles—*No!* I was not coming back—I had sold my house in Bel Air and was heading for the Plymouth Theatre in New York. Supremely confident and relaxed, sipping a gin and tonic, I lounged in a comfortable chair in my room at the Ritz Hotel, Philadelphia.

Eventually, I seemed to break through the clouds of dismay and bewilderment occasioned by my ingratitude, and I shall forever be grateful to Jules Stein for his acceptance of my decision—and his most generous attentions to my well-being on my return to New York, which eventualized in a contract that he made for me in 1947 to appear as Dr. Sloper in Jed Harris's memorable production of Henry James' classic *The Heiress.*

Ever since I said good-by to Mr. Sherlock Holmes there has lingered somewhere inside of me a sentimental attachment for this memorable character. I am not gifted enough to pay him the tribute I would—but a few years ago I made an attempt. And so by kind permission of Esquire Magazine, I give you

DAYDREAM

I had always loved the country of Sussex. It held for me some of the happiest memories of my life—my early childhood. Early in June I had slipped down, for a few days' much-needed rest, to the little village of Heathfield, to dream again of the past and to try to shut out, for a brief period at least, both the present and the future.

The last afternoon of my holiday I was walking across the gentle countryside when I was rudely stung by a bee. Startled, I grabbed a handful of soft earth and applied it to the sting; it's an old-fashioned remedy I had learned as a child. Suddenly I became aware that the air about me was swarming with bees. It was then I noticed the small house with a thatched roof and a well-kept garden, with beehives at one end, that Mrs. Messenger, my landlady, had so often mentioned. She had told me that "he" had come to live in the thatched cottage many years ago. As he bothered no one, no one bothered him, which is an old English custom. Now, in 1946, he had become almost a legend.

I saw him now, on this late summer afternoon, seated in his garden, a rug over his knees, reading a book. In spite of his great age he wore no reading glasses; and though he made no movement there was a curious sense of animation in his apparently inanimate body. He had the majestic beauty of a very old tree: his features were sharp, emphasizing a particularly prominent nose. He was smoking a meerschaum pipe with obvious relish. Suddenly he looked up and our eyes met.

"Won't you come in?" he called in a surprisingly firm voice.

"Thank you, sir," I replied, "but I have no right to impose on your privacy."

"If it were an imposition I should not have invited you," he replied. "Pull up a chair and sit down."

He gave me a quick glance of penetrating comprehension. As I sat down I had an odd feeling that I was dreaming.

"I'm sorry to see that you have been stung by one of my bees."

I smiled; the smile was intended to say that it didn't matter.

"You must forgive the little fellow," he continued. "He's paid for it with his life."

"It seems unfair that he should have had to," I said.

"No," mused the old man, "it's a law of nature. 'God moves in a mysterious way His wonders to perform.' May I order you some tea?"

"Thank you, no," I said.

"I used to be a prolific coffee drinker myself. I have always found tea an insipid substitute by comparison." He smiled. "Do you live here?"

"No, sir, I'm on a short holiday. But I was born near here."

"Really!" The smile touched his eyes. "It's a comforting little corner of the earth, isn't it, especially in times like these?"

"Have you lived here all through the war, sir?" I asked.

"Yes." The smile disappeared. Slowly he pulled an old Webley revolver from under the rug which covered his knees. "If they had come, six of them would not have lived to tell the story. . . . I learned to use this thing many years ago. I have never missed my man."

He cradled the gun in his hand and left me momentarily for that world which to each of us is his own.

There was quite a pause before I had the courage to ask, "Were you in the First World War, sir?"

"Indirectly—and you?" He replaced the gun on his knees.

"I'm an Inspector at Scotland Yard."

"I thought so!" As he spoke the book in his lap fell to the ground. I reached down, picked it up, and handed it back to him.

"Thank you. And how are things at the Yard these days?"

"Modern science and equipment have done much to help us," I said.

"Yesss." His hand went to a pocket and brought forth an old magnifying glass. "When I was a young man they used things like this. Modern inventions have proved to be great timesavers, but they have dulled our natural instincts and made us lazy— most of us at least."

"You may be right, sir. But we either go forward or back."

He put the magnifying glass and revolver back into two voluminous pockets of an old sports jacket which had leather patches at the elbows. Then he took a deep breath and released it in a long-drawn-out sigh.

"I've followed your career very closely, Inspector. The Yard is fortunate in your services."

"That's kind of you, sir."

"Not at all. I knew your father quite well at one time."

"You knew my father!" The words stumbled out.

"Yesss. He was a brilliant man, your father. He interested me deeply. His mind was balanced precariously on that thin line between sanity and insanity. Is he still living?"

"No, sir; he died in 1936."

The old man nodded his head reflectively. "These fellows with their newfangled ideas would have found him intensely interesting subject matter. What do you call them? Psycho—psychoanalysts!"

"Psychoanalysis can be very helpful, don't you think, sir?"

"No, I don't. It's a lot of rubbish—*psychoanalysis!* It's nothing more than a simple process of deduction by elimination."

We talked of crime and its different ways of detection, until a cool breeze crossed the garden with its warning of the day's departure.

He rose slowly to a full six feet and held out his hand. "I must go in now. It's been pleasant talking with you."

"I am deeply indebted to you, sir." I wanted to say so much more, but felt oddly constrained.

He held out the book in his hand, *The Adventures of Sherlock Holmes.* "Do you know these stories? They are often overdramatized; but they make good reading." Once again the smile danced in his eyes.

I acknowledged an intimate acquaintance with all the works to which he referred and he seemed greatly pleased by my references to "The Master." He accompanied me slowly to the road and we spoke briefly of S. C. Roberts, and Christopher Morley and Vincent Starrett.

"The adventures as written by our dear friend Doctor Watson mean a great deal to me at my time of life," he reflected. "As someone once said, 'Remembrance is the only sure immortality we can know.'"

On my return, Mrs. Messenger gave me an urgent telegram from Scotland Yard, requesting my immediate return. I didn't speak to her of my visit to "him." I was afraid she might consider me as childish as the youngsters in Heathfield who still believe "he" was the great Sherlock Holmes.

Which they did, until they reached an age when he was dismissed, together with Santa Claus and those other worthwhile people who, for a brief, beautiful period, are more real than reality itself.

RONALD REAGAN

Ronald Reagan (standing) in Knute Rockne—All American *(1940), Warner Bros.*

Born Ronald Wilson Reagan on February 6, 1911 in Tampico, Illinois . . . Nicknamed "Dutch" . . . Radio sportscaster . . . First film: *Love is on the Air* **(1937) . . .** *Hell's Kitchen* **(1939) . . .** *Knute Rockne—All American* **(1940) . . .** *Bedtime for Bonzo* **(1951) . . .** *Law and Order* **(1954) . . .** *The Killers* **(1964) . . . Elected Governor of California in 1966 . . . Married Jane Wyman 1940 . . . Divorced 1948 . . . Married Nancy Davis (daughter of prominent conservative) 1952 . . . Narrated military training films during WWII—his most memorable line: "Bombs Away!" . . . Reagan: "I'm a sucker for hero worship . . ."**

Win One for the Gipper

P eople come to Hollywood from many different places, and certainly are varied in their background and training, but all of them either bring one thing with them or acquire it upon arrival: the desire to see a certain story become a picture. I wanted to tell the story of Knute Rockne. I had no intention of playing Rockne. I had always seen Pat O'Brien as the logical star in the title role. I had something else in mind for myself—a fellow named George Gipp. No one could do the story of Rockne without devoting a portion of it to the great "Gipper."

It's hard to tell where legend ends and reality begins, but even the plainest, documented, factual story about Gipp still leaves him an extremely colorful character. In a day when college men observed the proprieties in dress, it is said that Gipp removed the cleats from a pair of football shoes which he wore daily, and his uniform in the classroom was usually a Notre Dame sweater worn over a sweatshirt with no shirt or tie. One night, filling time on a WHO broadcast, I had told the story of Gipp. As a freshman walking across the practice field, he had picked up a bouncing football and kicked it back toward the varsity players who were calling for it. He kicked it clear over the fence. Rockne persuaded this lackadaisical, easygoing stranger to don a football suit and then, irritated by Gipp's good humor, put him in the freshman backfield to carry the ball against the varsity—a varsity he had primed to murder the cocky freshman. Gipp went eighty yards for a touchdown, tossed Rockne the ball, and said, "I guess the fellows are just tired." The rest of his story is sports history. One of the all-time great stars, he died two weeks after his last game. At the time of his death, as an indication of his versatility, he had a signed contract to play major league baseball.

Being brand-new in Hollywood, I explored my idea openly, questioning all who would hold still about whom to see, whether simply to do a treatment, or try to write a script, until I was sure everyone at Warner Brothers knew that I was an actor with pencil in hand. One day I stopped talking long enough to read in *Variety* the announcement that Warner brothers were doing the life story of Rockne, starring Pat O'Brien. I rushed in to Brynie [Foy], clutching *Variety*, and sputtered that this was exactly what I had been trying to promote. He just grinned at me and said, "You talk too much." I suppose he thought I had some idea of charging plagiarism. The truth is, it had never occurred to me that one got money for story ideas: I just wanted them to make the picture so I could play Gipp.

When Brynie realized I was only excited about getting in the picture, he said, "Well, you'd better do something because they've already tested ten fellows for the part." I panicked. I knew I would hate whoever played this part. I went to see the producer. He was kind, but it was obvious he had no intention of even considering me for the part. Over and over again he kept saying, "Gipp was one of the greatest football players of all time." Finally it sank in: he was telling me I wasn't the type.

"But I played football for eight years," I protested. "I was able to go to college only because I played football."

Again came the answer: "But Gipp was the greatest player in the country."

My mind was beginning to function. "Wait a minute," I said. "You mean you think he has to weigh about two hundred pounds, and look like these fellows you see in the Coliseum?" He made a sort of shrugging gesture, and again repeated how great Gipp was. I was still too new in this business and too recent from the sports world to be polite. "You are producing the picture," I said, "and you don't know that Gipp weighed five pounds less than I weigh right now. He walked with a sort of slouch and a limp. He looked like a football player only when he was on the field." I wasn't getting any place. Then I remembered something a director had told me one day when we had been ordered to shoot a scene two different ways. I had thought it was a waste of time: we should decide in advance which version was correct and shoot only that one. The director had said, "You have to realize these fellows only believe what they see on film."

Without another word I left the producer's office, broke a few speed laws getting home, and dived for the bottom of my trunk. I came up with some photographs taken during my own college days (which weren't too many years back), and broke the same speed laws getting back to the studio. I barged into his office and slapped the pictures down on his desk. I must say the reaction was satisfying. Not very many fellows look like football players without the suit, and most do in the suit. I was smart enough to keep my mouth shut and let the photographs talk.

Holding them in his hand, he said, "Could I keep these for a while?"

I answered with one word, "Sure"—and headed home. I drove slower because it was hard to hold the wheel with all my fingers crossed.

I hadn't been in the house fifteen minutes when the phone rang. It was a call from casting: "Eight o'clock shooting—testing for the part of George Gipp."

Usually when a person is being tested for a role, some contract player is given the chore of playing the other part in the scene. You can imagine my gratitude when I arrived on the set and found that my assistant, complete with make-up, was Pat O'Brien, who already had signed for the Rockne part. It was a half a day's work he wasn't required to do, but he was there to give me all the tools possible to help me get the part he knew meant so much to me. I really didn't have to learn any lines; I had known Gipp's story for years. My lines were straight from Rock's diary. Our test scene was where Gipp, ordered to carry the ball at that first practice, cocked an eyebrow and asked Rockne, "How far?"

I got the part. It occupied only one reel of the picture, but in that reel it was a nearly perfect part from an actor's standpoint. A great entrance, an action middle, and a death scene to finish up. By way of frosting on the cake, in the last reel of the picture Gipp is recalled to the audience when Rock asks the team to win one for the Gipper, and reveals for the first time that this was Gipp's dying request.

We shot most of the football stuff at Loyola. My first scene was, oddly enough, my entrance in the picture. (I had learned that Hollywood usually shoots the last scene first.) Pat handed me a football and then, as Rockne had done many years before, said, "Can you kick another one like that?" My line was, "I think so." However, in staging the scene, I had to kick the ball at a high enough angle to miss the camera which was in close for our two-shot. Instead of pointing my toe, I kept my foot in a normal position and caught the ball well up on my instep so as to get height. Pat and I started doing our lines. I could see the effort he was making to hold his face straight, and I was beginning to strangle a bit with the effort to choke down a laugh. I think we exchanged at least four lines of dialogue before the ball I had kicked came down right between us, almost hitting Pat on the head.

A few days later, we reached the scene wherein I was to run eighty yards for a touchdown. In typical location style (which means everything gets more and more confused until we reach complete chaos, then we film it), I was told, "Get into the football suit," then, "Get out of the football suit, we're going to shoot something else." It was early morning, so I sent to the lunch stand that usually follows location troops. I had a nice, big, greasy bacon-and-egg sandwich, a can of pineapple juice, and coffee—at which point I was told, "Get back in the football suit."

Well fortified with a heavy lump in my midsection, I did eighty yards on a hot summer morning. Because it was a difficult dolly shot, I did the eighty yards all over again. Because the camera operator didn't like the way he had gotten the shot, I did eighty yards a third time. This time I didn't stop at the goal line: I just kept on going to the wooden fence where I was very sick. It's too bad I was several years ahead of my time. Today I could have gotten away with saying that throwing up was my own personal style of method acting.

The entire picture was a sentimental journey and a thrilling experience. Irish Pat—playing a Norwegian, coaching a team of all nations—chalked up an unforgettable performance. For inspiration Rockne's widow Bonnie was on the set every day as technical advisor. Between scenes most of our time was spent listening to reminiscences and stories of that great era when Notre Dame was the scourge of the football world. It was natural that Rock would one day use the story of Gipp's death to inspire a Notre Dame team. If the story had come out of his imagination, no one—including Bonnie—ever knew. To me the great significance was that Rock saved that story for eight years, and then didn't use it just to win a game, but used it to inspire a team that was losing mainly because of bickering and jealousy. For at least one half he gave his team, torn with dissension, the knowledge of what it was like to play together, and to sacrifice their individual quarrels for a common goal. As in every picture based on real life exploits, truth was stranger than fiction. There were scenes that couldn't be photographed because an audience wouldn't accept the truth, or it would appear too melodramatic. For instance, it is told that Jack

Chevigny, who carried the last touchdown over the goal in that game and then was carried off the field himself with a broken leg, looked up from the stretcher and said, "That's the last one I can get for you, Gipper."

Filmed in early summer, the picture was rushed to completion for fall release. In a surprisingly short time a sneak preview was held in Pasadena, in keeping with the Hollywood custom of running a picture unannounced before a theater audience, to get an "honest" reaction. Nervous as I was, I learned something unusual about watching myself. You can laugh at yourself on screen when you say something funny, but you can't make yourself cry. When I read Gipp's death scene I had a lump in my throat so big I couldn't talk. I can get the same lump just thinking about it, but suddenly there I was on the screen playing the scene, and I was as unmoved as if I had a cold in the nose. It was a terrible letdown and I went home thinking I was a failure. Actually, if I'd only been aware of it, the rest of the audience had the sniffles and I was unmoved simply because it is impossible to get worked up at your own death scene when you're sitting there well and healthy and very much alive.

Ronald Reagan and Norman Fell in The Killers *(1964), Universal.*

EDWARD G. ROBINSON

Edward G. Robinson in Little Caesar *(1930), First National.*

Born Emmanuel Goldenberg, December 12, 1893 in Bucharest, Rumania . . . Died in 1973 . . . Grew up in the Lower East Side of New York City . . . Briefly attended CCNY . . . Appeared in over forty plays before turning to movies, a medium he claimed to despise . . . First film, *The Bright Shawl* (1923), a silent. . . . *Little Caesar* (1930) . . . *The Sea Wolf* (1941) . . . *Double Indemnity* (1944) . . . *Key Largo* (1948) . . . *Cincinnati Kid* (1965) . . . *Soylent Green* (1973) . . . Blacklisted as a communist sympathizer . . . Later cleared . . . Built a multi-million dollar art collection.

Little Caesar

In late 1930 Hal Wallis asked me to his office to discuss my playing the role of Otero in *Little Caesar*—the best-seller by William R. Burnett, already recommended to me by Leah Salisbury [literary agent].

Yes, I said Otero. Not Rico (Cesare Bandello) the lead, but Otero, a minor part.

To this day I think it was a ruse. I think Hal had always meant for me to play Rico, and his ploy was to soften my rigid backbone. I've never asked him.

May I say a word about him? Hal Wallis is perhaps the least known of the movie moguls because actually he is not a mogul at all. Unlike the rest of the boys, he had (and has) instinctive taste. He loves making a buck, and he loves meaning and significance as well. Through the years he has gone from pictures about Becket and Queen Elizabeth (historically accurate and beautifully devised) to Elvis Presley and Martin and Lewis.

Maybe he saw in Presley a *Nouvelle Vague* (which he most certainly was) or in Jerry Lewis a clown in the great tradition (which the French intellectuals passionately believe him to be). Whatever his reasoning or his intuitions, he is a great producer, and you don't find his like around much anymore. (He also has a stunning collection of paintings, with two thrilling Fantin-Latours. I had nothing whatever to do with his collecting, but he had a great deal to do with mine. The money that bought them came from Warner's via Wallis.)

But on that day in his office I loathed him. In his cool, offhand and peremptory manner he handed me the script of *Little Caesar*, pointing out that the part of Otero was exactly right for me. I took the script back to my dressing room, read it, and decided not only that the part of Otero was exactly wrong for me but that the script itself was a literal and undramatized rendering of the novel.

I catch on fast, and I could see that the movies were, and by definition had to be, visual and not dependent totally upon verbal communication. This was a strange conclusion for one who had always depended upon words and dialogue. But it was now amply clear to me that a closeup could convey inner thought, that the technique of cutting could provide the aside. And it also came to me, not in a vision, but after careful study of the new sound movies, that movies had to move.

And what occurred to me with the utmost finality was that if I were going to get anywhere in this new medium, I was not about to play bits. I did not ask for star billing; I knew that was a danger to be avoided until the public (and I) considered me a star—but I also knew that third leads and bits were a graveyard.

So back I went to Wallis and announced pompously: "If you're going to have me in

Little Caesar as Otero, you will completely imbalance the picture. The only part I will consider playing is Little Caesar."

Hal was maddeningly patient, and I matched his patience. Rarely has there been so polite and well-managed double fury. But out of it I began to speak, to surface what I felt about the character in *Little Caesar*. It was not, I told him, merely a hokey-pokey cheap shot; it was rather a Greek tragedy. Inherent in it was the drama of the humblest, the most dispossessed, seeking to break his way out of the anonymity of ignorance, toward a goal in which he would not be one of many men but a man of his own. I even spilled some of my own longings that were parallel. Though Rico's goals were immoral and antisocial, and I had confined myself within stringent palings, we had this in common—somehow we would be different, above, higher. While I hoped the gods would not destroy me for my own ambition, they would surely destroy Rico, and in his death throes he would cry the eternal wail: "Mother of God, is this the end of Rico?"*

Hal listened carefully to my ravings, made a few notes, then reminded me that my contract gave me no approval of roles. Were I to refuse Otero, I could be put on suspension and no other studio would be able to use me—and no theatrical producer either.

Having made these points, thus asserting his contractual authority, Hal then said he would take the matter up with Mr. Warner, and within a matter of hours I was cast as Little Caesar. I think—and my memory may be faulty—that as a consideration I extended my contract. If I am wrong about this, I apologize to Hal. And I do now what I have never done before. I thank him for *Little Caesar*.

---

*That line, so often quoted, was actually shot two ways, and the way most of you hear it now on television and even in theaters then, is "Mother of *Mercy*, is this the end of Rico?"

Humphrey Bogart and Edward G. Robinson in Key Largo *(1948), Warner Bros.*

MACK SENNETT

Mack Sennett.

**Born Michael Sinnott on January 17, 1880 in Quebec Province . . . Parents
working-class Irish immigrants . . . Broke into burlesque as chorus boy . . . First
film: *Balked at the Altar* (1908) . . . Learned directing from D. W. Griffith
. . . Formed Keystone Studios in 1912 . . . At his "fun factory" created the
"Keystone Kops" . . . Produced 285-pound Fatty Arbuckle's best comedies
. . . Directed Charlie Chaplin, Buster Keaton, W. C. Fields, and Bing Crosby
. . . Perfected the quintessential American art of slapstick in *The Mistaken Masher*
(1913) . . . Awarded Special Academy Award in 1937 . . . Died 1960.**

How to Throw a Pie

When I started these recollections, I opened up with some remarks that might be taken as unbecoming and even downright immodest. I claimed that it had been a long, tired time since any citizens had been rolled in the aisles of a motion-picture house or had been doubled up with laughter while watching television comedians. I was implying, of course, that my own comedies truly murdered the people.

Don't get me wrong. It wasn't me, the Old Man, who was so funny; it was the comical people I had around me. I called myself "King of Comedy," a solemn and foolish title if there ever was one, but I was a harassed monarch. I worried most of the time. It was only in the evenings that I laughed.

I sat in a heavy, creaking rocking chair in the rear of my screening room at Keystone and examined our dizzy productions with a hard eye. When there was anything to laugh at I rocked back and forth with the contented rhythm of a broad-beamed Percheron in a bareback riding act. I seldom needed to say much to my writers, gag men, and actors. They watched the rhythm of the rocker. When I was in full gallop, they assumed that everything was as ridiculous as it should be. If I didn't rock and roar as the rushes went on the screen, everybody took it for granted that the work of art under eye was no good. Then we'd shoot scenes over again.

My main contribution to motion-picture comedy seems to have resided in my boiling point. I was equipped with a natural, built-in thermostat. It turned out that when I got up a full head of steam over a film and began to roll and spout, millions of movie-goers were likely to react the same way. I was a reliable one-man audience.

Since I did produce the Keystone Comedies, it turns out that I have been credited with considerably more inventiveness than I actually possessed. For instance, historians of the drama put me down for the creation of what was once a distinguished facet of cineplastic art—pie-throwing. I'd be glad to claim this honor, if I could claim it honestly, since a pie in the face represents a fine, wish-fulfilling, universal idea, especially in the face of authority, as in cop or mother-in-law. Also, those sequences in which we started building from the tossing of one pie, quickly increasing the tempo and the quantity until we had dozens of pastries in flight across the screen simultaneously, were wholesome releases of nervous tension for the people and made them laugh. But honor for the pie is not mine. It belongs to Mabel Normand.

Mabel was always shown on the screen as a comedy girl, usually poor and unfashionable, whose fate was to find herself surrounded by ruffians, villains and amiable boobs such as Ben Turpin, Ford Sterling, or 285-pound "Fatty" Arbuckle.

As our story would begin to release doses of our stock commodity, pandemonium, Miss Normand would invariably be caught in the middle.

But one afternoon in Edendale we were having trouble shooting the simplest possible kind of a scene. Ben Turpin had to stick his head through a door. Since Mr. Turpin's eyes were aimed in all directions, we thought the scene would be funny. It wasn't.

"Don't look into the camera," I instructed Ben. "This is the kind of quick scene we throw away, casual-like."

Turpin stared at me, or approximately at me, with the affronted dignity of a Wagnerian soprano ordered to conceal her tonsils.

"Shoot the eyes! Shoot the eyes!" he squalled. "What do millions of people go to movies for?"

If Turpin had ever seen the Mona Lisa he could have explained an ancient mystery. He would have claimed she was about to break out laughing at him.

Ben squinted, peered, and mouthed, but still the scene was not comical. Suddenly it was one of the funniest shots ever flashed on any motion-picture screen.

Mabel, who had nothing to do with this sequnce, had been watching. She was sitting quietly, minding her own business for once, when she found a pie in her hand. It was a custard pie.

Miss Normand was not startled. At Keystone you were likely to find anything in your hand from a lion to a raw egg. You were as likely to meet an ape on the sidewalk as Gloria Swanson. If you were unwary you were likely to get a shock treatment in the seat of the trousers, mustard in your make-up, or a balloonful of water on your head. We lived our art.

As it turned out, the projectile in Mabel's hand was neither a joke nor an accident. Two carpenters were having custard for dessert. Mabel sniffed, and was inspired.

She weighed and hefted the pastry in her right palm, considered it benevolently, balanced herself on the balls of her feet, went into a windup like a big-league pitcher, and threw. Motion-picture history, millions of dollars, and a million laughs hung on her aim as the custard wabbled in a true curve and splashed with a dull explosion in Ben Turpin's face.

No one expected this memorable heave, least of all Turpin. The grinding camera, going sixteen frames to the second, was full on him. When the custard smote him, Ben's face was as innocent of anticipation as a plate. His aplomb vanished in a splurch* of goo that drooled and dripped down his shirt front. As the camera held on him his magnificent eyes emerged, batting in stunned outrage in all directions.

Worse luck for scholars, I don't remember the name of the picture in which the first custard was thrown. The date would have been sometime in 1913. But if we failed in later years to understand the long words laid on us by heavy-duty professors who explain our art to us, we knew a good thing when we saw it, seized upon pie-

---

Splurch: A technical and onomatopoetic word coined by Mack Sennett; applies only to the effect of sudden custard in the puss.

throwing, refined it, perfected its techniques, and presented it to the theater as a new art. It became, in time, a learned routine like the pratt-fall, the double-take, the slow burn, and the frantic leap, all stock equipment of competent comedians. When the Turpin pie scene was shown that night in a screening room we saw at once why it was funny.

It was funny, not only because a pie in the face is an outrage to pumped-up dignity, but because Turpin received the custard without a flick of premonition. Non-anticipation on the part of the recipient of a pastry is the chief ingredient of the recipe. And it takes an actor with a stern artistic conscience to stand still and innocent, never wagging an eyelash, while a strong man takes aim at him with such ammunition.

If you don't run with show people you may find this incredible, but it is a fact that many actors are frustrated because they never had a chance to display their integrity and facial control by taking a pie. Franklin Pangborn, for instance, a gentle comedian and a fine artist, pined for many years to receive a custard. When he finally worked for me, we had to write in a scene for him in which he got splurched. Frank did well, too, but he said being pushed backwards into swimming pools while wearing top hat and cutaway was more in his line.

We became scientists in custard. A man named Greenburg, who ran a small restaurant-bakery near the studio, became a throwing-pie entrepreneur. Our consumption was so enormous that this man got rich. After several experiments he invented a special Throwing Pie, just right in heft and consistency, filled with paste, and inedible. He lost most of his eating customers when he began to sell them throwing custards by mistake.

Del Lord, my ace comedy director, soon became the world-champion pie tosser. And "Fatty" Arbuckle, who in spite of his suet was an agile man—the kind of fat man known as light on his feet—became a superb pie pitcher. Arbuckle was ambidextrous and had double vision like a T-formation quarterback. He could throw two pies at once in different directions, but he was not precise in this feat. The Christy Mathewson of the custard was Del Lord.

"This is a delicate and serious art," says Mr. Lord, "and not one in which amateurs or inexperienced fingers should try to win renown. Pie-throwing, like tennis or golf, which depend upon form, requires a sense of balance and a definite follow-through.

"Actually, you don't throw like a shortstop rifling to first base. You *push* the pie toward a face, leaning into your follow-through. Six or eight feet is the limit for an artistic performance.

"You must never let the actor know when you're going to give him the custard in the choppers. Even the most skillful actor, José Ferrer or John Gielgud, for instance, finds it difficult to conceal anticipation.

"The wisest technique is to con your victim into a sense of security and then slip it to him.

"In my day, when I was the acknowledged world-champeen pie heaver, I developed a prejudice for berries with whipped cream. After the actual whomp in the face, the berries trickle beautifully down the actor's shirt and the whipped cream besplashes his suit. This is muddy, frothy, and photogenic."

Soon after we discovered that a pie is as theatrical a device as Bette Davis's handkerchief or Cyrano's nose, we made a picture called *The Great Pie Mystery*. Pies are thrown every time the heavy would try to do dirt to the girl or the comic. Pies came from everywhere and the audience couldn't see who was throwing them. Our pay-off gag was that the fellow who began telling the story in the first scene was throwing the pies.

We also invented a way to throw pies around telephone poles. We did this by having an expert fly caster out of camera range atop a stepladder. After a little practice he could let fly with a nod and reel and make a pie do a figure eight before it hit a guy in the face.

As I was saying a while back, we demanded at least some kind of motivation in our pictures. Always the improbable, never the impossible. The introduction of pie-throwing was no stumbling block at all to our scenerio writers. They simply inserted a restaurant or a bakery into the scene whenever it seemed like a good idea to fling a pie.

Alma Burnett, Harry Gibbon and Harry Myers in The Great Pie Mystery *(ca. 1913), Keystone.*

OMAR SHARIF

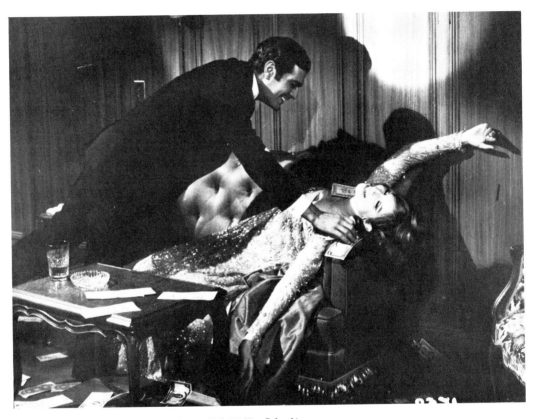

Omar Sharif and Barbra Streisand in Funny Girl *(1968), Columbia.*

Born Michel Shalhouz on April 10, 1932 in Alexandria, Egypt . . . Father a prosperous timber merchant . . . Converted to Islam . . . Broke into international films and received Academy Award nomination for *Lawrence of Arabia* (1962) . . . Other credits include: *Genghis Khan* (1965) . . . *Doctor Zhivago* (1966) . . . *Funny Girl* (1968) . . . *Che!* (1969) . . . *The Tamarind Seed* (1973) . . . One of the world's leading bridge players.

The Eternal Male

My kisses on the screen sometimes had terrible consequences.

The first kiss led to marriage; the second one practically cost me my citizenship.

In 1967, I was making a western in Hollywood—*Mackenna's Gold*—and I used to have lunch in the studio canteen every day. And every day producer Ray Stark and director William Wyler used to sit down at the next table. They were getting ready to do *Funny Girl* and had begun casting. Barbra Streisand, who'd created the play on Broadway, would be making her movie debut. They were looking for a co-star.

That wasn't such an easy assignment. The screenplay was built around Barbra. What actor would agree to play her straight man?

Fanny Brice sang, cracked jokes, fascinated the audiences; Nick Arnstein (her shady gambler husband) had to content himself with giving her her cues and looking good in a tuxedo, something that didn't improve matters at all. Apparently it was no cinch to find an actor who could look relaxed in a tuxedo. I just happened to be one of those rare individuals, something that started people in the studio canteen joking: "Why not Omar Sharif?"

You can't understand what made this such a big joke, unless you know that *Funny Girl* is set in a Jewish neighborhood of Brooklyn and that it's about a Jewish boy and a Jewish girl. But that didn't matter—they kept up the "Why not Omar Sharif?" campaign.

One day William Wyler reacted. "Well, *why not* Omar Sharif, anyway?" The question had its impact. Dumfounded, they all looked at him. So he repeated, "Yes, that's an idea. Why not? Think about it," he said, turning to me. "It's not such a bad idea at that."

We thought about it and, after thinking it over, became convinced that the idea was a good one. The producer of *Mackenna's Gold* agreed to speed up the shooting so I could be free sooner, and I signed my contract.

That was in 1967. A few days later Arabs and Israelis were locked in the Six-Day War. All the investments in the production were Jewish. The atmosphere of the studio was pro-Israeli and my co-star was Jewish.

Most of the newspapers backed Israel. And I was an Egyptian. An Egyptian from Nasser's regime, one of the Colonel's fellow citizens.

A wave of panic swept over the set. Barbra's mother declared outright, "My daughter isn't going to work with any Egyptian!" Ray Stark spoke of breaking my contract. Fortunately William Wyler, who was also Jewish, reacted strenuously: "We're in America, the land of freedom, and you're ready to make yourselves guilty of the same things we're against? Not hiring an actor because he's Egyptian is outrageous. If Omar doesn't make the film I don't make it either!"

Undecided up to then, Streisand agreed. The producers assigned me a P.R. man of my own. He was to watch over interviews that I'd do, check any statements I made, rectify any tactlessness, if there was any. I cheerfully consented.

The shooting of *Funny Girl* went ahead normally. No newspaper or magazine stressed my nationality; none tried to link my country, my role, and the Six-Day War. Everything went smoothly until the day Barbra and I had to rehearse a love scene.

A New York newspaper ran a photo of it and the photo wound up in Cairo. The Egyptian press got hold of the picture and mounted a campaign aimed at revoking my citizenship. I was declared a traitor to my country because I'd kissed a Jewish girl who'd given a gala to raise funds for Israel. The Cairo press knew nothing about our movie, but they still declared it pro-Israeli—just to make sure.

I got a phone call from the Associated Press.

"What do you think of those articles in the Egyptian papers?"

"I don't make a point of asking a girl her nationality, her occupation, or her religion before kissing her—either on the screen or off."

AP also asked Barbra the same question.

"You really think the Egyptians are angry?" she asked in reply. "You should see the letter I got from my aunt Rose." On the spur of the moment, she'd dreamed up an Aunt Rose who lived in Egypt.

Everybody played along with it. *Funny Girl* came out. I was very sad. All wars make me sad. I'm anti-nationalist and I disapprove of religious fanaticism. I hate racism. I hate anything that could lead one group of people to have contempt for another group of people.

The Six-Day War concerned me personally. I've got blood in my veins and that blood had something to do with the feelings that beset me. Yet I knew—I was convinced of it—that someone, something would stop the Israeli-Arab conflict. I tried to reason logically, dispassionately.

The racial question—what a good excuse! It's never raised in vain. Race? It's something we can see. We're born white, we're born yellow, we're born red. They drum color into our heads. And as if that weren't enough, they brainwash us with ideas about good and evil, ideas about wealth and poverty and what not. And, on top of family, class, and race, they add religion! I'm not talking about religious feeling or belief in God. I'm talking about what the various churches do to our feelings and beliefs.

I used to live in an Islamic world, and in catechism class they taught me that, without baptism, I would have kept the stigma of original sin! In that case, were my Mohammedan pals still tainted by the sin of Adam? The priest affirmed this with such authority and conviction that I came close to believing him.

It's the same with nationalism that brainwashes people with a scrap of cloth called a *flag*, with the infantile words of a childish anthem. Doesn't false patriotism creep into sports in the United States? I've never managed to go to a baseball game without hearing the national anthem played to remind everyone that America is the best country in the world. As if the United States wasn't a big enough country to forgo such nonsense! As if it made sense to give millions of people the idea that they enjoy some immense privilege simply by virtue of being born American!

How do we overcome this religious, patriotic, and racist conditioning? How? By love. By loving people. If we just tried to love one another a little, really . . .

As to carnal love, they've never found a substitute for it. Not that I place primordial importance on it. Not that it occupies such a big part in my life. No. For me, making love is something besides momentary pleasure. Don't get me wrong—it isn't something I could forgo. I'm not trying to pass myself off as asexual. But there's lots more to sex than mere gratification. It's never an end in itself.

In view of my reputation for being a lady-killer, this may come as a surprise. But I say, "Down with legends!" I can't understand why some men have to make conquests, unless it's a false virility or a lack of affection.

At the risk of being more candid than I'm given credit for, I'll say that the sex lives of my fellow men are completely shaped by the Oedipus complex. What man has never felt the need (or the desire) to cry on a woman's shoulder? What is the ultimate goal of the lady-killer, if not to find solace in a woman's arms? What have I been looking for? I have never been able to stick to the same woman for long! And yet each of those women has awakened in me love that was deep and sincere (perhaps even purified by physical love).

Making love? It's communion with a woman. The bed is the holy table. There I find passion—and purification. For me, one love drives away another and the woman who's inspiring that love at the time fills my entire world. She's never an object. Unless, perhaps, a sacred object that I put up on a pedestal.

If you believe what reporters make up about me on the basis of remarks taken out of context (but that's the name of the newspaper game, I suppose), I give the impression of making pat statements on the female world. Based on those articles, people could get the idea that I have contempt for the weaker sex. The truth is, I worship women . . . but a certain type of woman. The kind who can use both her intelligence and her femininity. A woman mustn't contradict me openly. She must prove to me, by some means which I prefer not to know, that I'm wrong, and make me change my mind. For instance, by saying to me, "You're right, dear, but don't you think that . . ." Confronting me head on, a woman gives me the impression that she's emasculating me.

On the other hand—and I don't think this can be written off as Middle Eastern atavism—I can contradict a woman because I'm a man and because arrogance is in the nature of men.

I don't understand militant feminism of the women's lib type at all, although I can see its historical justification. It's altogether likely that, if there were no women's lib, a good many changes, rational ones, would never be made. But I'm talking about my own life, my relationships with women, outside the general context, and in this respect I don't give a damn about the world. I'm only concerned with the circles that I move in and, in this limited sphere, I meet women I like. I try to get to know them and to go to bed with them. After tearing myself down, I must admit there's also a positive side to my maleness—I always succeed in having my way. And I make women happy, with the tenderness, love, and thrills I give them. The fact that I'm a movie star, my looks, my prestige—none of that counts. I'm going to be blunt: I get any woman I want because I give all of myself. And who can refuse so much human warmth? Giving, consoling, protecting, guiding—these are a man's privileges. Take them away and you take away his male prerogatives.

The woman, for her part, must give the impression that she needs the man . . . even if she's perfectly capable of running her own life. That's when a woman shows intelligence and femininity.

In this regard, there's one more thing I want to set straight with my fans. People would have them believe that Omar Sharif, the modern seducer, considers women inferior beings. That's untrue. I know from experience that a woman's intellectual level is often higher than her mate's. More than half of the world's learning comes to us from women. Having said this, I can't go along with the idea of a girl using her gray matter to compete with men. I'd say that she isn't being femininely intelligent.

That's one charge I can't level against Barbra Streisand.

Actually, while *Funny Girl* makes me remember an unfortunate political situation, it's also connected to a wonderful love story.

Barbra Streisand, who struck me as being ugly at first, gradually cast her spell over me. I fell madly in love with her talent and her personality. The feeling was mutual for four months—the time it took to shoot the picture. How many of my affairs seemed to last till the end of a shooting!

Barbra's villa served as our trysting place. At the time, my own villa housed my family. We spent our evenings, our weekends at her place. Our contracts ruled out any travel. The lives of movie stars—at any rate, their movements—are limited by the restrictions imposed by insurance companies that won't accept responsibilities other than those actually involved in making a film.

So, inside those Hollywood confines (about which aspiring young actors dream so much), we led the very simple life of people in love. Nobody could be more conventional, more discreet than a pair of lovers. That's something for prudes to think about.

We used to cook. When I'd used up all my Italian recipes—notably, ones for various pasta dishes which I can cook and season quite well—Barbra would heat TV dinners. I adore Italian food but only eat spaghetti in Italy or when I've cooked it myself. If I get the urge to order spaghetti anywhere else, I go back into the kitchen to supervise the operation. You see, pasta needs lots of room to swim around in a big pot full of water. That way, it doesn't all stick together. Any kind of pasta has to be tasted every few minutes so you can tell when it's been cooked enough. Sixty seconds too long and it's not fit to be eaten. I can't swear to it, but Sophia Loren's fine Italian cooking must have spoiled me.

So Barbra and I would enjoy simple food; then, relaxed in our armchairs, we'd watch television. We seldom went anywhere for supper. The first time, I recall, was at Gregory Peck's place. Greg and I had become friends in the course of making two pictures together. His wife, a Frenchwoman for whom I felt great affinity, had strengthened these bonds. I still see them both whenever I stop in Hollywood.

Like everyone else, Greg knew nothing about the affair Barbra and I were having, and he had invited me over. So I asked him if I could bring somebody with me. I knew he wouldn't let the news out. But if even one reporter happened to be there, that could have ended a romance which had been delightful (for me, at least)—and all too short.

The years have gone by and I say to myself that Fanny Brice loved the hero of the movie, that she didn't love Omar Sharif, that I loved the heroine . . . that I didn't love Barbra Streisand. It often happens that way. Isn't fiction more fascinating than reality? How pleasant, how easy it is to fall in love with my female co-stars: I've had so many of these ephemeral romances. Whenever I make a movie I become one with the character I'm portraying. Which amounts to saying that it's hard to stop loving the minute the director says, "Cut." It's hard to play love scenes all day and then drop into apathy at night. My co-star is beautiful, they ask me to love her for weeks, for months—and I'm supposed to change my feelings as I get back into my street clothes. Well, I can't always do it. You see, I'm in love because I'm available and sentimental. Because I'm in love with love.

But have I really loved? I don't know, since I've never suffered from love. They say I'm pathologically unfaithful. No. I'm never unfaithful. I simply fall in love a lot, often and fast.

ROBERT STACK

Robert Stack and Deanna Durbin in First Love *(1939), Universal.*

Born Robert Modini on January 13, 1919 in Los Angeles . . . Educated at University of Southern California . . . Socialite mother . . . Ad man father coined the slogan "The beer that made Milwaukee famous" . . . National skeet shooting champion at seventeen . . . Broke into movies with *First Love* (1939) as "the first boy to kiss Deanna Durbin" . . . Best known as Eliot Ness on TV's *The Untouchables* . . . Once shared an apartment with John F. Kennedy.

The Kiss Heard 'Round the World

Whenever I am asked about the beginning of my movie career in Hollywood, I have to say that I began not in Hollywood but in Universal City.

Universal City is unique in many respects. Perhaps the only city in the world founded specifically to produce motion pictures, it is located near Studio City, a Los Angeles suburb.

Today Universal City is also a major tourist attraction, with a large hotel and guided tours for the public. A ticket entitles the bearer to a tram ride around the lot, a chance to watch an exhibition of movie stunts and special effects, and even an opportunity to catch a glimpse of Universal's current reigning superstar, the shark from *Jaws*.

Universal City is not geographically part of Hollywood. It was founded in 1915 by Carl Laemmle, the president of Universal Pictures, whose private name for the studio's large tract of land in the San Fernando Valley was "the bottomless pit." The treaty which ceded California to the United States was signed on this location in 1847. On this historic piece of real estate, Laemmle proceeded to build a unique empire.

In the early days, tourists were invited to sit in grandstands and watch the filming. They could buy peanuts and watch the flocks of white chickens which were Laemmle's pride and joy. (Employees could buy eggs from the studio at a discount.)

As the head of the studio, Carl Laemmle was a feisty and colorful man who began his career in pictures by winning a legal battle with the monopolistic "trust," a group of pioneer film companies which controlled the fledgling movie industry.

Throughout the studio, everyone knew who was boss. Only five feet tall, Laemmle had provided Universal with its name after spotting a truck advertising "Universal Pipe Fittings." Even the signs which said Keep Off The Grass displayed his personal signature. Producers and directors had to mind their manners when talking to their office boys. Anyone on the lot might be a relative of the man known affectionately as "Uncle Carl."

One of Laemmle's unknown relatives was William Wyler, who went on to become one of Hollywood's most celebrated directors, and my boss at Liberty Productions.

Like most heads of studios, Uncle Carl enjoyed the limelight. On one occasion he was involved in negotiating the most unusual contract ever suggested in Hollywood—an on-camera appearance by Pope Pius XI. Uncle Carl was enthusiastic about the idea of photographing His Holiness making a Papal statement to the world. When the Vatican requested that the studio make a sizable donation to charity in lieu of compensation, Laemmle, in characteristic fashion, sent a telegram to his European representative: "Forget Pope!"

After running the studio for a number of years, in 1929 he announced his chosen successor, who was, not surprisingly, Carl Laemmle, Jr. He gave the studio to his son as a birthday present. The younger Laemmle, called "Junior" by everyone, was only twenty-one, but he was determined to leave his mark on the studio. It was during his regime that the studio produced such classic horror films as *Dracula* with Bela Lugosi and *Frankenstein* with Boris Karloff.

Eventually, the studio ran into a dire financial crisis and was sold in 1936 to a group of financiers. When I arrived at Universal in 1939 the studio was no longer in the Laemmle family. The new owners had discovered over seventy friends and relatives of Uncle Carl on the payroll—including more than one who would have had to come back from the great beyond to collect a paycheck. To replace the Laemmle regime, the new owners decided that the studio needed a major new asset, a superstar who could save Universal. They found one in a pretty twelve-year-old girl with an incredible singing voice. Her name was Deanna Durbin. Born Edna Mae Durbin, Deanna began her astonishing career in Winnipeg, Canada. In late 1935, MGM was searching for a girl who could play Ernestine Schumann-Heink, the celebrated opera singer, as a child. Deanna's voice had captivated everyone at Metro, including Maestro Andrés de Segurola, the Spanish opera singer and vocal coach consulted by the studio. A mustachioed bass who had toured Europe and directed Havana's national theater, de Segurola said that young Deanna had the voice of a fully mature adult. He became her teacher, and the studio was enthusiastic. Louis B. Mayer decided to dispense with the name Edna Mae, and since she was called D.D. by her friends, Deanna quickly acquired a new name.

Unfortunately, Ernestine Schumann-Heink died, the project was abandoned, and Deanna left MGM. She continued studying with Maestro de Segurola, however. She was given the lead in *Three Smart Girls*, and eventually turned up in a Universal feature *100 Men and a Girl*. This film, about a girl who organized an orchestra and persuaded Leopold Stokowski to conduct it, became a smash hit. At fourteen, Deanna Durbin became what is today called a superstar. Stores sold merchandise bearing her name. Toys and school supplies using her name or face were found everywhere. A national fan club which called its members "Deanna Durbin Devotees" began following her every move. A journal (naturally called *Deanna's Diary*) reported the tiniest details of her activities. Everything from what Deanna ate for breakfast to her handwriting (which was analyzed by a graphologist) was eagerly awaited by thousands of people. The school board assigned a private tutor to work with her because it was impossible for her to go to school without creating a major traffic hazard.

Away from the set, Deanna was quiet and reserved. It was understandable that she try to preserve whatever aspects of her private life she could, since the public was never far behind. To her fans, she was always the girl next door. But her home life could hardly be called that of the typical American girl. She lived in an Italian villa near the estates of W. C. Fields and Cecil B. DeMille. Her home was a maze of terraced gardens and lily ponds. There was a large swimming pool, and even an economic waterfall which turned on and off, courtesy of a handy push button.

For those of little memory or too young to recall, Deanna Durbin was a motion picture phenomenon. Barbra Streisand, Faye Dunaway, and Raquel Welch together wouldn't have had the impact she had as America's sweetheart, that darling girl with the golden voice. Perhaps the innocence of the late thirties in America had something to do with it.

Every parent wanted her for a daughter, and every young man felt sure he was the one to break through that curtain of sweetness and carry her off in his Hudson Terraplane. More to the point, she was "big box office." Universal Studios kept its gates open just because the bank held Deanna's contract as collateral. All America was up in arms over Deanna's growing up and having her first screen kiss.

Deanna had been maturing despite the studio's desperate measures. Nature was endowing her with a blouseful of goodies, as my racy older brother would say. The studio wardrobe department was doing everything possible to keep her thirteen years old forever. Suffice it to say, nature won! This presented a problem of monumental proportions. She was going to have to be allowed to grow up. Ninety percent of all child stars did not successfully make the transition into adult stardom, but every effort was to be made to carry Deanna through this dangerous time.

Someone came up with the idea of creating a Cinderella story around her. It wasn't exactly original, but it was suitable. Prince Charming had to be an unknown, prefabricated by the studio, a prince consort beyond reproach, or at least beyond any escapade reported by Louella or Hedda. Coincidentally, I was taking voice lessons from Deanna's singing teacher Maestro Andrés de Segurola. I managed to improve my sound from a bullfrog's croak to the mating call of an Irish wolfhound. In despair, the good maestro suggested that I visit Deanna on the set to hear how the human voice was capable of sounding. My eyes had hardly grown accustomed to the sound stage, when a short, sandy-haired gentleman sidled over to me and said, "Wunderbar, would you like to be in the movies?" I looked around, wondering who might be the subject of this query. When I realized he was looking at me, I said "of course," never giving it a second thought.

The man was Joe Pasternak, one of Hollywood's most powerful producers. No one could have been more surprised than I. Universal had been looking for months for Prince Charming, and Pasternak thought I was it. I didn't feel very charming when I overcame my initial delight and found out what was in store for me.

First came a photographic test. I sat on a piano stool, while someone lying on his back on the floor spun me around. Academy Award winner Joe Valentine was the cinematographer. He kept things moving with comments like: "My God, look at that profile. Okay, spin him around. Full face is no better. Okay, spin him . . . The other profile is worse . . . Spin him!" He went on and on and on! "At least the back of his head is okay," he concluded.

I felt a natural enough temptation to jump off the piano stool and give Joe Valentine a knuckle sandwich. But before I knew what was happening, I found myself being pulled onto a sound stage for an acting test. The girl assigned to test with me was Helen Parrish, one of Deanna Durbin's regulars, a gorgeous face with body to match. One look at Helen convinced me that I had been rewarded for not giving Joe Valentine a black eye. This was more like it!

When the verdict was handed down from the front office, the news was good. Universal had found a thoroughly unsuspecting Prince Charming, profile and all. Deanna Durbin had her first screen lover, and I had a new career. The year was 1939. The major stars who had known me as a champion skeet shooter were quick to recognize that Clark Gable and the other sex symbols had nothing to fear. ("We've lost a good shot and probably gained a lousy actor," said Spencer Tracy, expressing their basic point of view!)

On the set of *First Love*, Deanna was completely self-contained, courteous, private, almost aloof, off camera. On camera, she had the luster very few in our profession possess, particularly in musical numbers. The plots of her films were adjusted to give her a chance to sing a variety of arias. I remember her singing "One Fine Day," from *Madame Butterfly*. In this scene, Cinderella thought she had lost her prince. At the end of the scene, she saw me, the tears running down her face.

She rushed toward me, we embraced, and the film ended. It was a good thing the cameras were over my shoulder. The crew and I were welling up, right along with her. She could be very convincing. But all was not beer and skittles. Although a star is always present when his or her scenes are being shot, they sometimes leave the set if someone else is being photographed in close-up, and let the script girl read their lines. Deanna's penchant for leaving the set after her close-ups led to my first love scene with a blackboard.

Henry Koster was the director, a gifted man, and he did his best. He said, "All right, Bobby, do you see this chalk mark?"

I nodded.

"That's Deanna," he continued. "Now you see her. You notice she's pretty. Now she's beautiful. Now she looks at you."

The chalk mark didn't smile or say anything.

Koster continued to rhapsodize while he expected me to gaze at the chalk mark in rapt attention.

"You love her. You adore her."

No matter how many times I looked at that lousy cross, it never looked like Deanna to me. After a couple of hours, my right eye began turning in like a part-time Chester Conklin. This was my introduction to the world of illusion.

One of the reviewers of the movie later singled me out in this scene as the most promising new romantic lead to emerge in a long time. Happily, she attributed my myopic, slightly cross-eyed look, to passion, not confusion and boredom with a blackboard.

Movie makeup was full of surprises for a young man unaccustomed to worrying much about his looks. One day, before shooting began on *First Love*, I was ambling down the main street of Universal. I saw a white-smocked gentleman beckoning to me from a doorway. I walked over to see what he wanted and, instead of the customary "hello," he said, "Step in here and let me look at you." Curious, I obeyed him.

He led me by the arm to a sterile white operating room filled with what looked like hundreds of decapitated heads. On closer examination, the decapitated heads were wig stands on which makeup men stick the hair, beards, mustaches, and such, when actors go home.

"You know," he said, pushing me into a makeup chair, "no blond has ever made it as a leading man."

By now I began to get the queasy feeling I should have kept on walking.

"Wavy hair looks feminine," he added, pulling the mysterious tools of his trade from the many drawers that surrounded him. Finally, with eyes squinted, looking like a hawk who has spotted the hen-house door open, he said, "Did anyone ever tell you you have an inverted hair line?"

I was nearly convinced I was in the hands of a nut who had escaped from a nearby sanitorium, white smock and all. As I looked desperately around the room for means of escape, my eye stopped on a familiar golden statuette: FOR OUTSTANDING ACHIEVEMENT IN MAKEUP TO JACK PIERCE (the Oscar!).

I sighed a nervous breath of relief and settled back into the chair.

What other actors had the honor of having an Academy Award winner as makeup man? Jack Pierce was one of Hollywood's greatest makeup men, but his most famous creations were the title characterizations in *Dracula* (for Bela Lugosi), the *Invisible Man* (for Claude Rains), and those stalwart matinee idols in *The Mummy* and *Wolfman*. Jack Pierce's most famous creation was, however, the Frankenstein monster played by Boris Karloff.

At this time all the major studios tried to duplicate the trademarks of success. If Gable was king at the moment, ever new actor tried desperately to furrow his brow and do Clark's famous "Gable gargle." No matter what a young actor (or young actress) might look like, every effort was made to bend nature in the direction of a sure thing.

When Jack Pierce got his hands on me, Robert Taylor was the reigning star of the moment. With me in his clutches now, Pierce began casually enough with, "let me show you how you'd look with darker hair. Don't worry," he added, "it's only a rinse; it'll wash right out."

After a short procedure, there I was, a Latin with black, wavy hair and blue eyes.

"So far so good," said Mr. Pierce. "But that wavy hair ruins the effect. Let's take out some of that wave to give you more strength. Don't worry, it'll only last a few hours."

Now out came a device familiar to many a lady of an earlier period: a curling iron, or in my case, an uncurling iron. This seemed hardly the image for a character who spent his life playing polo, lifting weights, or shooting skeet, so I made him draw the curtains so no one would witness this last experiment. When he was finished the result was far from spectacular. My hair now had the texture of a wire brush, and my expression of muted horror did little to enhance the picture. Jack seemed to think it looked great, and maybe it did, compared to the lead in *The Phantom of the Opera*.

Rather desperately, I convinced him I thought it looked fine, but I argued that since the studio had signed me the way he had found me an hour before, I didn't want to give them a surprise, even such a nifty one, my first week at Universal.

With a smile worthy of Father Christmas, he instantly made preparations for the reparation. He washed my hair for a few mintues and then I heard a muted chuckle.

"Isn't that funny," he said. "I haven't done that since I was an apprentice."

My face was under water, so I let him go on.

"Most of the actors want the effect to last through a movie. I guess I forgot this was only a temporary job."

I finally surfaced and sputtered, "What?"

"You see," he explained, "I should have straightened the hair first. When you use a hot iron on the rinse it sets it like a dye."

"You mean . . ." I stammered.

"Yes, you now have straight black hair," he smiled encouragingly. "I think it's an improvement."

Over what? I thought.

"Well, anyway, now that we've fixed most of what's wrong," he said, "let's finish the job. Let's fix that inverted hairline."

My hairline had never been such an object of scorn before, but by now I figured, what the hell, why not?

He took a small triangular piece of black hair backed by hairlace, and after a few moments of adjusting and judicious trimming, he glued it to my forehead covering the offending inversion.

He stepped back, then crept toward me like a 35mm Mitchell movie camera coming in for a close-up, and then moved back again. Finally he spoke.

"*Now* you look like a movie actor!"

I opened my eyes, which I had held closed during this last experiment, and saw myself in the three-sided mirror. A complete stranger, someone I had never met but who looked vaguely familiar, looked back at me with an expression of wonder.

He looked—wait a minute—he looked just a *little*, a *very* little like Robert Taylor, seen through a funhouse mirror.

When I arrived for the first day's shooting of *First Love*, the assistant director called, "Places!" Henry Koster walked right past me yelling, "Where's Stack?" Then he turned to me and said, "Who are you?"

There was a long pause, worthy of Macready, the famous stage star whose trademark was a dramatic silence between phrases. "My God," he exclaimed, looking at the widow's peak. "What happened to you?"

On this note of confidence, I began my first motion picture. Other surprises were just around the corner. I quickly learned that *close-up* was the most magic of all show biz words, and also the most elusive. Established stars not only fought for them, but carefully considered which side of the face would be on camera, how much light shed on it, etc.

I seemed to be getting my share of close-ups in this first attempt. The studio, however, had forgotten to tell me about a time-honored Hollywood practice. All the film shot does not necessarily end up in the picture. Between the cup and the lip, slips occur in a clouded chamber called the editing room. The film cutter, or editor, as he likes to be called, does his best to see that the star of the flick is protected. Everyone else appears no more than is necessary. This is called "staying with the money."

The *First Love* premiere was unqualified madness. I prepared myself, went into shock, and the aftereffects still remain.

The studio did not allow any of us to see the rushes of *First Love*. The first time I appeared on screen that night, I had no idea who that black-haired idiot was. Whoever he was, I couldn't help wondering where he learned to speak in that weird, hollow voice.

Oh, my God, it's me! I thought to myself. *I don't look and sound like that, do I?* I contemplated sliding under my seat. But since nobody seemed to notice, I began waiting for those crucial close-ups. The camera cut in to pick up Deanna, and I leaned forward to see the shot of me that followed. I was nowhere to be seen. Suddenly, in a blinding flash, I realized that an entire scene can be played spotlighting the star, with just an astral voice and one ear representing the other actor.

The famous kiss turned out to be a bit of a letdown, too. Like a girl in a see-through blouse who keeps her arms crossed all evening, much was promised, but damn little was actually seen. The studio backed out at the last minute, cutting the kiss from a satisfying smooch of three seconds to a millisecond peck.

When *Life* magazine offered us its cover to feature the kiss, the studio turned it down as too controversial! This was the final straw. In *today's* Hollywood, Julie Christie and Warren Beatty could reprise their famous *in flagrante* love scene in *Shampoo* on the city hall steps without attracting attention from a national magazine.

As for public reaction to my debut, it followed a Hollywood tradition. The makeup department's attitude seemed appropriate for Mad Hatters and March Hares to me, but there was very definite method in their madness. The big studios felt that an actor, in order to reach the public, had to be represented in a specific mold. The mold might change from week to week, but if a specific image seemed to be working in the box office, every actor was expected to fit. If his ears, nose, or other features failed to conform, the makeup boys took over. When columnists described me as "looking like a young Robert Taylor," the studio purred with approval. Jack Pierce had succeeded.

Much of the motion picture business made no sense at all. I was accustomed to sports in which the best shot took home the trophy, and to be the best shot required a lot of practicing. But in the movie business, it's very possible for an actor to achieve the height of success before ever really learning his craft. Shortly after the premiere of *First Love*, I happened to be in a theater in New York, when a group of girls learned that Deanna's Prince Charming was in the audience. They tore down the aisles in pursuit. As I left the theater, they chased me out to the cab and, when I leapt inside, they lifted the wheels off the ground. Not entirely sure whether they found me irresistible or wanted to tear me limb from limb, I finally got away, wondering what I might have missed if I had let them catch me.

I had no idea what I had done to merit all this feminine attention, but I decided to enjoy it. In later years, I realized the incredible illogic of films. Stardom can be instant, but the phenomenon can disappear just as quickly. It depends on fate, luck, and all kinds of intangibles.

Another new element introduced in my life at that time was the fan magazine. Especially in the forties, these publications delighted in parading before the public the indiscretions and eccentricities of anyone whose face happened to appear on a movie screen. If an actor refused to be obligingly indiscreet, the magazines made up something. Any casual date could be turned into a heart-wringing passion. I'm glad that my mother saved many of these old articles about me. I enjoy them today. They're the funniest things this side of Mark Twain's Mississippi River, and their tales are twice as tall as any he ever wove.

One magazine dubbed me, "the Adonis on Wheels." Another introduced me as "the young man who committed an act of osculation with Deanna Durbin."

Sometimes, the studio publicity department planned "parties" to be attended by actors under contract and photographers. The actors were provided with noise-makers, hats, and everything else they needed to make it appear they were having a good time. The photographers would snap their pictures, and then everyone would pack up and go home. A really "wild" party might last ten minutes longer than the two hours normally required to take all the photos.

It's never a good idea to read things into photographs. At one point I had my picture taken with Lana Turner. We were supposed to be discussing Lana's interest in crocheting. (What else would a man be discussing with Lana Turner?) Lana was regarded as one of the most beautiful actresses in Hollywood. Since the premiere of *First Love*, the fan magazines had been madly speculating about the girls I dated. I asked Lana out and took her to see my racing hydroplane. The mechanics on the pier nearly fell off when they saw Lana (probably wearing one of the sweaters she crocheted) walking over to inspect my boat. Since I was involved in hydroplane racing up to my ears, I naturally assumed that Lana would be just as fascinated. I spent a marvelous evening getting the boat in racing condition. Unfortunately, I was so engrossed in what I was doing that I failed to notice that Lana—unaccustomed to being ignored, and not sharing my enthusiasm for camshafts, manifolds, and such— had simply picked up and left. (Lana and I should have stuck to crocheting.) . . .

Another vivid part of my life at that time was the Flag Room. It was on Whitley Terrace, a small curving street wandering into the Hollywood Hills, midway between Highland and Cahuenga. It came to rest in a cul-de-sac of jumbled apartments irregularly stacked on top of each other like building blocks put together by a drunk. Each apartment was perched dangerously on its neighbor. Over each apartment grew a luxurious, tangled web of vines creating a veritable Garden of Eden effect. It was here that I learned about the birds, the bees, the barracudas, and other forms of Hollywood wildlife. A friend of mine, Alfredo de la Vega, had come up with the idea that we should each convince our mothers we needed a hideaway for meditation and study. When our mothers surprisingly agreed to this arrangement, we promised ourselves to study our favorite subjects even harder than before.

One room in particular was the highpoint of our hideaway; it was guaranteed to stimulate a damsel's interest beyond anything as trite as etchings. The room itself was no bigger than a full-size bed; the ceiling was too low to allow an adult to stand fully upright. The walls and, in particular, the ceiling were plastered with flags from every nation. So no matter where you looked there was always something to hold your interest. I devised a game that required the lady of the evening to memorize the flags on the ceiling in a given time or pay the penalty. Since she was already in a horizontal position, paying the penalty was usually no problem.

Just to keep the game interesting, we kept switching the flags around so no ringers could ever memorize their order. Our landlord lived directly above us. He was a one-legged boozer of prodigious capacity who never seemed to mind the racket downstairs as long as the door was open. Around the shank of the morning, say two or three o'clock, we would hear the *clump, clump, clump* of his wooden leg as he came to collect his toll, a beer glass of straight scotch.

The Flag Room became as well known locally as the Pump Room in Chicago. De la Vega brought a nice-looking fellow to the studio one day, and introduced him as "Ambassador Kennedy's son John." I am happy to say that Jack Kennedy found occasion to further his geopolitical studies and gain future constituents at our little pad on Whitley Terrace. (When campaigning for the presidency and talking about his experience in international relations, he never publicly discussed the Flag Room. Yet Alfredo and I always believed ourselves responsible in some small way for Jack Kennedy's early interest in remembering which flag represented which country.)

In passing, I think it's worth mentioning that I've known many of the great Hollywood stars, and only a very few of them seemed to hold the attraction for women that JFK did, even before he entered the political arena. He'd just look at them and they'd tumble. I often felt like asking him why he wasted his time on politics when he could have made it big in an important business like motion pictures.

I'm not about to list the cast, since I still live in California, but suffice it to say that through those humble portals passed a guest list that ran the gamut from the chorus line to Academy Award winners to the great Oval Office.

Those were good times for me, but for all the charm and innocence of Hollywood's golden era, those times also produced unspeakable horrors and harsh realities. While I was kissing Deanna Durbin, Adolf Hitler was starting a war.

The invasion of one country after another by the Nazi armies was a stark contrast to the fresh optimism of Deanna Durbin's films. If Deanna was America's sweetheart, this reality of war was best illustrated by the fate of another young girl. In Holland, Anne Frank joined her family in a makeshift attic, to live in fear and cold terror as they hid from the Nazi barbarians.

Anne Frank is known throughout the world today for her diary, a document full of the kind of courage and strength that manages to discover love in a world riddled with hate. *The Diary of Anne Frank* was published in twenty-one languages and subsequently made into a motion picture. Anne Frank never had the opportunity to be a real-life Cinderella. She died in a concentration camp. But despite the horrors of war, she could write in her diary that people were really good at heart. Few of us remember that one of her fondest dreams was expressed in the caption for a small photograph of herself in her diary: "This is a photo as I should wish myself to look all the time. Then maybe I would have a chance to come to Hollywood." When the world discovered the possessions that this beautiful and optimistic child treasured during her family's hiding, they found my photograph. Anne Frank, like millions of other young girls, dreamed of finding her own "first love."

For all of Hollywood's departure from reality during those years, that very departure made it special. If, in some small way, the film industry brings a touch of magic to the Anne Franks of the world, our reward can only be measured in the intangible terms of human feeling.

Robert Stack and Glenn Ford in Is Paris Burning? *(1965), Paramount.*

GLORIA SWANSON

Gloria Swanson in Sunset Boulevard *(1950), Paramount.*

Born Gloria Josephine Mae Swenson on March 27, 1897 in Chicago . . . Met actor Wallace Beery by chance, married him in 1916 and went to Hollywood . . . Divorced 1919 . . . Queen of the Silent Screen in mid 1920s . . . Bank- rolled by Joe Kennedy, she made the notorious *Queen Kelly* (1928), original version unreleased until 1985 . . . *Prodigal Daughter* (1923) . . . *Sadie Thompson* (1927) . . . Early talkies unsuccessful . . . Retired 1934 . . . Made (second) comeback as Norma Desmond in *Sunset Boulevard* (1950)—Joe Gillis [William Holden]: "You were a big star once." Norma Desmond: "I'm still big. It's the pic- tures that got small."

Sunset Boulevard

When Mother and I arrived in Hollywood in January of 1949, I called my friend George Cukor before I phoned the studio and asked him if he thought it would be unreasonable of me to refuse to do a screen test. I told him I was terrible in them.

"Who's the director?" George asked.

"Billy Wilder, and the producer is someone named Charles Brackett."

"In that case, yes, it would be unreasonable. They're the brightest things at Paramount. They made *Lost Weekend* together, and *A Foreign Affair*. If they ask you to do ten screen tests, do them, or I'll personally shoot you."

Another dear friend, Alexander Tiers, gave me the same advice. So did William Powell. So did Clifton Webb. So did Allan Dwan. So did Mickey Neilan.

I was thoroughly subdued, therefore, prepared to submit to anything, when I met with Billy Wilder and Mr. Brackett the next day. Mr. Wilder and I chatted pleasantly but not at length about *Music in the Air*, our last picture together. I had had one other Hollywood failure in the fifteen intervening years, while he had become a leading writer-director who at forty-four was elfish, witty, confident, and a bit overactive. Mr. Brackett, quieter, more refined, the New York, Eastern type, was in his mid-fifties. They immediately said that I should think of the screen test as a formality, done mainly for the young man they had in mind for the lead.

"Who is that?" I asked.

"Montgomery Clift," Mr. Brackett said. "A promising new star. Excellent. Have you seen him?"

"No," I said. Then, changing the subject, I asked if I could see a script. They informed me that they had only a few pages. They were still working on the rest, they said, and hadn't even decided definitely how it would end.

"Well, what's it about?" I asked.

Mr. Brackett said it was based on a story he and Billy had written together, in which an ex–movie queen attempts to dominate a younger man, a writer, and return to pictures. There was a murder in it.

"Who murders whom?" I asked.

"We honestly aren't sure yet," Billy Wilder said. "Look over this short scene to get a feel of it," he added, handing me three typewritten sheets. "That'll be plenty for the test. We just want to have a look at you."

Several days later I ran the test with a blond young man, and Billy Wilder and Charlie Brackett registered total approval. In fact, they raved. We signed a contract a few days later. Then I rented a house on Mullholland Drive and settled in with Mother for a stay of three or four months.

Paramount soon asked me to report for some publicity pictures, and when I got there, they had me pose with Mr. Balaban, president of Paramount, and with Adolph Zukor, who was now chairman emeritus of the board. Mr. Zukor and I embraced and talked about the old days, and he said everyone was very excited about this new picture, which they were calling *Sunset Boulevard*. I asked Mr. Brackett if the script was finished, and he said not yet; in fact, they had decided to keep it very loose and compose it as they went along, adding and subtracting and changing as they saw fit.

"How about Mr. Clift?" I asked. "Is he here?"

They told me then that Montgomery Clift had objected, through his agent, to playing scenes of romantic involvement with an older woman. Therefore, they shyly asked, would I mind doing another screen test, since now their fear was that I looked too young for the man they had chosen to replace Montgomery Clift.

"And who's that?" I asked.

"William Holden," Mr. Brackett said. "Joe Gillis, the writer in the script, is supposed to be twenty-five and you're supposed to play fifty. But Bill Holden is thirty-one and nervous that you'll look too young. We may have to age you with make-up. Not too much. Just a little."

"But women of fifty who take care of themselves today don't look old," I said. "That's the point. Can't you use make-up on Mr. Holden instead, to make him look more youthful?"

They consented to try, if only out of tact, and after they looked at the test, they decided I was right. They changed Bill Holden's hair and adjusted his make-up and left me a spruced-up fifty, which was exactly my age.

By then they had more of the script for us. The story was narrated by the corpse of Joe Gillis, after it is fished out of a swimming pool on Sunset Boulevard. The script described my character, Norma Desmond, very sketchily: "She is a little woman. There is a curious style, a great sense of high voltage about her." The tone of the piece was a mixture of gothic eeriness and nostalgia for the old Hollywood of the twenties. For Norma Desmond's butler and ex-husband, they had signed Erich von Stroheim. For a group of old friends—referred to as "the waxworks" by Joe Gillis—who arrive to play bridge with Norma, they had signed Anna Q. Nilsson, H. B. Warner, and Buster Keaton.

"There's also a scene with Cecil B. De Mille," Mr. Brackett said, "and he's agreed to play himself. We're really going to mix up Hollywood then and now, real and imaginary. What do you think?"

"I don't know," I said, speaking the unveiled truth.

For Norma's house they had rented a marvelous twenties palace in the Renaissance style from Jean Paul Getty; and they were going to shoot the scenes of Mr. De Mille right on the set of the picture he was currently making, *Samson and Delilah*. Mr. De Mille's secretary told me he was having her cue him daily on his lines and that he was very nervous about appearing in front of a camera.

I told him, "Mr. De Mille, if you're just yourself, you'll be wonderful," and with that I grasped with fearful apprehension, for the first time, that the same certainly applied to me to a great extent, that I would have to use all my past experience for props, and that this picture should be a very revealing one to make, something akin to analysis.

Billy Wilder deliberately left us on our own, made us dig into ourselves, knowing full well that such a script, about Hollywood's excesses and neuroses, was bound to give the Hollywood people acting in it healthy doubts, about the material or about themselves, depending on their individual security. The more you thought about the film, the more it seemed to be a modern extension of Pirandello, or some sort of living exercise in science fiction. Early in the shooting, Bill Holden said that he needed to know more about Gillis in order to fill out the character, that the script was incomplete and unclear and therefore frustrating for him as an actor. "How much do you know about Holden?" was all Billy Wilder would say.

Edith Head and I together created perfect clothes for my character—a trifle exotic, a trifle exaggerated, a trifle out of date. For my scene with Mr. De Mille, I designed a hat with a single white peacock feather, remembering the peacock-feather headdress everyone was so superstitious about when Mr. De Mille and I made the scenes with the lions in *Male and Female*. When Billy Wilder and the set designer asked me for personal props from my own life, I thought twice but I supplied them: scores of stills in old frames; the Geza Kende portrait; an idea for a large plaid bow on my head in one scene, a bit like those Mother had me wear as a child, a bit like the ones Sennett bathing beauties wore; the fact that Mr. De Mille had usually referred to me as "young fellow."

In April, Erich von Stroheim arrived from France. We had long since reconciled our differences over *Queen Kelly*, but I hadn't seen him in eight or nine years, not since I had gone backstage in Chicago when he was in the touring company of *Arsenic and Old Lace*. He looked grand, and we reminisced for hours when Billy Wilder showed us a print of *Queen Kelly* and asked me if he could use a scene from it for a scene in *Sunset Boulevard*, where Norma and Joe are watching one of her old pictures. Of course I didn't mind, I said; it was a brilliant idea because almost no one had ever seen *Kelly*. Erich and I even decided it had weathered the years very well, glowed like a classic, and might actually be rereleased, in a version better than the one that had been tacked together in the early thirties for release principally out-side the United States.

Mr. De Mille took direction like a pro. Erich von Stroheim, on the other hand, kept adding things and suggesting things and asking if scenes might not be reshot— very much in his grand old manner of perfectionism regardless of schedule or cost. Billy Wilder always listened patiently to his suggestions, and took some, but more often he would say that he really didn't see how this or that change would improve the scene or further the story, and therefore he thought we should leave it alone. In one scene Erich, as Max, Norma's butler and chauffeur, drives her and Joe to Paramount in her old Isotta Fraschini with leopard upholstery. Erich didn't know how to drive, which humiliated him, but he acted the scene, and the action of driving, so completely that he was exhausted after each take, even though the car was being towed by ropes the whole while.

The scene where Norma plays bridge with a few old friends came closest to giving us all the creeps, but it reminded us too, once again, of exactly who we were. Anna Q. Nilsson and H. B. Warner had made several important pictures together, *One Hour before Dawn* in 1920 and *Sorrell and Son* in 1927, before Anna's career had been cut short by a riding accident. H. B. Warner had also been my leading man in *Zaza* and had played Christ in Mr. De Mille's great early biblical epic *King of Kings* in 1927. Anna had recently returned to the screen as a character actress and looked splendid, but H.B. appeared brittle, almost transparent, when he showed up. Buster Keaton, the fourth member of the bridge party, looked ravaged, as indeed he had been, by alcohol. The last time we had spent any time together, he was still married to Natalie Talmadge and I was the Marquise de la Falaise.

"Waxworks is right," Buster muttered in his unmatchable deadpan, as the four of us assembled for the scene, and we all howled with laughter.

In their brilliant script, which they unrolled for us day by day, Billy Wilder and Charlie Brackett had cleverly kept this ghostly world of oldies separate from the young Hollywood aspirants who form the other half of Joe Gillis' life; therefore, I had no scenes with Nancy Olson or Jack Webb. I only saw the rushes, and even that, in this Pirandello framework, was somehow perfectly appropriate. As for Bill Holden, he could not have been better. His craft and honesty impressed me more each day we worked together.

The atmosphere of the picture was a bit ghoulish, but Billy Wilder arranged for some marvelous light moments during the shooting. In one scene I did a Chaplin imitation, a bit like the one I did in *Manhandled* in 1924, and the wardrobe department brought in fifty derbies for me to choose from. As if that weren't funny enough, the next day when I walked on the set wearing the one I had picked, Billy Wilder and the whole crew were wearing the forty-nine that were left over. And two days later, when we shot a scene of Norma and Max burying Norma's pet chimpanzee, Mr. Wilder directed me to remove the Spanish shawl covering the chimp in the white coffin, and when I did so, the stuffed monkey was also wearing a derby.

As the weeks went by, I hated to have the picture end. None had ever challenged or engrossed me more. The final mad scene raised problems. I had to descend a grand staircase crowded with extras and a few real people like Hedda Hopper, in a state of derangement, and Billy Wilder wanted me to come down on the inside of the stairway where the steps were narrowest. On high heels I would have tripped for sure, so I played the scene barefoot. I imagined a steel ramrod in me from head to toe holding me together and descended as if in a trance. When Mr. Wilder called "Print it!" I burst into tears. I had a party planned for this last day, but then and there the cast and crew gave me one instead, right on the set. Everyone was in a great state of emotion, and Mother and Michelle and I said that night in our rented house on Mullholland Drive that there were only three of us in it now, meaning that Norma Desmond had taken her leave.

Not quite, it turned out. Preview audiences complained so strongly about the film's long opening—in which the corpse of Joe Gillis is taken to the morgue, where it converses by means of voiceovers with the other corpses and starts to tell the story—that Billy Wilder cut ninety percent of it, much as he liked the black humor of the material, and got some of us back to shoot a few replacement scenes.

That time we really did finish, and agreed unanimously that Billy Wilder had provided us all with the time of our lives. He had also brought in a blockbuster.

The evening of the first big screening in Hollywood, Louis B. Mayer had a dinner party for about twenty people. From there we went to the Paramount screening room, where the audience of three hundred people seemed to include everyone in motion pictures. I caught a glimpse of Mickey Neilan as we walked to our seats, and someone told me Mary Pickford was there. These affairs are known for being morbidly restrained, devoid of the slightest overt reaction, but that night the whole audience stood up and cheered. People clustered around me, and I had trouble moving up the aisle. Barbara Stanwyck fell on her knees and kissed the hem of my skirt. I could read in all their eyes a single message of elation: If she can do it, why should we be terrified? She's shown us that it can be done!

"Where's Mary?" I asked.

"She can't show herself, Gloria," someone said. "She's overcome. We all are."

The Paramount executives were so pleased with *Sunset Boulevard* that they asked me, long before the picture was ready for release, to do a publicity tour, ostensibly to promote one of the studio's new films, *The Heiress*, starring Olivia de Havilland, Ralph Richardson, and, ironically, Montgomery Clift. In fact, however, Paramount and all the other studios were pouring money and effort at a great rate into counteracting the bad publicity caused by the eruptions of scandal in the early months of 1950. The first of these was the nationwide uproar created by Oscar-winning Ingrid Bergman's giving birth to an illegitimate child, whose father was Roberto Rossellini, the Italian film director. Americans everywhere went purple at the thought that the good girl, the saint, the nun of pictures, should flaunt her adultery in their faces, and the studios were once again spending millions to prove that all Hollywood wasn't bad. The second source of fearful scandal was Senator Joseph McCarthy, who announced in Washington that he had lists of Communists all over America bent on the overthrow of our government. Hollywood was trembling. I personally admired Ingrid Bergman enormously for having gone ahead and had her baby, not to mention the fact that I considered her the finest actress to grace Hollywood since Greta Garbo—another Swede—had arrived in 1926. I also doubted that there were Communists hiding behind every corporation desk and director's chair. But while I spoke what I felt to my friends, I managed briefly to be a good-will ambassador for the industry, now that I had so recently, like the prodigal, returned to it, as if from the dead.

I took [my daughter] Michelle with me and toured America for Paramount, a bit as I had done with [my son] Henri in 1925. I shook hands and visited hospitals and spoke on radio and television and made appearances in movie theaters and hosted cocktail parties and posed for pictures. In Chicago I saw Virginia Bowker and talked to the media about our days at Essanay [Studios]. In Dallas I received the Neiman-Marcus Award for my contribution over the years to the world of fashion.

In Boston I had a private visit to make. I went to the gynecologist who had recommended a hysterectomy for me three years earlier. I asked him to examine me, and I studied his face intently as he did so.

"The tumor isn't there, is it?" I asked.

"No," he said uneasily.

"Don't you want to know how I got rid of it?"

"Yes," he said, "I do. How?"

"I went on a diet."

He threw back his head and laughed loudly.

"Obviously you don't understand," I said, without a trace of humor. "I stopped eating animal protein for three years and starved that tumor. If I'd listened to you, I'd be minus most of my female parts today and probably growing a beard. Therefore, I'm the one who should be laughing, Doctor, not you. Good-bye. And please, don't send me a bill."

By the time I finished the tour, I was famous all over America again. Then *Sunset Boulevard* opened at Radio City Music Hall and in theaters across the country in August 1950, and it was pronounced the best movie ever made about Hollywood. Instantly I had requests to make personal appearances everywhere, and I began to receive stacks of scripts to consider. In November I was asked to a Command Performance of *Sunset Boulevard* in London, and I took Michelle along. She was so impressed that she asked to stay on by herself and study drama, and I told her she could. In the meantime I returned to New York to begin a radio show, after signing a contract to make a film in London the following year.

I could hardly keep up with myself.

Seena Owen and Gloria Swanson in Queen Kelly *(1928, original version released 1985), United Artists.*

LANA TURNER

Lana Turner in The Postman Always Rings Twice *(1946), MGM.*

Born Julia Turner on February 8, 1920 in Wallace, Idaho . . . Discovered at a soda fountain—*not* Schwab's—while cutting typing classes at Hollywood High . . . The original "sweater girl" . . . First film: *They Won't Forget* (1937) . . . Other credits: *A Star Is Born* (1937) . . . *The Postman Always Rings Twice* (1946) . . . *Peyton Place* (1957) . . . *Imitation of Life* (1959) . . . *By Love Possessed* (1961) . . . Married first of seven husbands, Artie Shaw, in 1940 . . . Stephan Crane 1943 . . . Daughter Cheryl born in 1944 . . . Married Bob Topping in 1948 . . . Lex "Tarzan" Barker in 1953 . . . Met Johnny Stompanato in 1957 . . . "I expected to have one husband and seven babies!"

A Stab of Relief

T
he week after the Academy Awards I prepared to move into the house I'd
rented on Bedford Drive. Before I packed up my things I went through the house to
determine what else I needed. John was with me, and I mean *with me*. No matter
what I did, no matter where I went, he was a hovering presence. It was as though he
thought I'd escape somewhere if he freed me for more than an hour.

Although the house was completely furnished, even to glassware and some awful
china, I discovered there were no pots and pans or cutlery. So the day before I
moved, on March 31, I stopped by to pick up those supplies at Pioneer Hardware.
John helped me pick out the inexpensive silverware, an extra set of simple china
because mine was still in storage, and a set of kitchen knives, all to be delivered the
next day. I didn't bother to look at the carving set John selected—after all, knives
were knives to me, and he was the expert in that department.

Cheryl was on her Easter vacation from school, and she planned to spend a long
weekend helping me fix up the new house. John came with me to pick her up at my
mother's apartment. Once we got over to the new house another argument broke out.
It was the latest in the series about whether he would stay, or whether I could be
alone with Cheryl for the weekend.

Cheryl was up in her room putting some things away, and I knew she could hear us
quarreling. I kept telling John to keep quiet in case she was listening. But he got
angrier and angrier, and began to threaten me. Now I didn't doubt that Cheryl could
hear him. Finally I managed to get him out of the house, and Cheryl came down to
see me. Her little face was pinched and tight. I thought she might have been crying.

"Why does he say those things to you?" she asked. "Can't you just tell him you
don't want to see him anymore?"

"I've tried, Cheryl. Believe me, I've tried for some time."

"Then you're afraid of him. Does he hurt you, Mother?"

"Well, I never wanted you to know about it."

Then she said, "What happened that time when you were in London?"

I told her of his violent behavior, the constant threats he made, including threats
to harm her if I should leave him. Cheryl was reserved, a family trait, but her shock
and fear registered on her face. And I believe she was less frightened for herself than
she was for me.

"But why, Mother?" she kept asking. "Why can't you stop seeing him?"

"I wish it were so easy, Cherry," I said. "But he almost never leaves me alone. It
won't go on, but I must do it in a way that will be safe."

I talked with my mother about it, too. She insisted that I call the police, but I knew that press people hovered around the Beverly Hills precinct hoping for just such news. I thought that John might be reasonable if Cheryl moved in for a while. At least then if I wanted to keep him out I would have a plausible excuse.

Then came Friday, April 4, 1958. Earlier in the day I had gone shopping again— of course, John went with me—and we returned to the house about four-thirty in the afternoon. I was expecting Del Armstong to come by for a drink, and when we got home he was already there, with a friend we had met while making *Sea Chase* in Hawaii. The man's name was Bill Brooks, and I knew little about him, only that he was a businessman who traveled frequently around the islands.

As John took the bags to the kitchen, I sat down to chat. Bill Brooks turned to me with a thoughtful look. "Who did you say that fellow was?" he asked.

"John Stompanato."

"I believe I used to know him," Bill said.

"Really? Where?" I asked, as I made us drinks.

"If it's the one, we were at military academy together. Kemper, in Missouri, class of Forty-three."

Class of Forty-three? But John was older than that! Before I could press Bill about it, John returned.

"Remember me?" Bill asked, as they shook hands.

"Yes," John said. "Sure I do."

His response struck me as cool for someone meeting an old schoolmate after such a long time. And John did seem uncomfortable around Bill. After a short time he excused himself, saying he'd call me later. He'd mentioned something to Cheryl about seeing a movie,

"What's he like now?" Bill asked me after John had left the house.

Del and I exchanged glances, and Bill went on, "When we were at school together, he was bad news."

"What do you mean?"

"He caused a lot of trouble there. He was a thief. I'd be careful of him," Bill said.

I was not surprised by what Bill was saying. But I couldn't imagine why John had lied about his age. It was one more strand in that web of deception he'd been spinning and weaving around me. We chatted a while longer, and then the two got up to leave. Del suggested that I join them for dinner.

But the afternoon was fading, and I still had a lot to do. I'd hardly begun to unpack my clothes. My luggage from Acapulco was piled in the closet. I hadn't even looked at it yet. Once they were gone I spent a few hours sorting through boxes until John called around eight. I told him I was tired and wanted to skip the movie, adding that I'd turned down dinner with Del and Bill.

"But I might see them for dinner tomorrow," I mentioned conversationally.

"Without me?"

"Surely I have the right to see old friends," I said.

"I'm coming over and we're seeing a movie," John said, and hung up.

He arrived within half an hour, in a black mood. How long had they stayed, he wanted to know. Why had they stayed that long? I didn't want to argue so I went upstairs, where Cheryl was watching television. I hoped that John would cool off soon. But he followed right behind, still haranguing me about making plans without including him.

"Now look," I said, from the doorway of Cheryl's room, "I've told you time and again not to argue in front of Cheryl."

"Let her listen," he snarled. "I want her to hear the truth about you."

I could see it was going to be a serious fight. I don't know why, but I remember telling Cheryl explicitly what I was going to do. "I am going downstairs now. Then I'm coming right back up."

"Okay, Mother," she answered.

John followed me down to the bar, where I fixed myself a drink. "You break promises," he was screaming at me. "You said you would go to the movies but then you changed your mind. And now you're going to get drunk. You drink too damn much—"

"Just leave me alone," I interrupted.

But he wouldn't leave me alone. As I climbed the stairs his shouting echoed in the hall. He was right behind me when I went into my room, and he angrily slammed the door. ". . . And you'll do as I say," he was screaming.

"I don't want any more of this," I said. "Please get out of here." By then I was in tears, and seeing me cry enraged him even more. Suddenly I heard a tinkling sound in the hallway outside the door. I recognized the sound—it was the charms on a bracelet I'd recently given Cheryl.

"Cheryl," I called out, "is that you?" No answer came. "Cheryl, I can hear you. You *are* there. Please go to your room."

The tinkling faded away. Next to the bathroom there was a dressing room with a built-in vanity of pink marble. I lifted myself up onto it cross-legged and lit a cigarette to calm myself. But the cigarette didn't help. I was shaking, with anger, with fear, afraid to lash out at him but too unsure that I could keep my self-control. I needed a drink. I stubbed out the cigarette and started for the bedroom door.

"Where are you going?" John bellowed. "To the bar?"

"I'm not. But I *will* if I want to."

"Like hell," he fumed.

Before I could get the door open enough, he grabbed me and spun me around, then shoved the door shut with his foot. I thought he was going to hit me, but instead he shook me hard by the shoulders. I broke away from him, screaming, "Don't touch me! I have had it! Now get the hell out of my life!"

I was close to the door, and again I heard the tinkle of the charm bracelet. "Cheryl! Get away from that door! I'm not going to tell you again."

John was screaming back at me. "This time you'll get it. No one will ever look at that pretty face of yours again—"

I remember telling him to get out, something to the effect that "this is a new house and you're not going to be around in it."

There was urgent knocking on the door, and outside it, Cheryl was begging, "Mother, don't keep arguing. Let me talk to you."

Because we had originally planned to go out, John had brought over a shirt and jacket earlier in the day. They were on his own hangers, heavy wooden ones. Now, yelling abusively at me all the while, he went to the closet and took out his clothing, hangers and all. I felt a stab of relief. This meant he was going!

"Please," Cheryl persisted, outside the door. "Let me talk to both of you."

"Oh, all right," I called to her. "But the argument is over. John is leaving."

Cheryl opened the door.

What she saw was me sitting on the pink marble counter, and John coming toward me, his arms upraised, with something in his hand. She didn't grasp the fact that he was carrying clothing on hangers over his shoulder. Just that upraised, threatening hand, and what appeared to be some kind of weapon. And he was right in front of the door, his body unprotected.

Out of the corner of my eye I saw Cheryl make a sudden movement. Her right arm had shot out and caught John in the stomach. I thought she'd punched him. There was a strange little moment, locked in time, as each stood looking at the other.

"Oh, my God, Cheryl," John gasped out. "What have you done?"

I darted forward off the counter, afraid that John was going to punch Cheryl back. Cheryl was backing up slowly, staring at John. John took three little circling steps away from her, in slow motion. He didn't clutch his belly; he didn't cry out. Just those three little steps, and then he fell backward, like a board, straight to the floor. His eyes were closed. Weird gasping was coming from his throat, as though he couldn't breathe. At that moment I realized suddenly what Cheryl grasped in her hand. It was a carving knife, one from the set John had selected a few days before.

At that instant of consciousness, a wave of shock hit me. I stared at Cheryl as she dropped the knife and suddenly began to cry. Numbly I turned to look at John lying prone and motionless on the floor, then took Cheryl by the shoulder and sent her to her room. John was making dreadful, soft, choking sounds. I went to him and leaned over, but I didn't see a wound, not until I lifted his sweater. It was a small wound, only a little slice. Strangely there was very little blood. I don't remember going to the bathroom to get a towel to cover the wound, but since there was a towel there I must have. John's eyes were closed as though he were in a sound sleep. I moved in a dream. None of this could be real. What made me do it, I don't know, but I picked up the knife and dropped it into the sink.

Do something, my mind commanded. Call a doctor. Call my mother. But I couldn't remember the numbers for a while. Finally my mother's surfaced and I dialed it almost automatically. When she answered I had to struggle to ask for the doctor's number.

"Are you sick?"

"Don't ask me, Mother. Just give me the number."

"Lana, you sound dreadful. Is Cheryl all right? Tell me what's the matter."

I looked at John and saw no movement. After a long minute all I could say was, "Mother, John is dead."

I cut off her questions with another demand for the number, then hung up and dialed the doctor. I got Dr. McDonald's service, and he called me right back. Somehow I managed to choke out the message.

"Don't do anything," he ordered. "I'll be right there."

I tried calling my mother back then, but got no answer. Then I remembered poor Cheryl. I found her sitting on her bed, trembling violently. Sitting close to her, I held her, rocking her back and forth, trying to quiet her shaking. She began to sob again, but I didn't ask her questions. "Shhh, darling, don't cry, don't cry." I didn't know then that she had already phoned her father to tell him something terrible had happened. While I sat with her, soothing her, the doorbell sounded. I ran downstairs, and my mother rushed inside.

"What were you talking about?" she asked me, agitatedly. "Where is he? Where is Cheryl?"

She brushed me aside without waiting for answers and went straight up the stairs to Cheryl's bedroom. She gathered Cheryl, who by now was crying convulsively, into her arms. After a moment or two she turned to me and asked, "Where is he?"

I led her to the master bedroom. She started when she saw him, then looked at me. Then she dropped to her knees and listened to John's chest. I watched her as if in a trance. She went to the bed and got a pillow, then knelt down again and placed it under his head.

"Mother, don't touch him!" I cried.

She glared at me. "I'm doing the right thing."

Then she bent down and began to give him mouth-to-mouth resuscitation. I didn't want her mouth on his.

The doorbell rang. I raced down the stairs and let in Dr. McDonald, with a cry of relief.

"Where?"

"Upstairs. Mother's up there."

He went up with his bag, calling, "Mildred, Mildred."

"In here," she answered.

I realized later that he hadn't asked about Cheryl. He supposed I was the one who had done it.

In the pink bedroom he shrugged out of his jacket and threw it on the bed, and while opening his bag looked at John. He put his stethoscope to John's chest and felt for a pulse. Then he looked up at me. He didn't say a word. He just shook his head *no*.

Then reality broke in, like an explosion in my head. The haze gave way to a real horror. Now I watched Dr. McDonald take a syringe and lock an ampule of adrenalin into it. He plunged the needle into John's heart and pumped in the liquid. When he pulled out the needle he listened again for a beat through the stethoscope. As he waited for the sound he waved me toward the phone. "Call Jerry Geisler," he said.

I had to ask information for Geisler's number; after he answered I told him who I was and what had happened. I knew him only slightly from a few social occasions. He was the most famous lawyer in Hollywood, who had defended Errol Flynn and Charlie Chaplin, among others.

"John Stompanato is dead," I told him. "He's—he's here."

"I'll be right there," he answered. "Give me your address."

"Get me Geisler." That was one of the jokes at the time. If you were in trouble, you knew whom to call. Only now it wasn't a joke. It was something unspeakable, all too real.

Time was playing strange tricks on me. It seemed to stretch out long and then recede. Things were happening all the while that I didn't know about until afterward. For one thing, Stephan reached the house moments after Dr. McDonald. My mother must have let him in. The police arrived, and then the ambulance was there. And then Geisler. I didn't even notice them.

Meanwhile my mother sent Dr. McDonald in to see Cheryl, and Geisler came in to find me. I told him that Cheryl, thinking to protect me, had stabbed John with the knife. I took him into the bathroom and showed the knife still lying there in the sink. Then he and Stephan went to meet the police, and Dr. McDonald came in to check on me. And while he was doing that, Chief Anderson of the Beverly Hills police appeared at the door of the pink bedroom.

"Please," I said to him, "Let me say I did it . . ."

"Lana, don't," he said. "We already know it was Cheryl."

I learned the police had found Cheryl's charm bracelet on the landing outside the bedroom. She had taken it off so that I wouldn't hear the sound as she listened outside the door. And when Stephan came she had told him, "I did it, Daddy, but I didn't mean to. He was going to hurt Mommy."

The police poured in. So many police! I was stunned at the number of blue uniforms all over the place. Kneeling over John's body, circling it, standing over it, running upstairs and downstairs and into Cheryl's room. You'd have thought they were making a raid. Were they all there out of curiosity? Surely three or four would have been enough. Then the reporters came, clamoring outside, yelling to the police to let them in. I heard them shouting directions: "Bring a light." "Go around the back." The police photographers must have given pictures to the press, for later the newspapers printed shots of John's body lying on the floor. How cooperative with the press, the Beverly Hills police!

Cheryl had to dress because she was still in her robe, and we all had to go down to the police station. My mother was badly shaken, so one of the officers escorted her home. Geisler took Cheryl and me in his chauffeured car, while Stephan rode with the policemen. When we arrived at the stationhouse Police Chief Anderson ushered us into his office. He told Cheryl that he needed a formal statement and asked for her version of what happened.

"Don't ask her," I blurted out, "ask me."

"Lana," he said, "please be quiet. I want to hear it from her."

She told him but I hardly remember her words. Now in the glaring light of the police chief's office, I began to grasp the enormity of what Cheryl had done and began to understand why. She had heard John say he was going to destroy my face, and she had brought the knife to protect me. A young girl, a child, against a big man. The thrust of the knife piercing the aorta was fatal by chance. She had been trying to protect me. She was now in terrible trouble. Nothing seemed to matter except protecting her.

The matron stood there waiting, and Chief Anderson was explaining, "Cheryl, go with her. You'll be spending the night here."

"No!" I screamed, and I heard Stephan asking why.

"Because that's how we have to do it," Anderson said.

The events seemed to snowball, growing larger and larger, with no end in sight. "Let me go with her," I begged him.

"For a while you can," he said. "I'd like to talk to Steve."

I rushed after Cheryl and the matron. Down a corridor I saw the matron waiting, and when I reached her I saw Cheryl—behind bars. That vision is one that will never go away. My child's face, behind bars.

"Will you open that door, please," I ordered the matron.

She stared at me blankly.

"Open that door!"

Without saying a word she did it. Inside, I clutched Cheryl and she clung to me, then both of us sank to the cot and cried. "You'll be all right," I tried to reassure her. "You're the most important one in the world now, to all of us. Don't be afraid. You *will* be all right, and in the morning we'll come and get you. Chief Anderson said we could."

An officer arrived to lead me away. The matron stood at the door, holding it open. "You must leave," she said, and the officer took my arm as I stared back at my child. Cheryl stood there woodenly, impassive and silent.

When Stephan, Geisler, and I left the stationhouse, we saw why they were so anxious for us to leave. The press had gathered like vultures outside, cameras at the ready. And they got their damned pictures.

Geisler's limousine brought me home. What a horrible sight greeted me there! The ambulance attendants were removing John's body on a stretcher covered with a sheet. Still seated in the car, I watched the grisly procession on its way to the ambulance at the curb. I couldn't suppress a scream. Geisler held on to me, saying, "Stop it, Lana, stop it," and he shoved me down to the floor. He had seen the flashbulbs flaring as the body was carried away. When he got out of the car the reporters swarmed around him, as I hid, shaking, in the backseat. I heard him telling them that I had gone away for the night, and when the ambulance drove off the reporters followed it. Then Geisler came back to tell me the coast was clear.

I peeked out of the car. The street was empty. Quickly I ran into the house. There my friends had gathered, Del and the others, having heard the news on the radio. More questions, gentler this time. Yes, it was all true, but . . . All those kind faces, helpful, understanding, floated before me in a dream.

Diane Varsi and Lana Turner in Peyton Place *(1957), 20th Century-Fox.*

RUDOLPH VALENTINO

Rudolph Valentino and Agnes Ayres in The Sheik *(1921), Paramount.*

Born Rodolfo Alfonzo Raffaele Pierre Philibert Guglielmi on May 6, 1895 in Castellaneta, Italy . . . Arrived in New York as immigrant in 1913 . . . Arrested several times for petty theft . . . Became professional ballroom tango dancer . . . First film: *My Official Wife* (1914) . . . Reached Hollywood in 1917 . . . First box office success: *Four Horsemen of the Apocalypse* (1921) . . . Other films: *The Sheik* (1921) . . . *Blood and Sand* (1922) . . . *A Sainted Devil* (1924) . . . *Son of the Sheik* (1926) . . . Arrested for bigamy in Los Angeles . . . The Chicago Tribune called him "a painted pansy" . . . He challenged them to a duel . . . Died of a ruptured ulcer in 1926 . . . John Dos Passos: "The gigolo of every woman's dreams."

"You're a Hell of a Sheik"

New York is full of surprises! Think of it! One may walk through New York, even along the elegant stretch of Fifth Avenue from 34th Street to 59th Street, entirely unnoticed.

I am suddenly placed in the reverse of my usual position. It is I who notice people, and stare.

I stood in the lobby of the New Amsterdam bargaining for a seat to *"The Follies."* Hundreds of people passed me by without noticing me more than they noticed any other well-dressed young man who hadn't been thoughtful enough to provide himself with a seat in advance.

But from my corner, I noticed at least a dozen people whom I recognized and who had the grace not to recognize me. John Barrymore and his wife, Michael Strange, walked by entirely wrapped up in each other. I have never been introduced to Barrymore but I have been to parties with Miss Strange, whom her friends affectionately call Mike.

David W. Griffith came in to buy a seat. Instead of telling him, as he had told me, to wait until some tickets might be returned, the man at the box office gave him a box seat and absolutely refused to take money for it. It is different to be both great and recognized. Maybe if they recognized me, they would throw me out for fear of a panic. It would be just like my luck.

When I think what a delightful time I had last night, I can only think with a little scorn, of the patriarchs of Hollywood, who insist, to the point of tears, that the screen is bound to displace the theatre as a means of entertainment.

How much warmth and loveliness the maestro of the stage can get into a scene of his, for he deals with, not mere outlines, but flesh and blood automatons who have in them strange creative resources that shine out from their skins and their eyes.

"The Follies," as an institution, is in itself infinitely superior to the screen. For one thing, I enjoy it more. That should be sufficient.

I came home all tired out and flushed with the victory I had gained over my popularity. The Waldorf is not a very friendly hotel. It's rather old and cold and its splendor has let all the warmth seep out of it. Whatever charm the Waldorf has is absolutely unapproachable. I didn't bother to go to the desk, but stepped straight into an elevator and went directly to my room. I had no sooner opened it than I became aware of a peculiar presence. A young girl, who couldn't have been more than fifteen, was sitting in the red plush armchair, smoking a cigarette. "I beg your pardon," I said.

She looked up, exhaled some smoke. "Go right ahead. Make yourself at home."

I only put down my hat and went up to her as severely as I could. "Are you perhaps here by accident?" I asked.

"No," she answered, "I am here because you are here."

"Is that so?" I said. "Suppose, then, we both get out of here."

The child really looked too simple to be practicing blackmail. But blackmail has been known to take many strange disguises.

"It will be easier to talk here," she said.

"Oh, I see!" I exclaimed. "You are a reporter. I hardly expected a reporter at this hour of the night."

"I am not a reporter," she said with great decision. "I am only a very pretty young girl. Look carefully at me. You may be throwing away the opportunity of a lifetime."

I told her that I was never very much of an adventurer and that I was very sleepy. Even if she had been a reporter, I wouldn't talk to her. "How in the world did you ever get in here, anyway?" I asked.

"I walked in," she said simply.

I stared at her with amazement. "You walked fourteen flights?" I asked.

She smiled. "That was not at all necessary. I had the elevator take me up to the fifteenth floor. I simply walked down one flight."

"And now that you are here, what are you going to do about it?" I asked.

"Oh, I am prepared to do anything," she said.

"Tell you what," I suggested, "suppose I sign a copy of this book for you, will you leave me alone?"

"I don't care about your book," she said. "I looked through it before you came in. It's the lousiest poetry or anything else you want to make out of it. No, thank you, I don't want any of your books or autographs."

"Then what do you want?" I cried.

"I tell you," she said, looking steadily at me, "I came here prepared for anything. As a matter of fact, I needn't even go home," she added.

"That's fine," I said. "We'll arrange it immediately." I picked up the telephone and asked the desk to send up two porters.

"What do you want two porters for?" she asked.

"I'm sending you home," I told her.

"What for?" she asked.

"I don't know," I told her, "you are probably much safer here but I don't like you, in spite of your prettiness and I want to get you out of here as quickly as possible. I have known even little imps like you to make ejection hard for one porter. That's why I sent for two."

There was a knock on the door, and upon my response, two porters walked in. I pointed to the young woman and told them she was going home. She made no offer to resist, but at the door, she turned back to me spitefully. "You're a hell of a sheik," she said to me.

That was one night I slept.

Nita Naldi and Rudolph Valentino in A Sainted Devil *(1924), Paramount.*

MAE WEST

W.C. Fields and Mae West in My Little Chickadee *(1940), Universal.*

Born August 17, 1893 in Brooklyn . . . Father a heavyweight boxer, Battling Jack West . . . Her play *Sex* landed her in jail . . . A homosexual play was quickly banned . . . First film: *Night After Night* (1932) . . . *She Done Him Wrong* (1933) . . . *I'm No Angel* (1933) . . . *My Little Chickadee* (1940) . . . RAF named life jackets for her because "they bulge in all the right places" . . . Mae West: "It isn't what you do, it's how you do it."

My Little Chickadee

The compulsion to progress, without knowing where or exactly how I was to do so, bothered me. From now on I knew that I could trust myself only to material that would be "great" for my personality, though not necessarily great in a literary sense.

Whatever I did next would have to top my previous success. In the spring of 1938 I began a search for an idea or for material that would help me do so.

Personal appearances in connection with *Every Day's a Holiday*, and a tour booked by the William Morris Agency, did not interrupt that search. Wherever I appeared, mobs of fans demanded how soon I would make another picture. I put them off by saying, "As soon as I get back to Hollywood," but I was not sure myself.

While Chamberlain talked "peace in our time," Universal Pictures approached me with an offer to make a motion picture with W.C. Fields. It was a daring concept and a mad one, but the times were mad. A studio boss explained to me: "We have in mind with your combined comedy talents you two would tear audiences apart."

"Laughing, I hope," I said.

"We also have in mind we should do this as a comedy horse opera."

I asked, expressionless, "Whom do you have in mind for the horse?"

"This ain't to be a fantasy, Miss West."

I explained, "I was joking. I just intended to make sure no four-legged animal was going to grab top billing."

"Mr. Fields is a remarkable fella."

"I always enjoy his brand of comedy. There is no one else quite like Bill. And it would be snide of me to add, 'Thank God.' A great performer. My only doubts about him come in bottles."

"Under control. He's almost a tea-hound now."

"I never like to work with actors who drink on the job. They aren't dependable as a rule, and you can't tell when, inspired by some daffy alcoholic whim, they can ruin your performance."

"You'll see. Bill is on light wine and beer."

"Being a non-drinker myself, I'm sensitive to liquor fumes, especially when breathed over me at close range."

"He's in training for the part. It's a rugged, outdoor, manly role."

"I can't see Bill Fields as a two-gun man, but his dexterity as a two-bottle man is common knowledge. He is proud of it."

"He'll promise anything to work with you."

"He'll shudder with horror when I make it part of my agreement to do the picture that he lay off all alcohol while we are shooting."

"Not even a small beer?" Bill Fields was said to have whimpered as he signed.

Fields was a remarkable, difficult talent. A fine comic writer, a miser who had two hundred bank accounts under fictitious names all over the world—and a hater of dogs and children and civilization.

Bill's doctors had been after him to taper down to a quart or so a day. Realizing that his system must require some splashing ointment to keep away the shakes, I knew he would have difficulty staying on the wagon.

Eddie Cline, the director, a graduate of the Mack Sennett school of comedy, assigned members of the staff to keep a sharp watch that Bill didn't do any nipping between scenes. But Bill devised various stratagems to have his liquids handy, bringing it in disguised as a "Coke," done up in a parcel, wrapped in a napkin— anything that would prevent an accidental gleam of a bottle catching my eye. Once he complained, "Someone has stolen the cork out of my lunch!"

Ready to begin a day's shooting, I saw that Bill Fields was entertaining a large crowd of extras. He was in great form, and they were howling at him. Something told me that Bill was over-stimulated. The assistant director confirmed my suspicions. "I'm afraid Bill has slipped off the wagon this morning. He's telling the kid actors to go out and play in the traffic."

Another sign of Bill's condition was his comment on a hook-and-ladder fire engine on its way past the studio to fight a nearby fire. "Damn drunken house-painters."

I asked the director if there were scenes we could shoot without Fields. Eddie Cline checked the script and found there were.

"All right," I said, "pour him out of here."

The assistant director went over to Fields. "Bill, you can go home. We won't need you until tomorrow morning."

"Oh, ya-as?" His puffed, bloodshot eyes gave me a side glance. "Ya-as," he said again with an old-world courtesy, tipping his hat to me. And he walked out with a sheepish look.

Fields was brilliant and erratic in public as well as on the set. He once walked into a bank and grabbed a child in a cowboy suit, shouting, "A midget bank robber!"

Naturally, from the first, we had story problems. The studio had their story ideas, Fields had his story ideas, and I had mine. Bill and I had one thing in common: both of us disliked the studio's story. It was called *The Jayhawkers*, and amounted to little more than a formula western with jokes added.

Fields wrote me alarming letters. "I take, my dear, a very dim view of the studio's mental equipment, to put it mildly. It is up to us to take matters in our own firm hands concerning this dismal story. If we leave it up to the studio they will ruin us. Yes, ruin us. I say it again, ruin us."

I wrote a story of my own, which I gave the working title, *The Lady and the Bandit*.

We had more conferences at the studio. Everybody spoke his piece, Bill Fields and I speaking big pieces. Bill said, "And my last argument is we do Miss West's story or we do nothing."

So I wrote the screenplay, which became *My Little Chickadee*.

I did my very best to make Bill Fields' scenes as funny as possible. He was pleased with most of them, though he insisted on putting in some of his fine characteristic touches, which was no more than I would have done in his place—and have done in other times and places.

Once on the set, I thought of a line and a piece of business I hoped would be a tremendous laugh. I felt that Eddie Cline, the director, had a great comedy sense, maybe because he usually agreed with me.

"It's a wow, Bill—a buster."

When I turned to Bill Fields I was shocked to see his reaction. The big red-nosed man was so upset that he was shaking. From the look on his face I thought he was going to cry. Obviously, he didn't want me to get that big laugh. I realized he felt I was a little too fast for him.

"All right, Bill," I said, "if you don't want it in, I won't do it."

I think that under the grotesque ruin of a clown Bill Fields was tragically aware of the wreck he had made of himself.

While *My Little Chickadee* was still in work, Dr. Frank N. Buchman, the founder of the Oxford Movement, came to Hollywood to put on a huge Moral Re-Armament rally in the Hollywood Bowl. The philosophy of Moral Re-Armament—"Love Everything"—was catching on all over the world except in Germany. Dr. Buchman, a pretty good salesman, came up to see me at my apartment, to interest me in the gospel of the M.R.A. "To enlist, Miss West, your support of the movement."

"My own movement doesn't need any re-arming, Doc, but I am glad to help out the cause. I just happen to have a couple of press boys and photographers on hand. So let's take some pictures."

We did, under an oil painting for which I had posed of a reclining nude.

"I agree, Doc, that M.R.A. is a good thing, and a naughty world could use a lot of it. Have you met Bill Fields yet? Splendid raw material for you."

"No," he said, "but I'd love to meet him."

"You should," I said. "Moral re-armament is just what he needs. If you reform Bill, I'll let him win me body and soul in the picture. Give him your message. He'll go for it if you can put it into a bottle."

Dr. Buchman, good salesman as he was, failed with Bill Fields. "I'll take anything in a bottle," Bill said, "but I don't need re-armament. Just a stimulant. Besides, Herr Doktor, I believe in doing unto others as they do unto you—but I do it first. Care for a fruit juice cocktail—just a smidgin of gin?"

While working in the picture, I received a less philosophical visit than Dr. Buchman's. Ralph Capone and another brother of Al, the notorious "Little Caesar" of Chicago's rackets during the prohibition era, dropped by the studio "just to say hello." I had met all the Capones ten years before, when I first played *Diamond Lil* in Chicago. They had become ardent fans of mine. The Capone boys were rough and simple. Direct, too, and one had to be wary not to rile their primitive minds. Men of action—Dr. Buchman could have used them—they were vital.

Ralph said to me, "We are just passing through Los Angeles on our way to visit Al. He is in the new Federal prison at San Pedro. He's been transferred there from Alcatraz, where he's serving a twelve-year Federal rap Uncle Whiskers hung on him."

"So I heard," I said.

"For income tax evasion. Pretty sneaky, eh?"

I shook their hands. "Give Al my regards."

"Don't think we won't."

But Al Capone was small time in 1939. On September 1, Germany invaded Poland, and two days later England and France declared war on Germany.

Bill Fields said, "It's a fink world."

Closer to home in Los Angeles, state and county officials raided three gambling ships off Santa Monica Bay, where racket boy Tony Cornero held out aboard the *Rex* for a few days. He finally bowed to a court decision and surrendered the *Rex*, as an enemy warship.

The Townsend Old Age Pension Plan was knocked out in a test vote in the House. Old actors, hopeful for a weekly payoff, wept.

The sky over Los Angeles also wept, giving us 5.42 inches of rain in nineteen hours, after several days of record-breaking September heat, with a temperature of 107.2 degrees. Jim [Timony, West's manager] said, "Mae, you're still the hottest thing in town."

War came to the Hollywood studios. The motion picture industry had signed closed shop agreements with the International Alliance of Theatrical Stage Employees, and was faced with a strike, but the producers averted this by granting a 10 per cent wage increase.

Gangsterism in local labor unions had a strong leader. I remember Willie Bioff, the film union leader, a known shakedown artist, who held a pistol to the heads of the producers. He was wanted by police on an old Chicago warrant for pandering. They finally caught Willie and got him in a witness chair, and he sang like an off-key canary. This made a lot of trouble for "The Boys." They were very patient for a while. Then, much later, somebody attached an explosive charge to the ignition of his car. Exit Willie, not laughing.

We finally finished *My Little Chickadee*. One of the accepted gags I wrote in for Bill Fields was when Fields' Indian valet, Clarence, referring to me, asked, "Big Chief gottum new squaw?" Fields answered, "Ya-as, brand new. I haven't even unwrapped her yet."

Fields played the role of Cuthbert J. Twillie, an itinerant snake-oil salesman and card-sharp, trapped into a fake marriage with Flower Belle (me), who has been run out of a western frontier town and told not to come back until she is "respectable and married." On their "wedding night" Twillie begins to pet his bedfellow. "Are you wearing your caracule coat, my plum?" he asks. Then to his horror he discovers that Flower Belle has skipped and left a tied-up goat in her place under the covers.

To show her willingness to reform and cooperate in the community life of Greasewood City, Flower Belle takes over for the sick schoolmarm. Entering the classroom, she finds written on the blackboard: "I am a good boy. I am a good man. I am a good girl."

"What is this?" she queries. "Propaganda?"

The law catches up with Twillie, and he is about to be strung up. Asked if he has any last request, he says: "Ya-as, I'd like to see Paris before I die."

Through Flower Belle's stratagems, however, Twillie's innocence is proved, and he is spared; but he realizes he has no further place in Flower Belle's life. When he takes his leave, he invites her to "come up and see me sometime." Flower Belle, adopting his gravelly tones, says from the side of her mouth: "Ya-as, my little chickadee." As she mounts the stairs, "THE END" appears across her expressive posterior.

Over the years *My Little Chickadee* has been shown over and over again. Untold millions have seen it.

SHELLEY WINTERS

Shelley Winters in A Place In The Sun *(1950), Paramount.*

Born Shirley Schrift on August 18, 1922 in St. Louis . . . Grew up in Brooklyn . . . The "worst model on 7th Avenue" in '30s . . . First film: *What a Woman!* (1943) . . . Other picture credits: *The Great Gatsby* (1949) . . . *A Place in the Sun* (1951) . . . Oscars for supporting roles in *Diary of Anne Frank* (1959) and *A Patch of Blue* (1965) . . . *Lolita* (1962) . . . *The Poseidon Adventure* (1972) . . . Married Vittorio Gassman in 1952 . . . Divorced 1954 . . . Married Anthony Franciosa in 1957 . . . Divorced 1960 . . . Claims to have invented the "open mouth smile" that her roommate Marilyn Monroe perfected . . . Playmates included Marlon Brando, Errol Flynn, William Holden, Burt Lancaster.

"Follow Me to Shangri-la"

One day in the commissary Yvonne De Carlo, Universal's Brunette Sexpot, came over to me in one of her innumerable harem costumes and said, "Errol Flynn is making a swashbuckling picture on the back lot and was watching you work yesterday. Friday evening he's having an informal dinner party and would like me to bring you. He gives the most elegant small dinner parties. I think Clark Gable will be there, too. Do you want to go?"

DID I WANT TO GO!

In my excitement and confusion, I answered, "What will he serve?"

Yvonne looked at me strangely and replied, "Dumbbell. Wonderful food. And he'll run a new movie."

Trying to speak casually, I said, "Okay, but I'll follow you in my car, in case I want to leave before the end of the picture."

"You won't." She smiled and swished away in all her seven veils.

That Friday, when I went to work at 6:00 A.M., I brought with me a pair of black velvet Capri pants, red satin you-know-what shoes and a tailored white satin shirt. And gold hoop earrings, my first real ones.

At 6:00 P.M. Yvonne was waiting for me in a chauffeured limousine, and we got into quite a fight when I insisted on going in my little red Pontiac and following her. She really got annoyed and said, "Listen, Brooklyn, Errol is a perfect gentleman. Anytime you want to go home he'll send you in his limousine." She finally gave in. "All right, follow me to Shangri-la."

Aunt Fanny in the Bronx had knitted me a beautiful if enormous dark red shawl, which I casually threw around my shoulders, and I followed Yvonne. It was a little involved getting to Flynn's house. We went way up in the Hollywood Hills and finally went through some iron gates, which opened magically.

Mr. Flynn's house was surrounded by a six-foot stone wall, and there was an enormous pool on the front lawn. And guess who opened the car door. CLARK GABLE! I literally fell out of the car. He caught me, and while he was trying to straighten me out, his watch got caught in my shawl. I should have known from that New Year's Eve party never to wear shawls! I just don't have the élan to carry off any kind of shawl.

Gable stood me upright on my three-inch heels, took off his watch, and Yvonne disentangled it from the fringe while I got as red as the shawl. Then Errol Flynn came up, and he was handsomer than in the movies. Yvonne introduced me to both movie idols and another handsome gentleman, who turned out to be Errol's agent, and a beautiful statuesque redhead.

Flynn laughed. "That's one of the greatest entrances I've ever seen. Did you do it on purpose?"

Lying in my teeth, I said, "Of course, Mr. Flynn. At heart I'm a comedienne. I knew Mr. Gable would catch me."

Flynn told me to call him Errol and cautioned me not to depend on Gable's catching ability as he'd already had three double martinis. Gable made some joke like: "I could catch her anywhere, anytime, under any conditions." It wasn't so funny, but that sexy Gable growl made me giggle like a teenager.

We went into the den and sat in deep leather chairs. The butler handed me a double vodka martini in a silver goblet, and I began to feel as though I were in a stylish MGM movie. I noticed for the first time that Yvonne was wearing some gauzy gold harem pants and a sort of bikini top with full sleeves and, I suspected, nothing underneath. She was a knockout. I was a little confused as to who was my date, if it was a date. Both Errol and Clark were equally attentive and charming to all the girls.

We ate at a glass-top table in a sort of outdoor dining room surrounded by flowers and birds, and there were real gardenias floating in the pool. For once I can't remember much of what we ate because I was too intoxicated by the presence of these two men whom, when I was a kid, I had followed in movie theaters all over Brooklyn. I had seen *It Happened One Night* innumerable times in ten different theaters, and *The Adventures of Robin Hood* had thrilled my adolescent heart so that I would watch it until [my older sister] Blanche had to come and drag me out of the theater while Errol was up there swinging from balconies and saving damsels in distress. I looked at them closely, and they both looked as young and vital as they had more than a decade before. I figured they must have some youth secret that the rest of the world's male population didn't have.

While we were having Irish coffee and I was entertaining them with tales of the New York theater, a car drove up. A man who was obviously a doctor with a regulation black bag got out and said, "Hi," and went into the living room. Then, while we were talking and joking, all three men, one by one, went into the living room, and I heard each of them yell "Ouch!" A few minutes later they came back buttoning their shirts and rubbing their right shoulders.

After the second "Ouch!" I excused myself, sneaked down the hallway and peeked through the door into the living room. I saw Errol with his shirt off, and the doctor cut a little flap of skin on the back of his right shoulder, inserted some kind of capsule into it, then took a stitch in the skin, closing it. It seemed very weird, and to this day no regular doctor has been able to explain it to me. But that's what I saw.

I hurriedly got back to the table, beating Flynn by a minute, and lit a cigarette, in order to appear calm and blasé. The waiter filled my glass with rare wine, which I drank down as if it were Coca-Cola. While the gentlemen rubbed their shoulders and I choked on my cigarette, I was wondering how I could get the hell out of there. I had seen the Dracula films, too.

Yvonne hit me on the back and asked why I was smoking when I didn't know how, and I told her that the next film I was to do was Scott Fitzgerald's *The Great Gatsby* on loan-out to Paramount. Alan Ladd and Barry Sullivan would be in it, and Betty Field would play the good rich girl. I was to play the bad poor girl, and I felt it was necessary to learn how to smoke, or how else would the audience know I was a bad girl?

Flynn and Gable started to talk about Fitzgerald, whom they had met in Malibu bars, and Flynn asked me if I had read his books. I explained that I was getting cultural in alphabetical order, and I was only up to Theodore Dreiser, although I had cheated and skipped to the *W*s and read all of Thomas Wolfe. Flynn told me he had all of Fitzgerald's first editions, and he would lend me *The Great Gatsby*, as I really ought to be familiar with all of his work before I did that film. He added wistfully, "I wonder why no one ever offers me films like that." I assured him that he gave millions of people delight and enjoyment and thrills. He looked at me shrewdly and said, "Would *you* be content with that kind of career?"

I started to lie a compliment and then stopped. He was too honest and elegant and nice a man. I told him that I felt that the function of films and the theater was to bring joy, as well as to enlighten people's lives. I then quoted something from one of George Bernard Shaw's critiques: "Theatre [or Film] is at its finest when it is an elucidator of social consciousness, a recorder of the mores of its time, a historian of the future, an armory against despair and darkness, and a temple in the ascent of Man."

The table got very quiet, and for a minute I felt as if I had made a gigantic faux pas and brought reality into never-never land. I guess in a way I had. Flynn held my chin in his hand and said, "You've got a lot between your ears beside those blonde curls, haven't you, Shelley?"

I grinned with pleasure and said, "I hope so. I never finished high school, and I'm trying very hard to make up for it, and I'm directing a wonderful play called *Thunder Rock* at the little Circle Theater."

The conversation suddenly turned serious and interesting. Gable asked me if he hadn't seen an English film called *Thunder Rock* with James Mason and Michael Redgrave. I said, "Yes, it was made in England after the Spanish Civil War, and it's about hope."

Flynn's agent asked about the plot—never mind the message. I told him it was a play by Robert Ardrey about a man who takes a job as a lighthouse keeper on an isolated island in the Great Lakes, disillusioned after fighting with the Loyalists during the Spanish Civil War. The democracies had given little help to the Spanish Democratic Republic while the Fascist forces had fully supported the Franco coup.

In the lighthouse the man sees a plaque, dated 1850, with the names of the people sailing from England whose ship went down on the rocks off that island. All the characters from the novel he's trying to write come to life in it, but walk in a slanty, distorted manner and speak in phony, stilted words. Only when the man is shocked into truly looking at his characters is he able to see that these people who were drowned in 1850 really project hope to the audience. There's a woman who has been deported from England for fighting for women's suffrage; a starving child who has escaped from a Welsh coal mine; a Scottish workingman who has been crippled during a strike for a twelve-hour day. Despite the seeming hopelessness at any given moment in world history, when man's future seems lost and hopeless, these characters show that everything they died for, which in their lifetime seemed impossible, came about in less than 100 years. And man's condition improves, and he survives.

I hadn't meant to get on a soapbox, but I was directing the play weekends and nights, and my heart and mind were full of it. Flynn looked at me ruefully and said that he had flown to Barcelona with Hemingway to try to do research for the film *The Sun Also Rises* but had developed a case of cold feet when he realized they were using real bullets and he couldn't yell, "Cut!" But someone had told me he had helped Hemingway run guns from Crete to the Loyalists, so I kissed him, and he put his arm around me, and we all trooped into the long, narrow living room. We sat down at one end on a big white curved sofa and were served enormous goblets of champagne and brandy.

Errol yelled at some invisible person over his head, "Thread up and start."

Yvonne stood up and said, "Could you wait a couple of minutes for the ladies to use the ladies' room?" The redhead and I took the hint, and we traipsed into the gold and crystal bathroom. While she was answering the call of nature, Yvonne turned both faucets on full force and whispered in my ear, "Which one do you like the most, Gable or Flynn?"

"Do I have a choice?"

Yvonne said she thought Errol really liked me, so she would sacrifice herself and take Gable. But she advised me not to show my brains too much. "I've noticed at Hollywood parties, the handsome leading men like to talk to the intelligent women writers, but they go home with the dumb blond starlets." I got her message. But I wasn't sure if I wanted to play by those rules.

When we got back, Flynn was sitting on the right side of the ten-foot sofa and pulled me down next to him. Gable was to my left, Yvonne sat next to him, the handsome agent was far left and the redhead proceeded to sit on his lap.

As the lights went out and the MGM lion roared on the screen, I suddenly realized I really was sitting between CLARK GABLE and ERROL FLYNN! Mr. Flynn handed me my goblet, and I gulped the champagne. As he put his arm around me, all I could think was, this must be some sex fantasy I'm having at the Loew's Pitkin movie theater in Brownsville. I stared at the screen with complete concentration without the slightest idea what the picture was. Mr. Flynn took my empty goblet.

I never knew a man who smelled as wonderfully as he did. I don't know if it was the cologne or his soap or maybe it was a combination of both and especially his own outdoorsy smell. I almost swooned like a heroine in a Victorian novel.

When we got about an hour into the film, something shiny caught my eye. Mr.

Flynn must have pressed a button because a twelve-foot sliding panel had slid open, and there on a raised platform was a huge bed covered with cream-colored satin sheets and pillows, the top sheet turned back, ready. As I gazed in stunned fascination, I saw that around the bed there were plants, books, scripts, telephones, a small wet bar, and on the other side were an icebox, a radio and a phonograph. On the ceiling above the bed was a huge mirror, and as I watched, the mirror slid away, and I could see the stars and the moon through a flowering magnolia tree.

I looked at the other people in the room, but their eyes were riveted to the screen except for Gable, who was kissing Yvonne's neck. Mr. Flynn just held my hand a bit tighter. I noticed he had rather large hands, quite calloused for an actor. He whispered some sweet nothing in my ear, and all I could think of to answer was: "I wonder what the poor people are doing."

He burst into laughter and the panel slid back in place. Dammit! Maybe I had dreamed it all. There wasn't much light from the movie, so how could I tell the sheets were cream-colored?

The movie ended, and the other two couples got up and started to leave. I think I tried to, but Flynn's arm kept me in my seat. Maybe I wasn't trying too hard. As everyone began to disappear, he said to Yvonne, "I'll see that Shelley calls home."

"Remember she has to be at work six-thirty Monday morning." What the hell was she talking about? This was only 11 P.M. Friday night!

In those days, when the film industry considered a scene censorable, the camera would pan to such things as the fireplace, or waves pounding on a beach, or fireworks exploding.

So . . . cut to:

A fire roaring in a fireplace,
Waves pounding a beach,
Fireworks exploding,
Tchaikovsky's 1812 Overture, complete with cannons.

Index